Lyndon B. Johnson School of Public Affairs
Policy Research Project Report
Number 142

Technology-Based Solutions to Workforce Service Delivery

Project directed by

Robert W. Glover

Christopher T. King

Francis Dummer Fisher

Lodis Rhodes

A report by the
Policy Research Project on
Workforce and Technology
2002

The LBJ School of Public Affairs publishes a wide range of public policy issue titles. For order information and book availability call 512-471-4218 or write to: Office of Communications, Lyndon B. Johnson School of Public Affairs, The University of Texas at Austin, Box Y, Austin, TX 78713-8925. Information is also available online at www.utexas.edu/lbj/pubs/.

Library of Congress Control No.: 2002110950
ISBN: 0-89940-755-2

Cover design by Doug Marshall
LBJ School Office of Communications

Policy Research Project Participants

Students

Tanya M. Cruz, B.A. (Spanish and Sociology), University of Wisconsin-Madison

Cao Yong, B.A. (International Studies), Beijing Foreign Studies University

Anthony De Lawyer, B.A. (Public Justice), St. Mary's University

Michael G. Faust, B.S. (Mathematics and Statistics), Miami University, Ohio

Christine Ghabel, B.A. (Political Science), Virginia Technological University

Vanessa Garza, B.A. (Economics), The University of Texas at Austin

Kevin Heinz, B.A. (Political Science), DePaul University

Cassius O. Johnson, B.A. (Political Science), Texas Tech University

Vanessa Mitra, B.A. (International Relations), St. Mary's University

Svetlana Negrustuyeva, B.A. (Public Administration), Moscow State University

Marlene Romanczak, B.A (Industrial and Labor Relations), Cornell University

Daniel Starr, B.A. (Public Research and Communication), Evergreen State College

Piper Stege, B.A. (Spanish), Carlton College

Kathryn M. Supinski, B.A. (Spanish Literature), Whitman College

Jema Turk, B.A. (Economics), Southwestern University

Madge Vásquez, B.A. (International Studies), Southwestern University

Susan Vermeer, B.A. (English), University of Colorado, Boulder

Project Directors

Robert W. Glover, Ph.D., Research Scientist, Ray Marshall Center for the Study of Human Resources, Lyndon B. Johnson School of Public Affairs, The University of Texas at Austin.

Christopher T. King, Ph.D., Director, Ray Marshall Center for the Study of Human Resources, Lyndon B. Johnson School of Public Affairs, The University of Texas at Austin.

Francis Dummer Fisher, J.D., Senior Research Fellow, Lyndon B. Johnson School of Public Affairs, The University of Texas at Austin.

Lodis Rhodes, Ph.D., Professor, Lyndon B. Johnson School of Public Affairs, The University of Texas at Austin.

Table of Contents

List of Tables

List of Figures

List of Acronyms

AACC	American Association of Community Colleges
ACAP	Army Career and Alumni Program
ACC	Austin Community College
ACE	American Council on Education
ACIN	America's Career InfoNet
ADD	Attention Deficit Disorder
ADL	Advanced Distributed Learning
AFDC	Aid to Families with Dependent Children
AIM	Academic Improvement Management
AISD	Austin Independent School District
AJB	America's Job Bank
ALX	America's Learning Exchange
ARIES	Austin Regional Industry Education Systems
ASALFS	Automated Student and Adult Learner Follow-up System
ASL	America's Service Locator
ASTD	American Society for Training and Development
ASVAB	Army Service Vocational Aptitude Battery
ATI	Austin Technology Incubator
AUAO	Army University Access Online
AWS	America's Workforce System
AWTS	America's Workforce Technology Solutions
BLS	Bureau of Labor Statistics, U.S. Department of Labor
CAEDD	California's Employment Development Department
CARE	Commonwealth Access and Resource System

CATF	Capital Area Training Foundation
CAVE	Computerized Automatic Virtual Environment (an Army program)
CBI	Computer-Based Instruction
C-BIRD	Cross-Border Institute for Regional Development
CBO	Community-Based Organization
CCC	Captain's Career Courses (term used in the National Guard)
CCRS	College Credit Recommendation Services
CDR	Career Development Resources, Texas Workforce Commission (formerly Texas State Occupational Information Coordinating Committee)
CELF	Clinical Evaluation of Learning Fundamentals
CETA	Comprehensive Employment and Training Act of 1968
CHRM	Center for Human Resources Management
CPS	Current Population Survey
CTTC	Community Technology and Training Center
CUX	Corporate University Xchange
DHS	Department of Human Services (Texas)
DL	Distributive Learning
DoD	U.S. Department of Defense
DOL	U.S. Department of Labor
DSL	Digital Subscriber Lines
DSP	Digital Signal Processor
DTTP	Distributive Training Technology Project (a project of the National Guard Bureau)
DVI	Digital Video Interactive
ERA	Employment Retention and Advancement (a project in Texas)
ES	Employment Service
FETPIP	Florida Education and Training Placement Information Program

FRED	Florida Research and Economic Database
FRS	Functional Requirements Specifications
FSE&T	Food Stamp Employment and Training Program
FY	Fiscal Year
GPS	Global Positioning Satellites
HACU	Hispanic Association of Colleges and Universities
HRIS	Human Resource Information Systems
HT	Houston-Tillotson College
HTML	Hyper-Text Markup Language
ICT	Information and Communication Technologies
ICT	Institute for Creative Technologies
ID	Infantry Division
IMS	IMS Global Learning Consortium (initially entitled Instructional Management System)
IP	Internet Protocol
ISD	Independent School District
IT	Information Technology
ITV	Interactive Television
I-TECC	Incubator for Technology Enterprise in Corpus Christi
JTPA	Job Training Partnership Act of 1973
LWDB	Local Workforce Development Boards
MDTA	Manpower Development and Training Act of 1962
MCSE	Microsoft Certified Systems Engineer
MHMR	Texas Department of Mental Health and Mental Retardation
MOS	Military Occupational Specialty
NAPA	National Academy of Public Administration

NAS	National Academy of Sciences
NASWA	National Association of State Workforce Agencies (formerly known as ICESA)
NCO	Non-Commissioned Officer
NGB	National Guard Bureau
NSF	National Science Foundation
NTSA	National Training Systems Association
NWCET	National Workforce Center for Emerging Technologies (formerly Northwest Center for Emerging Technologies)
O*NET	Occupational Information Network
OJT	On-the-Job Training
OKI	Open Knowledge Initiative
OSOS	One-Stop Operating System (developed by the U.S. Department of Labor)
PERSCOM	Personnel Command (the Army's equivalent of a Human Resource Office)
PUC	Public Utility Commission of Texas
SACS	Southern Association of Colleges and Schools
SCORM	Sharable Courseware Object Reference Model
SESA	State Employment Security Agencies
SKIES	Skills Knowledge Information and Employment System
SOICC	State Occupational Information Coordinating Committee (in Texas) (now entitled Career Development Resources, Texas Workforce Commission)
SREB	Southern Regional Education Board
TACC	Texas Association of Community Colleges
TACL	Test of Auditory Comprehension of Language
TAMU-CC	Texas A&M Corpus Christi
TANF	Temporary Assistance to Needy Families
TASP	Texas Academic Skills Program

TCWEC	Texas Council on Workforce and Economic Competitiveness
TDCJ	Texas Department of Criminal Justice
TDED	Texas Department of Economic Development
TEA	Texas Education Agency
TEC	Texas Employment Commission
THECB	Texas Higher Education Coordinating Board
TI	Texas Instruments
TIF	Texas Infrastructure Fund
TIERS	Texas Integrated Enrollment Redesign System
TOLD	Test of Language Development
TSSB	Texas Skill Standards Board
TSTCS	Texas State Technical College System
TWC	Texas Workforce Commission
TWIST	The Workforce Information System of Texas
TYC	Texas Youth Commission
U.S. DoD	United States Department of Defense
U.S. DOL	United States Department of Labor
UMET	Use Your Military Experience and Training
UWORKS	Utah Workforce System
VCT	Virtual College of Texas
VTC	Video Teleconferencing
VETS	Veterans' Employment and Training Service
W3C	World Wide Web Consortium
WAGES	Work and Gain Economic Self-Sufficiency
WGU	Western Governors University
WIA	Workforce Investment Act of 1998

WILMA   Washington Interactive Labor Market Access

XML   Extensible Markup Language

Foreword

The Lyndon B. Johnson School of Public Affairs has established interdisciplinary research on policy problems as the core of its educational program. A major part of this program is the nine-month policy research project, in the course of which two or more faculty members from different disciplines direct the research of 10 to 30 graduate students of diverse backgrounds on a policy issue of concern to a government or nonprofit agency. This "client orientation" brings the students face to face with administrators, legislators, and other officials active in the policy process and demonstrates that research in a policy environment demands special talents. It also illuminates the occasional difficulties of relating research findings to the world of political realities.

This investigation of the applications of information technology to improve workforce development services in Texas was conducted by a policy research project in 2000-2001, sponsored by the office of the Texas Comptroller of Public Accounts in connection with its E-Texas initiative and by the Entertech Project of the IC^2 Institute at The University of Texas at Austin. Recommendations from the project aim to highlight ways that information technology can be implemented to increase the efficiency, effectiveness, and equity in the Texas workforce development system, administered by the Texas Workforce Commission and local Workforce Development Boards collaborating with employers, workers, and their organizations, education and training providers, and other community organizations.

The curriculum of the LBJ School is intended not only to develop effective public servants but also to produce research that will enlighten and inform those already engaged in the policy process. The project that resulted in this report has helped to accomplish the first task; it is our hope that the report itself will contribute to the second.

Finally, it should be noted that neither the LBJ School nor The University of Texas at Austin necessarily endorses the views or findings of this report.

Edwin Dorn
Dean

Acknowledgments and Disclaimer

We want to thank the Texas Comptroller of Public Accounts, the Entertech Project of the IC² Institute, and the LBJ School at The University of Texas at Austin for assisting in the financing of this project. Various individuals associated with these sponsors provided assistance, comments, and guidance in the development of this report. In this regard, Sidney Hacker and Kimberlee Harper Hanken of the e-Texas Workforce Task Force at the Office of the Texas Comptroller of Public Accounts, and Deaton Bednar and Melinda Jackson of the Entertech Project were especially helpful. Dean Edwin Dorn of the LBJ School made helpful initial contacts for us in the United States military and U.S. Department of Defense.

We also want to acknowledge and thank the numerous individuals who generously shared their time, energy, and expertise with us. Several individuals came to meet with us and made presentations to our group, including Nora Sabelli of the National Science Foundation, John Fitzpatrick and Rip Rowan (Executive Director and Operations Director of the Capital Area Training Foundation), Suzanne Hershey (Consultant and Trainer with Knowbility), Darin Hartley (formerly director of E-Learning at Dell Corporation and currently on the staff of the American Society for Training and Development), David Groening (Private Consultant and Project Manager), and John Horrigan (Senior Research Specialist, Pew Research Center Internet Project). Frank Fisher (Senior Research Fellow at the LBJ School of Public Affairs) joined our meetings as a key advisor throughout the year, prodding us with many good and often difficult questions.

Also especially helpful were staff of the Central Texas Workforce Development Board and its contractors, especially Susan Kamas, Linda Angel, and Jerry Haisler. Bill Grossenbacher (ACS State and Local Solutions, Inc., formerly Lockheed Martin Corporation), Daniel O'Shea (Ray Marshall Center for the Study of Human Resources), Richard Froschele (Texas Workforce Commission), Dr. Dale McCollough and Mary Jo Sanna (Capital Tech-Prep Consortium), John Dorrer (National Center on Education and the Economy), and many others provided information in interviews and various other communications with us.

We want to thank all who shared with us their knowledge, ideas, suggestions, and comments on this exciting project. At the same time, we want to remind the reader that any errors remaining in this report are the responsibility of the authors alone.

This report was edited by Robert Glover, with assistance from Tina Ghabel, Chris King, Frank Fisher, Lucy Neighbors, Karen White, Trish Norman, Kevin Hendryx, and Sue Carter.

Chapter 1. Introduction

The New Economy, characterized by globalization, technological innovation, and rapid labor market change, has increased pressure on both employers and public institutions to educate and train workers more quickly and efficiently. These forces have also led to changes in training content. Workers must possess broad-based competencies, including the ability to communicate, to learn, and to work in teams, as well as technical skills, if they are to succeed in today's labor market. Most workers will need basic computer skills to enter their chosen occupation as well as additional specialized training in field-specific applications to advance. As Harry Holzer, former chief economist for the U.S. Department of Labor, put it: "Technology skills are becoming increasingly essential in today's workplace."[1]

This report examines three important areas: technology, the New Economy, and workforce development policy. Our concern is primarily with their intersection, the point at which workers and employers access information and workforce services in order to compete successfully in labor markets. Highly interrelated changes are under way in each of these areas that are truly global in scope.

Rapid and dramatic changes in these areas have put pressure on governments, employers, and service providers to deliver workforce services more effectively, more efficiently, and more equitably. Effectiveness, efficiency, and equity—the "three E's"—serve as important underlying themes for the chapters that follow. On the one hand, we *must* deliver services more effectively, efficiently, and equitably because of economic and other pressures. On the other hand, we are going to deliver them more effectively, efficiently, and equitably simply because we *can*. To some extent, invention has become the mother of necessity.

These changes are also placing greater responsibility for workforce development on individuals and families. Increasingly, workers are expected to identify, arrange, and finance their own opportunities for learning. They are also expected to foster their own career development over time.

In this chapter, we discuss these three areas and their intersection. We then offer an overview of key issues that comprise the separate chapters of the report.

Technological Change

Information and communications technology (ICT) has undergone rapid and remarkable changes. In only two decades, personal computers and the Internet have become ubiquitous both in the workplace and at home. And, while these changes are clearly evident here in the United States, they certainly are not limited to this country. Recent books and reports published by the International Labour Organization suggest that technological changes are widespread, extending to nearly all parts of the globe and affecting developing as well as developed countries.[2]

The Internet is a worldwide group of private and public computers linked together for the purpose of rapid information exchange. No one person or organization can claim sole credit for the advent of the Internet. However, the first ideas of a "Galactic Network" concept were written in a number of memos by MIT's J. C. R. Licklider in 1962.[3] He envisioned a global network through which everyone could share and access data and programs. A few months later, Licklider joined the United States Department of Defense's Advanced Research Projects Agency (ARPA), the institution that largely spearheaded and funded the Internet's development. In late 1969, the first test of an ARPANet was made at UCLA and then later at Stanford. Email and the Internet made their first appearance in 1972 at the Internet Computer Communication Conference. Over the years, the role of managing the Internet changed hands from ARPANet to the National Science Foundation in 1990, and then to a consortium of commercial providers in 1995.[4]

According to NetRatings, an Internet media and market research firm, Internet penetration has reached 60 percent in the United States, with more than 168 million people having Web access either in the home or in the workplace. At-home users accounted for 58 percent of that total, or 162 million, and at-work users accounted for 14 percent, or 41 million people.[5] The U.S. Department of Commerce reported that more than half of all households (51 percent) had computers by 1999.[6]

The rapid uptake of new information technologies is occurring among most groups of Americans, regardless of income, education, race or ethnicity, location, age, or gender, suggesting that digital inclusion is a realizable goal. Even groups that have traditionally been digital "have nots" are now making dramatic gains. The gap between households in rural areas and households nationwide that had access to the Internet was 2.6 percentage points in 2000. In rural areas for 2000, 38.9 percent of the households could access the Internet, a 75 percent increase from only 22.2 percent in December 1998. Americans at every income level are connecting at far higher rates from their homes, particularly at the middle-income levels. Internet access among households earning $35,000 to $49,000 rose from 29.0 percent in December 1998 to 46.1 percent in August 2000. Access to the Internet is also expanding across every education level, but particularly for those with some high school or college education. Households headed by those with some college showed the greatest expansion in Internet penetration of all education levels, rising from 30.2 percent in December 1998 to 49.0 percent in August 2000.

African Americans and Hispanics still lag behind other groups, but have shown impressive gains in Internet access. African American households are now more than twice as likely to have home access than they were 20 months ago, rising from 11.2 percent to 23.5 percent. Hispanic households have also experienced a tremendous growth rate during this period, rising from 12.6 percent to 23.6 percent. The disparity in Internet usage between men and women has largely disappeared. In December 1998, 34.2 percent of men and 31.4 percent of women were using the Internet. By August 2000, 44.6 percent of men and 44.2 percent of women were Internet users. Individuals 50 years of age or over experienced the highest rates of growth in Internet usage of all age groups: 53 percent from December 1998 to August 2000, compared to a 35 percent growth rate for individual Internet usage nationwide. All of this progress is very favorable news for those advocating technology solutions for workforce service delivery.

Despite these hopeful statistics about the rise of Internet access and computer ownership among almost all groups, various digital divides remain. Recent data show that divides still exist between those with different levels of income and education, different racial and ethnic groups, old and young, single-and dual-parent families, and those with and without disabilities. People with a disability are only half as likely to have access to the Internet as individuals without a disability: 21.6 percent compared with 42.1 percent. While just under 25 percent of people without a disability have never used a personal computer, close to 60 percent of people with a disability fall into that category. Among people with a disability, those who have impaired vision and problems with manual dexterity have even lower rates of Internet access and are less likely to use a computer regularly than people with hearing difficulties.

Large gaps also remain regarding Internet penetration rates among households of different races and ethnic origins. Asian Americans and Pacific Islanders have maintained the highest level of home Internet access at 56.8 percent. At the other end of the spectrum, large gaps for African Americans and Hispanics remained when measured against the national average Internet penetration rate. The divide between Internet access rates for African American households and the national average rate was 18 percentage points in August 2000. That gap was 3 percentage points wider in August 2000 than the 15-percentage-point gap that existed in December 1998. The Internet divide between Hispanic households and the national average rate was 18 percentage points in August 2000, 4 percentage points wider than the 14-percentage-point gap that existed in December 1998.

With regard to computer ownership, the divide appears to have stabilized, although it remains large. The August 2000 divide between African Americans households and the national average rate with regard to computer ownership was 18 percentage points (a 32.6 percent penetration rate for African American households, compared with 51.0 percent for households nationally). Similarly, there was a 17-percentage-point difference between the share of Hispanic households with a computer (33.7 percent) and the national average.

Broadband services, a relatively new technology used by only 10.7 percent of online households, showed urban-rural disparities. In August 2000, rural areas were lagging behind central cities and urban areas in broadband penetration at 7.3 percent, compared with 12.2 percent and 11.8 percent, respectively.

Technology is the great facilitator/enabler for workforce service delivery. Without widespread computer and Internet access, important technology-based approaches to delivering workforce services when and where needed simply would not be possible. At the same time, it appears that the advent of these technologies may be leading workforce customers—job seekers and employers alike—to demand even faster, better, and cheaper services than currently exist.

The New Knowledge-Based, Global Economy

In many respects, the New Economy provides the larger context for our analysis. Key components of the New Economy include the following elements (Cappelli et al. 1997; Ganzglass et al. 2000):

1. globalization—increased relatedness of world markets;

2. technological change–computerization, miniaturization, advances in ICT, among others;

3. new management practices and forms of work organization—for example, economic value added, high-performance work organization;

4. new business strategies, including pursuit of "niche" markets, smaller more flexible production runs, and so on; and

5. new financial institutions and mechanisms.

These changes have brought increased emphasis on speed, flexibility, and collaboration. They have also led to widespread enterprise restructuring, greater job instability/insecurity, flattened management structures and truncated career ladders, a shift from company career ladders to community career ladders or "climbing walls," increased labor market segmentation and growing inequality, and the demise of the "social contract."

The New Economy is apparent in Texas and several of its metropolitan areas. In short, Texas has been transformed from an economy based largely on natural resources, including oil and gas, cattle, lumber, and crops, to an economy that is knowledge based. The state and several of its major metropolitan areas have become advanced New Economy prototypes with strong ties internationally. Austin has become a center for software development, computer assembly, and semiconductor manufacturing. Likewise, Dallas has become a locus of firms in high technology. A focus on biotechnology and medical applications is developing in San Antonio.

In 2001-2002, the economic downturn hit high-tech markets and various sectors of the New Economy especially hard. Some have referred to the "dot.com bust" in the stock market. But, most analysts firmly believe that the New Economy will rebound strongly in upcoming years and is here to stay over the long run. Returning to the old ways of doing business in the economy and the labor market is simply not an option.

Workforce Systems in a Changing Policy and Program Context

Workforce development is a process that assists people in acquiring the skills and knowledge needed to participate in productive work. Workforce systems aim to provide individuals with better skills so they can connect to the labor market and advance in their careers. Workforce systems include education and training programs for workers, those preparing to go to work, and job seekers, delivered through formal and informal means that are designed to enhance the skills of people to maintain or improve their socioeconomic status. This includes programs for new entrants into the labor market (the emerging workforce), for unemployed and dislocated workers and others experiencing labor market problems (the transitional workforce), and for currently employed workers (the incumbent workforce). This comprehensive definition specifically includes technical and occupational courses in the for-credit curriculum of community colleges, as well as the noncredit customized training they offer for business and industry. Additionally, it includes employment and training programs for the temporarily dislocated and long-term unemployed.[7]

In Texas, the Texas Workforce Commission (TWC) is charged with overseeing and providing workforce development services to employers and individuals.[8] The TWC is responsible for training services that are delivered through contracts with a network of 28 local workforce development boards whose members are appointed by local officials. In addition, at least seven other state agencies, 50 community and technical colleges, 35 public universities, and 1,042 school districts provide services that support the state's employers and employees.[9] Four guiding principles of the Texas workforce system are local control over centralized solutions, integrated workforce services, focus on employer needs, and accountability for real-world results.[10]

The *workforce system* refers to a broad range of employment and training services whose purpose is to enable job seekers, students, workers, and employers to access a wide range of information about jobs, the labor market, careers, education and training organizations, financing options, skills standards or certification requirements, and needed support services. In Texas, one-stop workforce centers provide job seekers and employers with access to employment and training services at particular locations or through electronic linkages.[11]

Workforce Development: Reforms and Emerging Expectations

Structures and approaches for delivering workforce services have been undergoing dramatic changes over the last decade.[12] In Texas, these changes began with passage of two major reform packages: Senate Bill 642, passed by the Texas legislature in 1992, and House Bill 1863, passed in 1995.[13]

Subsequent reforms at the federal level, including the Workforce Investment Act (WIA) of 1998, were modeled largely on Texas legislation.[14] Texas H.B. 1863 mandated the creation of local workforce boards, which are responsible for redesigning, implementing, and overseeing a local workforce delivery system responsive to local needs and conditions. WIA requires states to streamline and consolidate their job training systems by creating a "one-stop" approach to workforce service delivery.[15] Each of the 28 workforce boards in Texas utilizes workforce centers, or one-stop centers, to provide services to individuals and employers in a centralized location.[16]

The system of workforce centers or "one-stop" centers is the cornerstone of the Texas workforce system for the delivery of employment-related services across the state. This system is the organizing vehicle for transforming the fragmented array of employment and training programs into an integrated and consolidated service delivery system for job seekers and employers.[17] The centers, which provide access to employment and training services, are designed for use by the general public and are often the starting points for individuals seeking workforce services.

Note that local workforce boards in Texas enjoy a much broader scope than local boards in most states. Like Michigan, Florida, and a few other states, Texas has devolved responsibility for a broad array of federal/state workforce programs to its boards. In Texas, local boards administer programs under WIA, Welfare-to-Work, TANF, Food Stamp Employment and Training, and even child care. Fewer than one in ten local boards nationwide has such far-reaching responsibility and authority. Most boards in other states primarily operate only WIA programs.

Additional federal reforms came in welfare-to-work policies and programs under the Personal Responsibility Act of 1996 and the Balanced Budget Act of 1997. The primary focus of these welfare reforms was to assist families help themselves move from welfare to work by promoting family responsibility, accountability, and self-sufficiency through work. The Personal Responsibility Act also transformed welfare into a program of temporary assistance.[18]

The 1996 federal welfare reform law marked a historic shift in social policy by devolving to states the authority to develop and implement innovative approaches to welfare reform. In partnership with Congress and the Clinton administration, governors reached an agreement to end the individual entitlement to cash, and to instead accept federal funds in the form of the Temporary Assistance for Needy Families (TANF) block grant.[19] The TANF block grant provided states the flexibility to implement innovative welfare reform programs based on work requirements and time limits, along with the ability to use TANF funds to provide needed work supports for low-income working families.

States have enacted policies and programs to help individuals move into work and have provided them with work-related supports. Success in the workplace depends largely on an individual's ability to stay connected to other work supports and related benefits, such as child care, transportation, Medicaid, and Food Stamps. Texas is striving to create a more comprehensive system to assist individuals with workforce services and related benefits.

One-stop centers have helped Texas integrate its workforce programs while ensuring that they comply with the requirements of federal law. The Texas workforce system still needs greater coordination among the seven state agencies that are responsible for most of the state's workforce services.[20] In addition, workforce-related programs at three additional agencies—the Texas Department of Criminal Justice (TDCJ), the Texas Youth Commission (TYC), and the Texas Department of Mental Health and Mental Retardation (MHMR)—would benefit from improved coordination.[21] As a recent report of the Texas Comptroller pointed out:

Despite the reform efforts of the 1990s, Texas' system still needs improvement, due in large part to the difficulties inherent in coordinating its many components. This fragmentation of effort makes the system unwieldy and incapable of adapting quickly to changing circumstances in the job market.[22]

The Texas workforce system is still evolving and adapting, both to the needs of the New Economy and to the availability of new and innovative technologies.

Technology, the New Economy, and Workforce Service Delivery—The Intersection

The story begins to get interesting at the intersection of these three areas. Technological innovations and intense pressures of the New Economy are rendering traditional approaches workforce service delivery—for example, applying in person for unemployment benefits, filling out and submitting numerous job applications by hand, looking up job openings in newspaper want ads—obsolete. Emerging workforce service delivery approaches that exploit new technologies mean that employers no longer have to wait for days to place and fill job orders and can better respond to the competitive pressures they face to tailor their products and services and get them to market just in time.

The State of Texas and many of the actors that comprise its system for workforce development have pioneered not only new workforce policies but also new workforce service delivery models, taking considerable advantage of new technologies as they respond to the imperatives of the New Economy. Examples of these Texas-based initiatives include the following, among others:

1. the use of Web-based tools generally;

2. the development and dissemination of LMI and computer-assisted career guidance and counseling tools for training and work-related education, for example, OSCAR and CAREERS, two innovative tools developed by the Career Development Resources[23] staff of the Texas Workforce Commission;

3. state-of-the-art one-stop centers that place a premium on appropriate uses of technology (e.g., Killeen, Dallas), including hand-held devices (e.g., Palm Pilots) as well as computers;

4. the Virtual College of Texas and distance learning initiatives in the state's community and technical colleges, still a relatively small but growing initiative to provide distance learning statewide;

5. telephone-based and Web-based UI application and claim processing and labor exchange kiosks, many of which have been located in shopping malls, where residents are more likely to use them; and

6. the EnterTech[TM] Training Project—recently renamed eLearning and Training Labs—launched in 1997-1998, which has made extensive use of the latest technologies for developing and delivering employer-driven, competency-based

learning, while constantly measuring performance (for more information, see www.entertech.org and www.eltlabs.org).

Texas is at forefront of workforce reform *and* the use of ICT to deliver workforce services. Texas is at the leading edge of "next-generation" workforce systems, serving as a model for other states. Still, there is room for improvement, as was noted by the Texas Comptroller's Office in its recent (2001) *E-Texas Report*. The *E-Texas Report* analyzed a number of important trends in the labor market, among them rising employer expectations, greater corporate commitment to training, and increased use of technologies for training delivery (the Internet, company intranets, satellite transmission, videoconferencing, and CD-ROMs). This report offered a number of recommendations for improving the Texas workforce system to make its services more efficient and less costly via the application of information technology.

As indicated earlier, other countries of the world are not standing still while Texas moves forward on this front. Even developing and transitioning countries are embarking on technology-based initiatives for workforce service, despite facing challenges such as a less reliable and less comprehensive communications infrastructure. Two such efforts are a computer-based literacy project operated by several nongovernmental organizations in Ghana and a distance learning project in Fiji.[24] Technology-based solutions to workforce service delivery are very advanced in Texas communities, but they are rapidly becoming the norm in the rest of world as well.

Organization of This Report

A number of issues and concerns surfaced from examining research and best practice in the use of technology for workforce service delivery in Texas and elsewhere. Ultimately, these issues and concerns became the organizational framework for our report, which begins with a discussion of two cross-cutting issues that are fundamental to the effective use of information technology in workforce services. Chapter 2 deals with assuring effective access to information technology for all Texans, and Chapter 3 explores developing instruction based on sound pedagogy. Next, applications of information technology in three arenas of the workforce system are discussed—in online labor exchange (Chapter 4), in the one-stop workforce centers (Chapter 5), and in the training of workforce staff, especially case managers (Chapter 6). Chapters 7 and 8 focus on secondary and postsecondary education in preparing the Texas students for work in the New Economy. Lessons from the use of technology for learning in the military and innovative applications in the workforce systems of other states are raised in Chapters 9 and 10. Chapter 11 discusses the use of partnerships to implement information technology in workforce systems. Each chapter focuses on an important dimension of information and communications technology and its application to improve an aspect of workforce service delivery.

Notes

[1] Leslie Eaton, "Labor Department Study Describes Need for IT Skills for Most Workers." *New York Times* (October 20,1999). Online. Available: http://www.nytimes.com/yr/mo/day/news/national/regional/ny-computer-skills. Accessed: November 20, 2000.

[2] For example, see International Labour Office (ILO), *World Employment Report 2001: Life at Work in the Information Economy* (Geneva, 2001). This report is rich with examples of technology applications for work and preparation for work throughout the world. See also Torkel Alfthan, Christopher T. King, and Gyorgy Sziraczki, eds., *Global Restructuring, Training and Social Dialogue* (Geneva: ILO, 2001).

[3] C/Net Coverage website. *Who Started the Net?* Online. Available: http://coverage.cnet.com/Content/Features/Techno/Networks/ss05.html. Accessed: April 24, 2001.

[4] Ibid.

[5] Tim McDonald, February 14, 2001. *Internet Penetration Sets New U.S. Record.* News FactorNetwork. Online. Available: http://www.newsfactor.com/perl/story/7497.html. Accessed: April 24, 2001.

[6] U.S. Department of Commerce, Economics and Statistics Administration, and National Telecommunications and Information Administration (October 2000). *Falling through the Net: Toward Digital Inclusion. A Report on Americans' Access to Technology Tools.* Online. Available: http://www.ntia.doc.gov/ntiahome/fttn00/Falling.htm. Accessed: April 2, 2001. Statistics quoted in subsequent paragraphs come from this report.

[7] G. Stephen Katsinas, *Community Colleges and Workforce Development in the New Economy* (Winter 1994). Online. Available: http://scholar.lib.vt.edu/ejournals/CATALYST/V24N1/katsinas.html. Accessed: April 2, 2001.

[8] The Texas Workforce Commission Website. *The Workforce Investment Act (WIA) of 1998.* Online. Available: http://www.twc.state.tx.us/svcs/jtpa/wiajtpa.html. Accessed: April 1, 2001. Also, see Daniel O'Shea and Christopher T. King, *The Workforce Investment Act of 1998: Restructuring Workforce Development Initiatives in States and Localities* (Albany: The Nelson A. Rockefeller Institute of Government, Rockefeller Report No. 12, April 2001).

[9] Texas Comptroller of Public Accounts, *E-Texas Report.* Online. Available: http://www.e-texas.org/report/ch08/. Accessed: April 2, 2001.

[10] Ibid.

[11] Karin Martinson, "Coordination and Integration of Welfare and Workforce Development Systems." *Literature Review on Service Coordination and Integration in the Welfare and Workforce Development*

Systems (January 1999). Online. Available: http://aspe.hhs.gov/hsp/coord00/appa.htm. Accessed: April 2, 2001.

[12] See Evelyn Ganzglass et al., *Transforming State Workforce Systems: Case Studies of Five Leading States* (Washington, D.C.: National Governors Association, Center for Best Practices, 2001); and W. Norton Grubb et al., *Toward Order from Chaos: State Efforts to Reform Workforce Development Systems* (Berkeley: National Center for Research in Vocational Education/University of California, MDS-1249, January 1999).

[13] For a review of these reforms, see Lyndon B. Johnson School of Public Affairs, *Building a Workforce Development System for Texas . . . A Funny Thing Happened on the Way to Reform,* Policy Research Project Report Series, no. 126 (Austin, Tex., 1997).

[14] Christopher T. King, "The State at Work: The Workforce Investment Act of 1998 and What It Means for Texas," *Texas Business Review* (October 1999); and Christopher T. King, "Federalism and Workforce Policy Reform," *Publius: The Journal of Federalism*, vol 29, no. 2 (Spring 1999), pp. 53-71

[15] Ibid.

[16] Ibid.

[17] U.S. Department of Labor Employment and Training Administration Fact Sheet. *The One-Stop Center System.* Online. Available: http://www.doleta.gov/programs/factsht/one-stop.htm. Accessed: April 2, 2001.

[18] Virginia Department of Social Services, *Temporary Assistance for Needy Families.* Online. Available: http://www.dss.state.va.us/benefit/tanf.html. Accessed: April 5, 2001.

[19] See Richard P. Nathan and Thomas L. Gais, *Implementing the Personal Responsibility Act of 1996: A First Look* (Albany: The Nelson A. Rockefeller Institute of Government, State University of New York, 1999); and National Governors Association, *Welfare Reform Policy.* Online. Available: http://www.nga.org/nga/legislativeUpdate/policyPositionDetailPrint/1,1390,554,00.htm. Accessed: April 3, 2001.

[20] Texas Comptroller of Public Accounts website, *E-Texas Report* (online).

[21] Ibid.

[22] Ibid.

[23] And its predecessor, the Texas State Occupational Information Coordinating Committee. For at least 20 years, CDR/Texas SOICC has been a nationally recognized leader in the design, development, and implementation of user-friendly tools for state and local planners and training providers, including employers.

[24] International Labour Office, *World Employment Report 2001*, pp. 209-216.

Chapter 2. Improving Access to Information Technology in Rural Texas

It is the policy of this state to ensure that customers in all regions of this state, including low-income customers and customers in rural and high cost areas, have access to telecommunications and information services, including interexchange services, cable services, wireless services, and advanced telecommunications and information services, that are reasonably comparable to those provided in urban areas and that are available at prices that are reasonably comparable to prices charged for similar services in urban areas.[1]

Introduction

While computers and the Internet have the potential to be great equalizers in providing convenience and access to millions of Americans, rural communities still lag behind urban areas. Information technologies, such as computers, personal digital assistants, cell phones, and pagers, are becoming increasingly important to social, political, and economic life. New uses of technology are permeating all facets of life, such as online shopping, banking, communication, learning, and work. In addition, the ability to use technology in the workplace and to acquire skills through distance learning technology is revolutionizing the way we deliver workforce services. Information technology offers potential solutions to some of our most challenging workforce delivery issues, especially in rural, underdeveloped communities. Now more than ever, distance learning is becoming a viable alternative—or at least a desirable and considerable complement—to traditional classroom learning. Computer-based applications, including simulated work environments for more effective training, can be delivered using distance learning systems.

As the use of distance learning in workforce training expands and improves, assuring access to information technology becomes a more critical issue. Barriers to access include cost, racial and ethnic disparities, gender bias, and disabilities such as visual and speech impairment, conditions that restrict physical movement, learning disabilities, language barriers, and lack of infrastructure (both equipment and trained staff) in rural areas. All of these factors may impede access to information technology. This chapter focuses on issues and barriers in bringing improved distance learning to rural Texas. It makes recommendations to optimize the use of distance learning in order to improve the workforce system in rural Texas.

Digital Divides

Information technology applications are revolutionizing the way workforce training services are delivered. However, as advances in technology continue, the digital divide continues to widen. Although rapid technology improvements have contributed to the digital divide, technology, coupled with sound public policy, can also help resolve the equity and access issues our nation faces.[2]

Awareness of digital divides is necessary for any thoughtful discussion or policy recommendations regarding technology and workforce training. In our emerging economy, the Internet will serve as the central nervous system for training and continuous development. New and evolving technological shifts promise a level playing field, but will not come with a guarantee of equal access or training on the networks and devices that will make learning anywhere, anytime an option for all Americans. While technology has arguably improved the quality of life for most, many people still do not have access to computers and the Internet.

There are many "digital divides" which reinforce one another. The main features of the divide are education, income, and race/ethnicity, as well as geography. Better educated Americans are more likely to be connected to the Internet. In 1998, those with a college degree were more than 8 times as likely to have a computer at home and nearly 16 times as likely to have home Internet access as those with an elementary school education.[3]

Those with higher incomes are more likely to have access to information technology. In 1998, households with incomes of $75,000 or higher were more than 20 times more likely to have access to the Internet than those at the lowest income levels, and more than 9 times as likely to have a computer at home. The existence of a digital divide between the affluent and the poor has been fueled by inadequate access to quality computing facilities, network devices, infrastructure, and the scarcity of training opportunities in low-income communities.[4]

Whites are more likely to be connected to the Internet than African Americans or Hispanics. African American and Hispanic households are two-fifths as likely to have home Internet access as white households.[5]

The Geographic Divide

Many of the divides listed above are exacerbated in rural areas because these communities experience all the above issues in addition to the challenges of distance, lack of infrastructure, and isolation. Rural residents are less likely to be connected than urban residents regardless of income. Rural communities lag behind in computer ownership and Internet access. In some income levels, rural households are 50 percent less likely to have Internet access than those earning the same income in urban areas. Low-income households in rural areas are the least connected, with connectivity rates in the single digits for both computers and Internet access.[6]

Putting equity and access aside, rural America is still a vital part of the U.S. economy. Twenty-one percent of the U. S. population resides in rural communities, 18 percent of jobs are rural, and the earnings of rural residents comprise 14 percent of national earnings. According to William Galston, rural-urban divergence can be measured along a number of key dimensions. Rural employment is growing at a slower rate—10.6 percent compared to 23.8 percent in metropolitan areas between 1979 and 1989. Unemployment rates in rural areas were between 1 and 2.5 percent higher in rural areas than in metropolitan areas during the same time period. Per capita income in rural areas is at an all-time low, with average annual earnings per job falling 8 percent in rural areas compared to 2 percent in urban areas. Lastly, poverty in rural areas is up to 50 percent higher than in urban areas.[7] While most programs to improve these numbers focus on schools and libraries as natural places for technology training, it has become clear that schools and libraries in low-income, rural areas have problems, too. Only 14 percent of the schools in rural areas are connected to the Internet. By comparison, nearly 80 percent of schools in more affluent areas are connected. Lack of teacher training and know-how have made it difficult for schools in these areas to transfer technology skills. Similarly, community libraries in poor areas typically do not have the available staff or equipment to teach marketable information and technology literacy skills to their patrons. Rural areas are plagued by what technology experts call the "last mile" problem.[8] The cost of laying cable in rural areas for high-speed connections limits inhabitants to the use of only dial-up connections. Many rural communities lack a sufficient customer base to provide the economies of scale for cost-conscious telecommunications companies to make investments in infrastructure. Given this picture, rural-area school children and adults using community libraries for computer access are at a disadvantage when it comes to developing the information and technology literacy skills that can help them to become self-sufficient.

Distance from metropolitan areas has been a defining feature of rural Texas. Without ready access to the varied markets, urban populations, and support networks for human capital development, and support systems for business development, rural areas have long relied on an economy based on natural resources. Capitalizing on the natural resource base of rural Texas—including its row crop and animal agriculture, oil and gas, wildlife, scenic and historic features—will continue to be important. Yet future growth in rural Texas may well depend on innovations in telecommunications technology.

The expanded use of computers and the Internet offers promising solutions to workforce training in rural areas. Yet certain populations remain left behind. Ironically, it is often the same groups that workforce development initiatives target. So, how can technology help workforce development if its use is already inadequate in the populations the workforce system is trying to reach?

Barriers to Training

In addition to digital divide issues, three notable barriers deter individuals who wish to pursue additional training: difficulty of scheduling courses, required time commitment, and cost. According to U.S. Department of Education, the most common barriers to participation reported by nonparticipants who knew of offerings were lack of time (47 percent) and high cost (30 percent).[9] Low-skilled workers are especially affected by cost factors. Compared with their counterparts in other states, Texas' working poor are more likely to lack a high school education. In the mid-1990s, 15.6 percent of Texas working families with children lived below the poverty line—one-third higher than the national rate of 11.5 percent. In Texas, full-time workers were found in 37.1 percent of poor families with children, more than one-and-half times the national average of 25.8 percent.[10]

Other barriers include (1) individual/psychological issues on the part of the learner; (2) lack of knowledge of the opportunities available; (3) poor facilities, inadequate spaces, insufficient numbers of qualified teachers, inconvenient time schedules; and (4) transportation/distance issues, affordability, barriers to participation by disabled individuals.

All these barriers impede workers from participating in training programs, which tends to keep them in low-skilled, low-paying jobs. These problems also affect many minority workers in inner-city areas.

Distance Learning

Distance learning has become a focal point of hope in discussions about bridging geographical divides. Distance learning provides a timely and cost-effective means of continuing education and lifelong learning. Utilizing a network infrastructure and a combination of multiple technologies, motivated adults can be trained and even earn college credits, certificates, or degrees at home or in other learning environments through satellite and computer networks. Through distance learning, everyone can have equitable access to information. With learning opportunities readily available, people can acquire the necessary knowledge to become productive members of the workforce and advance in their jobs because of this advanced training. Distance learning can overcome some significant barriers that prevent workers from obtaining the training they need. Specifically, distance learning involves advantages in terms of cost, pedagogy, flexibility, and access. Cost is an important factor. Distance learning can reduce students' training costs by eliminating or reducing the need for travel, accommodation, and/or other expenses.

Distance learning can also make a significant contribution to improvements in teaching and learning. Teaching through information and communications technology (ICT) can help students by actively engaging them in learning through using information and materials to construct their own understanding and knowledge. Students learn by doing, and teachers become navigators or guides rather than being sources of knowledge. Teachers do this by providing students with self-paced, self-directed, and problem-based learning experiences, and then follow up by testing students in new interactive and interesting ways.[11] Combining multimedia (text, graphics, audio, and video) in interactive environments offers opportunities to provide immediate feedback and to simulate real-life scenarios. Learners retain more of the course material than with traditional classroom versions of courses, and instructors are better utilized. For instructors, better control over course management is meaningful. Instructors may limit or extend training opportunities to small or large groups of students; security codes and passwords allow them to maintain confidentiality while tracking student progress. There is sufficient evidence to support the claim that ICT-mediated instruction can be as effective as conventional instruction and can provide students opportunities to learn in information-rich environments.

For many, learning at a time and place of their choice and convenience provides the ultimate flexibility and is an ideal solution to the barriers to receiving advanced training and education. Faster completion of training courses is possible through distance learning. Moreover, self-paced learning allows learners to control their learning experience. They can work at a pace that suits them best, as well as bypassing training that is not relevant. Furthermore, the growth and demand for flexible, part-time training is ideal for the adult learner. Rapid changes in the workplace will require rapid delivery of training. Such training must be high speed, low cost, and capable of reaching both small and large groups. Traditional ways of delivering training are time-consuming, labor intensive, socially disruptive, and costly. Distance learning offers flexible solutions.

Distance learning is also more accessible. Learners do not have to wait until the course is scheduled; they can take a course whenever and wherever it suits them. For marginalized populations who reside in remote areas, distance learning offers a promising alternative to travel costs and time constraints. Barriers such as time and distance are eliminated, and the ability to learn from the best teachers becomes feasible even in the most deprived communities and individuals.

Distance Learning in Texas

Distance learning offers potential solutions to three critical issues facing skills development in Texas: (1) distance learning can overcome rural-urban gaps in access to training and education; (2) it can eliminate geographical barriers, and (3) it can provide access to new technology to deliver training to those with demonstrated skills gaps.

Progressive legislation has put Texas in a leadership position in distance learning. Distance learning has benefited from Texas state government actions to promote access and to help remedy inequities. Specifically, proceeds from an education tariff imposed on the sale of telecommunications services are used to broaden access and to support distance learning. H.B. 653 grants qualified educational institutions reduced rates to meet the distance learning needs of the state. In addition, the Texas Interactive Multimedia Communications Fund Demonstration Program (H.B. 1029) helps finance the acquisition of multimedia technology and services by school districts. Initiative H.B. 183 encourages cooperation among educators, government, and private industry for demonstration projects related to distance learning.[12]

The 75th session of the Texas Legislature sought to increase the use of distance learning systems to reduce travel costs and increase the amount of time in the work site, while ensuring a highly trained and technologically proficient workforce. In Article IX, Section 14, subsections 13-16 of the 1998-1999 General Appropriations Bill, the legislature required agencies to "utilize teleconferencing and other telecommunications technologies to the maximum extent possible in order to reduce agency travel expenditures." This mandate included interactive television and videoconferencing facilities and emphasized a need to conserve taxpayer resources while using the best combination of training strategies, delivery methods, and distance learning systems to ensure that employees master the required tasks and skills.[13]

Telecommunications Infrastructure Fund (TIF)

The Telecommunications Infrastructure Fund (TIF) and the TIF board were created under Section 3.606 of House Bill 2128, the Public Utility Regulatory Act of 1995. Recognizing the rapid changes taking place in the telecommunications industry on a national level, the reform sought to create economic opportunities for Texans and to overhaul the telecommunications industry. The mission of the TIF board was to "help the citizens of Texas deploy an advanced telecommunications and information delivery infrastructure by stimulating universal and scaleable information and applications access for elementary and secondary school campuses, institutions of higher education, public libraries, academic health science centers, and public and not-for-profit healthcare facilities. [The] priority [would] be given to rural and underserved populations."[14] TIF's ultimate goal is to "assist all citizens of Texas in achieving equitable access to information and education resources, irrespective of their socioeconomic condition or geographic location."[15]

Through annual assessments of 1.6 percent on gross revenues of both local phone companies and mobile communications providers (excluding Internet services), the TIF board provides grants to TIF-eligible entities. These entities, established by the legislation, are public schools, higher education institutions, libraries, and nonprofit health-care facilities. The annual assessments, totaling an estimated $150 million per year, will be collected for 10 years, ending in 2005. The funds are separated into two accounts. The first is dedicated specifically for Texas K-12 public school districts and campuses (the Public Schools Account). Under this account, grants are provided to purchase equipment, including computers, printers, computer labs, and video equipment, as well as other items necessary to support connectivity within the campus. The second fund provides monies to Texas K-12 public school districts and campuses, colleges and universities, and nonprofit health-care facilities (the Qualifying Entities Account). The grants under this account include funding for items and services such as equipment, wiring, material, program development, training, installation, or any statewide telecom network.

The grants are awarded both on a noncompetitive and on a competitive basis. The noncompetitive grant programs include technology advancement, distance learning, and telemedicine, which offers basic telecommunications packages, including networking and telecommunications equipment such as routers and hubs, computers, and two-way videoconferencing. The grants also cover training and installation costs. Competitive grants are made under the Collaborative Community Networking and Discovery Program, which aims to promote innovative projects demonstrating collaboration and/or creative uses of technology. These grants encourage high-level technology solutions to community needs and also support and extend existing advanced projects. The goal is to allow the four types of entities eligible for TIF funding "to involve a broad range of community residents and organizations in a multi-purpose and community-based network."[16]

TIF has had a mixed record of success. It has achieved notable success in wiring schools, libraries, and nonprofit health-care facilities across Texas. As of March 1, 1999, $202 million in telecommunications grants were provided to 1,018 school districts and charter schools (out of a total of 1,145), 57 community colleges (out of 57), 592 public libraries and branches (out of 789), and 330 public and not-for-profit health-care facilities (out of 742).[17] Of these awards, TIF has awarded grants to 566 of the 574 rural public school districts and to 355 rural public libraries.[18]

As of November 2000, the total assessments collected were $759,434,564 and the total disbursements were $621,869,344. The allocation of funds across various types of entities as of November 2000 was as follows: 52 percent to K-12 public schools, 18 percent to agencies (funds allocated to public projects through board approval), 9 percent to nonprofit health-care facilities, 7 percent to libraries, 7 percent to higher education, and 6 percent to discovery and community collaboratives. Of the total spent that year, only 1 percent was spent on operations.[19]

For FY 2000, the total amount awarded to public schools was $112,164,014; to libraries a total of $23,241,021; to public health care a total of $33,678,228; to Discovery a total of $4,391,697; and to Community Network Grants. FY 2000 was the first year for TIF to offer the Competitive Community Networking Grants. In the initial year, a total of $18,488,336 was distributed among 36 grantees.

According to Wendy Latham, a grant administrator at TIF, "The agency has funded all 10 academic health science centers; all of the higher education institutions except the total of community colleges; and 99 percent of public districts, of which 51 percent of campuses have been funded."[20] She further commented that in FY 2001, the agency planned to target those libraries that had not yet been wired.[21]

Despite these significant gains to provide the infrastructure and the access to technology for people across the state, the agency experienced a number of internal challenges. The first stems from the fact that the agency is unique to Texas and to the United States, and thus the allocation of monies each year has been a learning process for the staff and the board. The evolving nature of the agency has led some to question the future of the agency.

The slow start for the agency did not help matters. Though TIF was created and the TIF board members were appointed in November 1995, formal operations did not begin until June 1996, when an executive director was hired. TIF did not award its first round of grants until November 15, 1996.[22]

Under the direction of this new leader, the agency and board began to award grants to the eligible entities. However, the board took the definition of "infrastructure" very literally and in essence, limited monies to providing the equipment and often did not include or cover the cost of training on how to use the new technology. This limited interpretation would later prove to be a big mistake for the agency.

In April of 2000, the executive director resigned and it was not until October 2000 that a new executive director assumed the helm. Under the new leadership, several programs have been implemented to improve the operations of the agency and restore its image in the public eye. A needs assessment process, which includes surveying grantees for their input on the operations and grant process of TIF, has been established to produce more appropriate applications and more effective results.[23] Technology working groups, composed of TIF board members, TIF staff, and individuals from the technology industry, also have been established to investigate minimum standards for scaleability and sustainable equipment for their constituencies.[24] The mission of the organization was also slightly modified "from connecting buildings to the Internet, to connecting the people who use the technology within those buildings."[25]

Barriers to Distance Learning

Before distance learning becomes the buzzword for the new millennium, it is necessary to examine its limitations. These include bandwidth issues, cost, media limitations, pedagogy, and public policy.

Broadband Access

High-speed Internet access can greatly enhance entertainment, education, workforce training, and economic development opportunities to rural Texas, as the state moves into the 21st century. Until now, the common belief has been that high-speed Internet services simply would not be available to rural Texas in the foreseeable future. Although the Internet can be accessed through a dial-up connection, the speed is extremely slow. Many websites and Web-based training programs, as well as videoconferencing, require high-speed access to be effective and meaningful to the learner. If the goal is to provide training through distance learning, a significant barrier lies in the speed of the delivery mechanism.

Policy makers have struggled with how to entice cable television and telephone companies to spend millions of dollars deploying their services in high-cost, difficult-to-serve rural areas. Promoting broadband access for all citizens is clearly necessary. However, when the cost of infrastructure is weighed against the future benefits, legitimate questions can be raised. In addition, satellite or other wireless technology may soon make cabling or other wired facilities unnecessary. All of these considerations make for a lively and contentious policy debate. Telecommunications companies do not want to be forced by the government to provide expensive cabling and infrastructure to connect rural areas, where there are insufficient economies of scale to justify the investments.[26] During the 77th Texas Legislature, much discussion centered on including technology-neutral language that would allow telecommunications and other high-speed Internet providers to utilize other means, such as satellite technology, to make high-speed Internet access available to rural areas. Legislation proposed in the session called for communications firms to answer requests for high-speed Internet in rural areas through a bidding process.[27] Along with the Texas Legislature, the Lieutenant Governor's Office, the Department of Agriculture, and the Public Utility Commission all are studying advanced communications concerns for rural Texas. Specifically, they seek to establish broadband and Internet connectivity in rural areas.

While existing phone lines can accommodate most e-commerce, Texas policy makers acknowledge that there is a growing demand for faster Internet connections in rural areas, especially if distance learning is to be realized. The phone companies and cable companies are upgrading their lines with hopes of connecting rural Texans with high-speed services. Unfortunately, they will not reach everyone in the near future. For those who have not been connected to the information superhighway, there are alternatives. The most promising is satellite or wireless service. However, satellite connections are still slower than Digital Subscriber Lines (DSL) and cable, even if they are faster than dial-up connections. Furthermore, the monthly cost of wireless service may be comparable to DSL, but the satellite dish and modem may cost customers more than a DSL modem.[28] Finally, satellite technology is limited by nature. Signals can be interrupted by storms, humidity, or clouds.[29]

There is no doubt that consumers and representatives of rural communities will continue to advocate for high-speed service in rural areas. However, thus far, the telecommunications lobby has been effective in preventing passage of any legislation that coerces telecommunications and cable firms to provide broadband access to rural residents across Texas. In this case, technology itself may have to become the equalizer through satellite services for rural areas.

Cost

While concerns regarding access continue in any discussions about distance learning, equally important will be the cost of this provision to users (students) and the providers, whether they are individuals, corporations, colleges, or universities. Coopers and Lybrand, a consulting firm, in an analysis of the cost of producing a distance learning course in 1998, concluded that software that captures the many facets of the learning process and that can substitute for campus-based learning is not yet on the market.[30] Coopers and Lybrand estimated a cost of approximately $3 million for software and an additional $500,000 annually for maintenance to produce a high-quality distance learning course. This cost estimate does not include marketing and distribution or the cost of faculty. From the students' point of view, aside from basic tuition, there may be additional hardware costs, software costs, Internet connection and subscription costs, paper costs, books, and so on. The cost to the low-income user becomes unaffordable very quickly.

Limitations of Media for Delivery

No single distance learning system can meet the essential requirements of a training program. Training professionals have found that technology is not the answer for every problem. Numerous criteria determine the type or combination of distance learning system that is appropriate for a particular need. Each type of delivery method has its own advantages and disadvantages, as illustrated in Table 2.1.[31]

Table 2.1
Advantages and Disadvantages of Various Media for Delivery of Distance Learning

Medium	Advantages	Disadvantages
Videoconferencing. Television screens at all sites with camera and microphones to transmit visual images and audio. Trainer and participants can see and hear each other at multiple sites. Data and graphics can also be transmitted.	Two-way video, audio, and data; very interactive.	Cost to purchase equipment can be high; consider renting.
Desktop videoconference. Same as group videoconference, but participants sit at a computer with camera and microphone attached. Can see trainer, other participants, and data on computer screen and hear/participate in all conversations.	Participants can take part at their own desks; very interactive.	New technology; not readily available, but low cost.
Internet, Intranet, email. Training via email or the Internet. Training material sent to participants online; they read and respond via online discussions (one-way: copy each other on responses, or two-way: use a "live chat" function and "talk" at same time online).	Easy to design and implement; very effective for small classes.	Must have email or Internet access; need accountability for participation.
Computer disk/CD-ROM/laser disc. Mail out with course. Participants respond to trainer via phone, fax, email, or computer disk.	Simple to implement; inexpensive.	Need good course design; participants must be motivated to finish.
Satellite. Training program delivered via satellite link. Participants watch, then respond via phone, fax or email.	Good for short, informational-type courses with wide audiences.	Can be boring if not designed correctly; old method.
Two-way satellite. Television cameras at participants' end offer two-way video and audio. Similar to videoconferencing, but with different equipment.	Two-way video and audio; very interactive.	Very expensive; rarely done.
One-way satellite with an electronic keypad as a response tool for participants. They respond to the trainer by selecting their choice on the keypad. Answers are displayed on a TV screen at all sites.	More interactive than one-way satellite w/o keypad; participants prefer it.	Cost goes up with keypads; installation issues.

22

Cable/broadcast television. Same as one-way satellite/ microwave, but with cable television. Instructor teaches from a TV station. Materials sent in advance; participants respond via phone, fax, or email. Used by many universities for home study.	Good for short, informational-type courses with wide audiences.	Can be boring if not designed correctly; old method.
Videotape. Mail out videotape with course. Participants respond to trainer via phone fax, or email.	Simple to implement; inexpensive.	Need good course design; participants must be motivated to finish; old method.
Printed materials. Send printed materials with course lesson. Participants mail responses back. Trainer provides feedback via mail or phone. This is the model commonly used in correspondence courses.	Simple to implement; inexpensive.	Need good course design; participants must be motivated to finish; old method.
Audioconference. Training through telephone connection. Audio only; no visual. Send pre-work via mail, email, or fax in advance. Discuss as a group in an audioconference with multiple sites.	Inexpensive and relatively easy to set up.	No visual cues.
Audiographics. Computer and phone linkage. Participants listen and respond to the trainer via speakerphone, while observing computer screen training. They respond with a writing whiteboard linked to their computer screens. All sites linked "live" at same time. All linkage via phone lines.	Includes visual and auditory components; very interactive.	Requires purchase of software and whiteboard; need expert to set up.
Audiotape. Mail out audiotape with course. Participants respond to trainer via phone, fax, or email, or they make own audiotape response.	Simple to implement; inexpensive.	Need good course design; participants must be motivated to finish; old method
Voice mail. Trainer sends out material in advance, then asks participants to leave responses on voice mail. Trainer responds to each via voice mail. Can also set up so all participants hear each other's responses and have discussion.	Easy to implement; low cost; good for short classes.	Need good course design; must install voice mail.
Radio. Course is broadcast via radio waves. Participants respond via mail or phone. Used in Australia to teach students in the outback.	Can reach many people across vast distances.	Outdated method; new alternatives have replaced it.

Virtual reality. Participants placed in a realistic situation to learn a new skill where they must respond verbally, visually, and kinesthetically. Involves computer simulation of some type. A flight simulator is a good example. Other equipment includes virtual reality technology.	Taps into all senses and learning styles; exciting experience.	Technology very new; costs very high; not yet readily available.

Source: The State of Texas Human Resources Management, *The Report on Distance Learning* (2000).

Table 2.1 provides just one perspective on different delivery mechanisms. Other ways to look at these media include from learner perspectives, type of content, or group learning/individual learning perspective.

Policy Barriers

Policy makers and elected officials in particular tend to view the digital divide as an opportunity to pass legislation focusing on their districts or a particular segment of the population. Federal policies on workforce development are spread across the Departments of Labor, Education, and Commerce. Attempts to coordinate the efforts by these agencies to address access issues have been uneven. The incongruity is simply a result of different agencies implementing different policies for different industry groups and occupations. In addition, because implementation takes place at the state and local levels, access to training differs from state to state and from city to city. "The state is the system designer, a service provider, a funding sponsor, a partner, and a regulator. In fact, its many missions sometimes even contradict one another."[32] In this light, public policy is failing to bridge gaps across all areas of the country. A critical role for the federal government should be to streamline the current "patchwork" of workforce development services it provides. The need to build a comprehensive workforce system is crucial to addressing the efficiency of public sector programs as they vary across the states.[33]

Successful Programs

Despite the barriers to implementing distance learning technology, successful programs do exist. Numerous programs highlight people and communities grappling with access issues. Programs targeting youth, low-income households, and the disabled are currently available. Economic development and educational opportunities are determining factors of income, poverty, and employment rates. These factors are pervasive among the most challenging populations served by the workforce system. Most of the issues affecting rural areas are also repeated among underserved populations in the urban areas. If rural areas are not provided access to education and economic development, they will continue to suffer the effects of low income and unemployment.

From a public policy perspective, one of the biggest contributions government can make to workforce development is to take advantage of and implement the wealth of knowledge and technology accumulated by the military. The National Guard Bureau (NGB) has been designated by Congress as the executive agent to conduct the NGB Distributive Training Technology Project (DTTP). This effort is a distributive learning (DL) project designed to meet the increasing educational and training needs required to ensure National Guard troop readiness. In addition, the learning and information delivery system devised for readiness purposes will be used to provide guardsmen and members of their communities broad access to education, training, and information for development of new skills, lifelong learning, and enhanced quality of life.

The DTTP includes the development, operation, and maintenance of linked distance learning centers in state-designated facilities. The NGB is responsible for overall design and implementation of the network, software, equipment, installation, integration, and courseware availability. The program has the additional responsibility of establishing and promoting civil and governmental shared usage of the DL sites on a space-available, reimbursable basis.

The core business concept of the DTTP is the idea of public-private partnerships through shared usage. By sharing the costs of operating these technology-supported learning centers, each site can become financially self-sustaining. Revenue generated through shared use of equipment and services can offset operational and maintenance costs while providing the sites with state-of-the-art technology.[34]

Clearly, programs such as DTTP are bridging the geographical divide through distance learning techniques. It would be advantageous to emulate these ideas in the civilian sector so that a comprehensive training plan can be achieved. Table 2.2 illustrates applications of distance training using diverse technologies, including online courses, live interactive video teletraining, electronic coaching, and video satellite broadcasting.

Table 2.2
Organizations Meeting the Challenge through Distance Learning

Organization	Function	Headquarters	Number of Trainees	Geographic Training Area	Distance Learning Tool Used
U.S.Army Intelligence Corps	Military Training	Fort Huachuaca, Arizona	3,000 active and reserve soldiers	Worldwide	WWW, print
SBC Communications	Telecommunications	San Antonio, Texas	120,000	Worldwide	Classroom. videoconferencing, desktop CBT
MCI WorldCom	Telecommunications	Clinton, Mississippi	NA	United States, Canada	WBT
GAO	Audit	Washington, D.C.	4,500	Nationwide	Videoconferencing, interactive television, email, CBT
Reseau INTERACTION Network	Consulting in training at a distance	Ottawa, Ontario	Fluid workforce: 20-60 per year	Mainly North America	Audio conferencing, WBT, videoconferencing
U.S. RIS	Tax admission	Washington, D.C.	105,000	Nationwide	Video teletraining, online courses
FORDSTAR	Auto	Dearborn, Michigan	215,000	North America	Videoconferencing, CD-ROM, multimedia classroom
American Red Cross	Disaster relief	Washington, D.C.	Over 1.3 million	Mainland United States	Internet and Intranet, interactive television
U.S. Postal Service	Mail delivery	Washington, D.C.	800,000	Nationwide	Audiographics, satellite, PBS videotapes, CD-ROM, WBT

Source: Adapted from L. Zane Berge, *Sustaining Distance Training* (San Francisco: Jossey-Bass, 2001), pp. xv-xxv.

Recommendations Made by the Public Utility Commission of Texas (PUC)

Others in Texas have been examining rural equity issues. Figuring the most prominently in this endeavor has been the Public Utility Commission.[35] The PUC conducted a study entitled "Availability of Advanced Services in Rural and High Cost Areas," which recommended the following policies to help resolve problems of rural Texas in accessing advanced services:

Implement technology neutrality—encourage the deployment of advanced services to rural Texans in a technology-neutral and cost-effective manner.

Avoid excessive regulation—if regulation is necessary, it should be the least intrusive means available.

Encourage local solutions—policies that encourage local solutions are more likely to result in the efficient use of resources and better meet the needs of rural communities.

Avoid "one-size-fits-all" solutions—develop a "tool kit approach" that allows communities to select the program that best fits their needs. The differing capabilities of broadband technologies do not always provide the best answer in all locations and circumstances. As an example, consumers in remote areas may be more cost-effectively served by fixed wireless or satellite services rather than by existing telecommunications or cable infrastructure.

Promote "demand aggregation"— join small customers (e.g., local school districts, local government entities, small businesses, and individual residents) interested in broadband services into a single customer that is large enough to warrant private investment in providing the service.

 Facilitate *"anchor tenancy"*—utilize large consumers of telecommunications services (local government, schools, and libraries) to guarantee a certain level of consumption, thus mitigating the risk of making the relatively high fixed investment.

Encourage community networks—expand community network initiatives undertaken by TIF to encourage participation by other than existing TIF stakeholders.

Provide tax incentives—offer tax relief for companies agreeing to provide advanced services in rural areas.

Deploy fiber optic cables in state's rights of way—adopt a policy that allows the State of Texas to contract with a private advanced services provider to install and maintain a public/private fiber optic network along the state's highway rights of way. This network, in turn, could be leased to providers of broadband services.

Recommendations and Conclusions

The application of distance learning for education and training in this decade will continue to be relevant to development and planning of a wider delivery strategy for workforce services. Distance learning has the ability to connect communities of learners and teachers in various locations. The promises of distance learning are limited only by the imagination and capacity of the people who participate in it and benefit from it. Access to that promise should not be limited to the wealthy, or those who live in information-rich urban areas. Skills, knowledge, and support to use the tools should be provided to the many citizens who need education and training enable them to escape from traps of deprivation. To benefit the many, we must get some things right about online education, at both the state and local levels.

Recommendation 2.1: As a matter of state policy, Texas should promote effective access to information technology for all Texans. Universal access needs to be a fundamental public policy concern in this arena.

Recommendation 2.2: Texas state agencies should implement the specific recommendations of the Texas PUC made in its January 2001 study, "Availability of Advanced Services in Rural and High Cost Areas." The Texas PUC has taken a leadership position in this arena with thoughtful and informed recommendations that deserve further consideration and action by the State of Texas.

Recommendation 2.3: The State of Texas should allow local governments to compete for grants from the TIF. This measure would open greater flexibility for local governmental entities with the initiative and commitment to pursue ICT access for their areas.

Recommendation 2.4: Texas should allow cities and counties to fund telecommunications-related initiatives by giving them the authority to issue bonds or increase local sales taxes for such projects.[36] Rural Texas needs the same level of ICT access available to individuals in urban areas if its economy and workforce development are to remain healthy.

Recommendation 2.5: To promote access to distance learning, the State of Texas should require providers of telecommunications and Internet services to make special provisions (such as free supply of appliances, connections, etc.) for marginalized groups so that they can benefit from distance learning courses. Enlisting the support of private vendors who benefit from public policy decisions to assist marginalized groups in rural areas would help widen access to ICT.

Many barriers exist in using information technologies to implement workforce service delivery strategies. Various digital divides limit the effectiveness of workforce strategies, especially in rural areas. Rural communities in Texas have been the focus of the workforce system and distance learning is emerging as a possible alternative to promote skills training in these communities. Distance learning has proven to be cost-effective in addressing geographical divide issues. Improvements in pedagogy also offer promising solutions in the delivery of distance learning programs. Furthermore, distance learning provides increased flexibility and access to the learner.

Texas has consistently promoted the development of distance learning as a public policy priority. The Texas Infrastructure Fund seeks to connect rural Texas and provide necessary conditions for distance learning to occur.

Several barriers limit the effectiveness of distance learning. Public policy needs to coordinate efforts to address these barriers and to promote broadband access. The issue of how to bring broadband technology to rural areas is currently under debate, especially whether or not telecommunications and cable providers should be forced to provide access in rural areas. Overcoming barriers to provide broadband access to rural Texas is necessary to make workforce training initiatives effective. Rural areas are integral parts of Texas, and the ability to train rural workers through technology is dependent on the availability of adequate technology in those areas.

Notes

[1] Public Utility Regulatory Act, TX. UTIL. CODE ANN., Section 51.001(g) (Vernon 1998 and Supp. 2000), as cited in Public Utility Commission of Texas, *Report to the 77th Texas Legislature: Availability of Advanced Services in Rural and High Cost Areas* (Austin, Tex., January 2001).

[2] Gary Chapman, "Industry Needs New Take on the 'Digital Divide,'" *Austin American-Statesman*, (February 23, 2001).

[3] William Galston, "The U.S. Rural Economy in Historical and Global Context," in *Back to Shared Prosperity: The Growing Inequality of Wealth and Income in America,* ed. Ray Marshall (Armonk, NY: M. E. Sharpe, 2000).

[4] Ibid.

[5] Ibid.

[6] "From Digital Divide to Digital Opportunity: The Importance of Bridging the Digital Divide." The White House. Online. Available: http://clinton4.nara.gov/WH/New/digitaldivide/digital3.html.

[7] Galston, "The U.S. Rural Economy in Historical and Global Context," pp. 387-388.

[8] Mary Ann Zerh, "Rural Connections," *Education Week,* vol. 20, no. 35 (May 10, 2001).

[9] See National Center for Education Statistics, U.S. Department of Education. Online. Available: http://nces.ed.gov/pubs98. Accessed: June 30, 2002.

[10] Center for Public Policy Priorities, *Working but Poor* (Austin, Tex., March 1999).

[11] C. Blurton, *Human Development: Information and Communication Technologies and Social Processes* (New York: United Nations Development Program, 2000), pp. 46-50.

[12] Daniel Minoli, *Distance Learning Technology and Applications* (Norwood, Mass: Artech House, Inc., 1996), p. 175.

[13] The State of Texas Human Resources Management, *The Report on Distance Learning* (Austin, Tex., 2000).

[14] The Telecommunications Infrastructure Fund (TIF) Mission Statement. Online. Available. http://www.tifb.state.tx.us. Accessed: May 1, 2001.

[15] The TIF Board Annual Report (January 2001), p. 3. Online. Available: http://www.tifb.state.tx.us/other/Annual%20Report%20Jan15.00.doc. Accessed: May 2, 2001.

[16] Ibid., p. 12.

[17] "Texas Libraries Receive Technology Funds" March 1, 1999 (press release). Online. Available: http://www.tifb.state.tx.us/grantloan/LibraryInfo/LB3PressRel.htm. Accessed: May 2, 2001.

[18] Email from Whitney Sklar on behalf of Sam Tessen, executive director, Telecommunications Infrastructure Fund Board, November 27, 2000, as cited in Public Utility Commission of Texas, *Report to the 77th Texas Legislature*.

[19] The Telecommunications Infrastructure Fund (TIF) Board Annual Report (January 2001), p. 55. Online. Available: http://www.tifb.state.tx.us/other/Annual%20Report%20Jan15.00.doc. Accessed: May 2, 2001.

[20] Interview by Tina Ghabel with Wendy Latham, grant administrator for the Telecommunications Infrastructure Fund (TIF), May 1, 2001.

[21] Ibid.

[22] The TIF Board Annual Report (January 2001), p. 3. Online. Available: http://www.tifb.state.tx.us/other/Annual%20Report%20Jan15.00.doc. Accessed: May 2, 2001.

[23] Ibid.

[24] Ibid., p. 49.

[25] Ibid., pp. 49–50.

[26] Vikas Bajaj, "Bills Seek to Close Rural Divide," *Dallas Morning News* (April 6, 2001).

[27] David Sibley, Relating to the Regulation of Telecommunications Services, Feeds and Programs. Texas Senate Bill 1783, 77th Legislature, 2001.

[28] Vikas Bajaj, "Bills Seek to Close Rural Divide."

[29] Burt S. Barnow and Christopher T. King, "Information and Communications Technology and Workforce Service Delivery: A Comparative Look" in *Global Restructuring, Training and the Social Dialogue*, edited by Torkel Alfthan, Christopher T. King, and Gyorgy Sziraczki (Geneva, Switzerland: International Labor Organization, 2001).

[30] Coopers and Lybrand, *Transformation of Higher Education in the Digital Age* (Boston, 1998).

[31] The State of Texas Human Resources Management, *The Report on Distance Learning*.

[32] Texas Comptroller of Public Accounts, "Texas at Work: Developing an Information Age Workforce," in *Education, Excellence, Efficiency, Effectiveness: Report of the e-Texas Commission* (Austin, Tex., December 2000), p. 148.

[33] Christopher T. King, "Federalism and Workforce Policy Reform," *Publius: The Journal of Federalism,* vol. 29, no. 2 (Spring, 1999), pp. 53-71.

[34] Distributive Training Technology Project, Army National Guard, 111 South George Mason Drive, Arlington, Va. 22204-1382.

[35] Recommendations from the Public Utility Commission of Texas, *Report to the 77th Texas Legislature.*

[36] Tom Powers, *TIF: Progress and Future.* Keynote address to the Texas Distance Learning Association Conference, 1999.

Chapter 3. The Importance of Pedagogy to the Future Success of Computer-Based Training and Education

The Promise of Information Technology to Revolutionize Learning

Computer-based technologies hold great promise both for increasing access to knowledge and for promoting learning. Computer-based education and training offer potential for workers and the unemployed everywhere to achieve the skills necessary to become and remain gainfully employed. The concept of using the computer to deliver education is powerful. Learning can become available anytime, anywhere, to anyone with access to a computer. Instruction can be individualized and truly learner centered. Computer-based instruction can be self-paced. Patterns of errors can be recognized and tutorial sequences can be tailored to the needs of individual learners. The Internet offers rich potential for inquiry-driven learning as well as an effective means to connect with experts outside of traditional schools and classrooms. Computers can deliver information in multiple languages or assist visually impaired users with audible assistance to navigate through a program. Information technology provides advanced communication tools for classroom presentation and for improving other communications between instructors and learners and among learners. Computers offer possibilities for new methods and measures to assess what people know and are able to do.

Despite the enormous potential, good software applications in education and training that are based on a full understanding of principles of learning have not yet become the norm. As researchers from the National Research Council recently concluded: "Software developers are generally driven more by the game and play market than by the learning potential of their products."[1] A former U.S. secretary of education similarly has argued that most so-called computer-based educational programs promote glitz, glamour, and graphics instead of serious learning.[2] Considering that the computer was recognized over 40 years ago for its promising application to education and training, his perspective begs the question: Why aren't serious computer-based education programs ubiquitous in 2001? The dearth of computer-based instructional programs using advanced pedagogical approaches can be attributed to a number of factors, described later in this chapter.

Computer-based instructional programs, regardless of their applications, can be divided into three components: pedagogic approach, technology, and content. *Pedagogy* refers to the teaching principles that underlie the program and address questions about how people learn. Technology comprises the computer hardware, software, and networking capabilities and is the medium through which courses are delivered. Content is the information about the subject that is being taught by the computer-based program, be it geometry, accounting, biology, or workplace-specific tasks.

Pedagogic approach is at the core of effective computer-based instructional programs. The issue of pedagogic effectiveness is especially critical for low-skilled adult learners, including under- or unemployed workers, participants in welfare-to-work programs, and individuals whose skills have become obsolete. The United States is rapidly becoming a knowledge economy in which basic skills such as using computers and other technologies, interpersonal skills, working effectively in teams, problem solving, and communication are critical for every employee—from entry-level workers to the chief executive. In knowledge economies, people must continually increase their learning power in order to sustain their earning power.[3] Education via the computer may be a solution to this demand because courses can be taken anytime, anywhere, and can be as effective as traditional methods of teaching and learning. However, these educational opportunities may not be accessible to individuals without computers and Internet connections.

The Effectiveness of Computer-Based Instruction

Recent research has confirmed what many have long believed about the effectiveness of computers for education: computer-based instruction works. Learners who use computers can learn more in less time. With well-designed learning programs, student achievement increases; students undertake more ambitious projects; and students have a more positive attitude toward classes that use computers for instruction.[4]

Computers used in education and training are helping many students who do not succeed in conventional classroom settings. Students who learn slowly can establish their own pace on a computer and benefit from the computer's infinite patience. Peer pressure and embarrassment is nearly eliminated because students cannot tell what other students are studying or how well other students are doing. Students are able to begin and complete their education based on their own schedule. For employed persons or individuals with families to care for, this may make the difference between being able to take a class or not.[5]

Computers are also expanding educational opportunities for physically impaired students. Advances in computer hardware, such as enlarged keyboards, voice recognition software, and the ability to make software programs audible, have increased access for those with visual and mobility impairments. These advances open new opportunities for instruction of the disabled.

Examples of Well-Designed Courseware

Finding examples of courseware that is mindful of pedagogic approach and effectiveness can be a difficult task. Absent an industry-wide rating system that gauges educational effectiveness, it is necessary to collect information anecdotally, from research papers, and the Internet to identify potential candidates for further study. Two entities, the EnterTech Project and Scientific Learning, offer examples of programs that are pedagogically effective.

The EnterTech Project

The EnterTech Project is a simulation-based e-learning program developed to rapidly impart the knowledge, skills, and attitudes to succeed in entry-level jobs in technology manufacturing and related industries.[6] Managed by the IC[2] Institute at The University of Texas, the project operated as a collaborative effort involving Texas businesses, educators, government, and community-based organizations. Although EnterTech integrates or blends several types of learning environments, about 70 percent of the training involves computer-based simulation of high-tech work environments in warehousing, materials handling, and assembly.[7] The curriculum's target learners are individuals in transition from welfare to work. Students learn basic employment skills such as work ethics, communication, and time management. They also receive training on tasks such as processing customer orders for computer components.

What makes the EnterTech Project different from other software programs is the careful attention staff paid to researching effective instructional and evaluation methods during the development phases. The developers of the program acknowledge that assessment and evaluation are inextricably linked to curriculum development and are essential in the development of any effective instructional program.[8] EnterTech incorporated assessment instruments into its program and used the results to make informed decisions about instructional design. The findings were compiled into a series of papers, including "Report on Assessment and Evaluation Strategies for the Learner," "Report on Evaluation Strategies for the Program," and "General Characteristics of the Target Learner."[9] The results are also summarized in a final report on the EnterTech Project.[10]

EnterTech staff researched the general characteristics of their target learners to assist in the development of appropriate and effective instructional strategies, learning activities, and materials. The target learners for Entertech were primarily women in their 20s and 30s, most of whom had children. For this population, common barriers to employment include lack of employability or "soft" skills, low basic academic skills, substance abuse, health limitations, depression, a child needing chronic medical attention, lack of dependable transportation, and inadequate child-care services. With this knowledge, EnterTech added support models into its program to assist individuals in coping with barriers. For example, individuals receive assistance in making connections to social service agencies. In addition, a "soft" skills component was included, which covers work-ready skills such as appropriate attire, communication, and time management skills.

EnterTech staff also systematically engaged the intended learners in the development process by obtaining feedback through focus groups in user testing, beta testing, and pilot site testing.

EnterTech staff researched methods used to assess student progress and program effectiveness. For the learner, the program was designed to include a combination of assessment strategies, including authentic assessments (performance in real work-related situations), portfolio assessments (ongoing collection of completed work), embedded assessments (computer assesses skill level and prescribes higher level or remedial exercises), and achievement test assessments (traditional standardized tests).[11] The program is evaluated by ongoing formative and summative evaluations.[12] The main function of formative evaluation was to identify and correct any design flaws during the development process. Summative evaluation occurs when the program is in use as intended. Summative evaluation often addresses the informational needs of program stakeholders, in this case learners, employers, funding sponsors, and program developers. EnterTech has continuously modified and improved its approach, based on lessons learned.

Scientific Learning Corporation

Scientific Learning Corporation in Berkeley, California, has developed a family of computer-based reading programs for children and adults. The programs are based on over 25 years of neuroscience research on how the brain learns. A program entitled Fast ForWord develops the fundamental language and reading skills for kids. The ReWord training program is designed to develop language and organizational skills for adults.

The research behind Scientific Learning's programs was performed by scientists at Rutgers University and the University of California at San Francisco beginning in the 1970s. The learning methods developed by these researchers were patented and Scientific Learning now holds the worldwide license. Scientific Learning Corporation was created in 1996. A year later, the company launched its first training program, Fast ForWord Language, a program that uses the Internet and a CD-ROM to develop fundamental language skills that are the building blocks for the development of reading skills.

Extensive in-house testing has shown that the reading programs have improved language and reading skills for ESL students, at-risk middle and high school students, at-risk African Americans, and children with attention deficit disorder (ADD).[13] For each of these populations, Scientific Learning ran controlled experiments and compared scores achieved on standardized, nationally normed language tests before and after training on Fast ForWord programs. For example, ESL students tested on the Test of Auditory Comprehension of Language (TACL) improved their performance from below average to average. At-risk African American students, tested on the CELF (Clinical Evaluation of Learning Fundamentals) and the TOLD (Test of Language Development) also improved their performance from below average to average.

Third-party assessments of Fast ForWord have indicated that the program is effective for some learning impaired students. In 1997, the Collier Center for Communication Disorders at the University of Texas at Dallas began using the program to treat students with language-learning impairments.[14] It found that Fast ForWord Language did not aid each child in the same skill area or to the same degree. Some children exhibited great improvement after completing the program, while others showed only minimal gains. The Center recognized the value of the program to certain learning-impaired students, but concluded that it was not a substitute for language therapy.

There is no easy way to determine how effective the programs offered by EnterTech and Scientific Learning have been for others. In fact, this author had to search their respective websites extensively to learn about the pedagogic underpinnings of the programs as well as what each company is doing to evaluate effectiveness. This illustrates a fundamental problem facing the success of computer-based education.

Unless consumers can readily assess the level of expected effectiveness for computer-based instructional programs, the market for such programs may be diminished. Society may lose the opportunity to reap the full potential of learning via the computer.

Barriers to Developing Good Programs

Knowledge about how people learn promises to unlock the vast and highly anticipated potential of computer-based education. Many companies engaged in the computer-based instruction industry have prioritized the development of subject-specific content and glamorous presentations because developing effective pedagogical techniques for computer-based learning requires large investments that may not be recoverable. Cost and other barriers to the development of effective programs have so far prevented the industry from reaching its full potential.

High Costs

Researchers recently observed that some computer-based adult basic education programs are not well designed and implemented because shortcuts were taken to avoid the expense of developing the courseware, which can easily add up to several million dollars.[15] The EnterTech Project and Scientific Learning are exceptions. They did not take shortcuts. EnterTech spent $3.5 million over three years for activities including the targeting of learner characteristics, technology infrastructure surveys, evaluation, instructional design, prototype development, production of multimedia and software code, implementation testing, learner feedback, program revisions and improvements, dissemination, and sustainability planning.[16]

This level of intensity of research and development is prohibitive in most private-sector companies, and thus many private-sector e-learning businesses are engaged in distributing curriculum through "portal" websites rather than engaging in research and development (R&D) and developing content.[17] A learning portal centralizes information about educational programs and course offerings from various locations on a single website. Examples of portals for educational programs include click2learn.com, University.com, and eMind.com. These sites help to organize a large variety of programs, but consumers will find it difficult to discern the quality of course offerings.

Developing effective pedagogic technology is an R&D activity requiring much testing and evaluation and made much more difficult because there are no universally agreed upon criteria with which to evaluate these types of programs. As an R&D activity, the most promising educational technology products we enjoy today are the result of federal government investments in R&D since the 1960s, made through the military or through agencies such as the National Science Foundation (NSF).[18]

The government has been a leader in supporting the development of pedagogical technologies. Starting in the 1960s, the U.S. military realized the value of computers for training and used them for drill-and-practice and simulation exercises.[19] Since the 1960s, federal investments funded the development of the most promising educational technologies, yet these investments were quite modest.[20] The federal government continues to fund such activities today, albeit at a low level, as a commercially viable alternative has not been found. In 1999, the United States spent about $313 billion on public K-12 education and invested less than 0.1 percent of that amount to determine what educational techniques actually work and to find ways to improve them. By contrast, the United States allocated about 23 percent of the $77 billion spent on prescription and nonprescription medications for research and development aimed at discovering new drugs and evaluating their effectiveness.[21]

U.S. Patent Law

The process by which a patent is obtained under U.S. patent law may not provide adequate protection for investors in pedagogic technology. According to R. Anthony Reese of The University of Texas Law School, the value of patents for software is very low because the economic life cycle of most software programs is quite short, about two to five years, and a patent may not even become effective within this time period. It currently takes an average of two years to file for a patent. Litigation or infringement challenges may add two to three years. If the company seeking patent protection must pursue litigation to recover damages, costs will increase further and their investment may never be recovered.[22]

Lack of Consensus on Evaluation Criteria

The evaluation criteria used by consumers guide producers of instructional programs. If producers of computer-based education programs do not know the criteria purchasers use to evaluate programs, incentives that would otherwise draw producers into a market keep them away.

Linda Roberts, former director of the Office of Educational Technology at the U.S. Department of Education, acknowledges the difficulty in evaluating computer-based instructional programs.[23] She agrees that there is no single agreed upon set of criteria that are used to evaluate these programs. For computer-based programs used in K-12 education, educators look to measures such as changes in student performance in standardized test scores, increases in graduation rates, and reductions in absenteeism rates. Mindy Jackson, project manager at the EnterTech Project, suggests using similar criteria for training products, such as standardized testing, promotion rates, and absenteeism rates.[24] Alternatively, industry researchers Wilson, Golas, and O'Neil argue that design is critical. Computer-based instruction offers significant advantages over traditional classroom instruction in assessment, diagnosis, and prescription. They argue that one of the surest ways to determine the quality of a computer-based instructional program is to examine the feedback for each possible alternative error response that a student may make to a given question. Then determine whether the feedback adequately addresses the errors that a student makes.[25] The quality of the diagnosis and feedback process is just one of the areas in which any computer-based program needs to be judged. As long as agreement is not reached on criteria to properly evaluate computer-based instruction, advances in pedagogic techniques for computer-based learning will be slow in coming.

Learning from the Market for Textbooks

Another potential barrier to the development of pedagogic technology is market dynamics. If the textbook market for K-12 education is any indicator, the quality of instructional software is in doubt. The incentive structure driving the development of textbooks is perverse. According to a representative of the NSF, a textbook has a slim chance of survival in the national textbook market unless it conforms to the curriculum standards set by California, Texas, and Virginia, all of which use centralized statewide selection and procurement processes for textbook acquisition.[26] Curriculum standards are content driven. Therefore, textbooks are often written to deliver content without sufficient consideration of the way people learn. This situation has led to widespread criticism of the quality of textbooks; although they cover the content of the subject, they are often not pedagogically effective. At this point, it is unclear whether the perverse characteristics of the textbook market will carry over into the market for instructional software. The important lesson to draw from this example is that criteria developed to evaluate the quality and effectiveness of any computer-based instructional program should include pedagogic effectiveness.

Recommendations

Well-designed computer programs developed for instruction are a small minority of the vast selection of currently available instructional programs. Given the potential of the computer to revolutionize the training and education industry and the tremendous benefits to be gained by those who have found it difficult to succeed in traditional classroom settings, more needs to be done to improve and verify the pedagogic effectiveness of computer-based educational programs. The situation is a classic case of market breakdown. The rewards are simply inadequate to offset the high costs of developing good programs with high-quality, effective pedagogy, nor do consumers have adequate information to judge the effectiveness of products available to them. The following suggestions are made to help remedy these problems.

Recommendation 3-1: The federal government should increase research and development (R&D) funding to support the development and dissemination of effective pedagogical instruction. Support for continuing research and development is critical to produce highly effective programs. Such federal support in the past has come through funding from the National Science Foundation and the military. The federal government should increase funds available to universities and others for research and development. The EnterTech Project would not have been possible without substantial financial support from the Texas governor's office. Scientific Learning is notable for the substantial university-led research that underlies its learning programs. Increasing access to effective pedagogical techniques can reduce the costs of development, thereby greatly increasing the number and diversity of effective educational programs for the computer.

Recommendation 3-2: The federal government should establish a standards body to develop and publish criteria for pedagogical effectiveness and for use in rating instructional programs. The federal government could establish a standards body, perhaps through the National Research Council, to determine criteria for pedagogical effectiveness and to rate instructional programs. Such a standards body could be composed of cognitive psychologists, academicians, and other experts, with the input of representatives from education and training providers, software developers, instructional technologists, and others with relevant expertise.

Recommendation 3-3: Educational institutions and the public sector should increase the demand for pedagogically effective programs. The market for computer-based adult basic education and job skill programs is unlikely to produce innovation in pedagogic techniques based solely on overall growth in the economy and expansion of the Internet. Therefore, a vital role that the public sector can play is to increase demand for these programs in public schools and universities by increasing the funds they have available to purchase, implement, monitor, and maintain computer-based instructional programs. Computer-based instruction with effective pedagogy merits increased investment by creating incentives to promote its spread via private markets.

Notes

[1] John D. Bransford, Ann L. Brown, and Rodney R. Cocking, eds., *How People Learn: Brain, Mind, Experience and School.* Chapter 9, "Technology to Support Learning" (Washington, D.C.: National Research Council, 1999), pp. 194-218.

[2] William J. Bennett and David Galernter, "Improving Education with Technology: Why Two Former Skeptics Have Joined the Revolution," *Education Week* (March 4, 2001), p. 68.

[3] Lois S. Wilson, Katharine Golas, and Harold F. O'Neil, Jr., "Basic Skills Training," in *Training and Retraining: A Handbook for Business, Industry, Government, and the Military,* ed. Sigmund Tobias and J. D. Fletcher. (New York: Macmillan Reference USA, 2000), p. 492.

[4] See U.S. Department of Education, *E-Learning: Putting a World-Class Education at the Fingertips of All Children* (Washington, D.C., December 2000), p. 21. Also, see John D. Bransford, Ann L. Brown, and Rodney R. Cocking, eds., *How People Learn: Brain, Mind, Experience and School*, chapter 9, pp. 194-218.

[5] Wilson et al., "Basic Skills Training," pp. 514-515.

[6] E-Learning and Training Labs, *The EnterTech Project: Changing Learning and Lives* (Austin, Tex.: IC² Institute, The University of Texas at Austin, 2002), p. 1.

[7] Ibid., p. 38.

[8] Melinda Jackson, "Report on Assessment and Evaluation Strategies for the Learner." Online. Available: http://www.utexas.edu/depts/ic2/et/eval/stueval.html. Accessed: April 24, 2001.

[9] EnterTech, *EnterTech Reports*. Online. Available: http://www.utexas.edu/depts/ic2/et/report.html. Accessed: February 4, 2002.

[10] E-Learning and Training Labs, *The EnterTech Project.*

[11] EnterTech, *Report on Assessment and Evaluation Strategies for the Learner* (online).

[12] EnterTech, *Report on Evaluation Strategies for the Program* (online).

[13] Scientific Learning Corporation, *Results*. Online. Available: http://www.scientificlearning.com/scie/index.php3?main=results_intro&cartid=. Accessed: April 22, 2001.

[14] Shannon Turner and Donise W. Pearson, "Fast ForWord Learning Intervention Programs: Four Case Studies," *Texas Journal of Audiology and Speech Pathology*, vol. 13 (Spring/Summer 1999). Online.

Available: http://www.scientificlearning.com/scie/index.php3?main=abs/sciepublished&cartid=. Accessed: April 22, 2001.

[15] Wilson et al., "Basic Skills Training," p. 515.

[16] E-Learning and Training Labs, *The EnterTech Project*, p. 20.

[17] *E-Learning Magazine: Content, Technology, Services.* Online. Available: www.elearningmag.com. Accessed: March 20, 2001.

[18] Office of Technology Assessment, "Power On: New Tools for Teaching and Learning, Summary" (Washington, D.C.: Government Printing Office, 1989), p. 23.

[19] Andrew S. Gibbons and Peter G. Fairweather, "Computer-Based Instruction," in *Training and Retraining: A Handbook for Business, Industry, Government, and the Military*, ed. Sigmund Tobias and J. D. Fletcher. (New York: Macmillan Reference USA, 2000), p. 411.

[20] Office of Technology Assessment, *Power On*, p. 23.

[21] Web-Based Education Commission, *The Power of the Internet for Learning: Moving from Promise to Practice* (December 2000). Online. Available: http://www.webcommission.org. Accessed: March 22, 2001.

[22] Class presentation by R. Anthony Reese, assistant professor, University of Texas Law School, at the IC2 Institute, The University of Texas at Austin, February 20, 2001.

[23] Interview by Kathryn Supinski with Linda Roberts, former director, Office of Educational Technology, U.S. Department of Education, Austin, Texas, February 26, 2001.

[24] Interview by Kathryn Supinski with Mindy Jackson, project manager, EnterTech, Austin, Texas, February 21, 2001.

[25] Wilson et al., "Basic Skills Training," p. 516.

[26] Interview by Kathryn Supinski with Nora Sabelli, National Science Foundation, Austin, Texas, March 6, 2001.

Chapter 4. Job Finding and Matching through the Internet

Introduction

The Internet is having sweeping effects on labor markets worldwide, many of which are still unfolding.[1] It is dramatically transforming labor markets, altering the way job seekers look for and secure employment as well as the methods that employers use to recruit, screen, and hire workers.[2] Although there were more than 2,000 Internet-based job search sites in 2000, little is known of their effects on labor markets.[3] Government workforce agencies are attempting to understand and adapt to this rapid move toward the Internet in order to improve the delivery of workforce services to customers. For decades, state workforce systems have connected employers with needed workers through traditional techniques. Widespread introduction of advanced information technology, including the Internet, provides opportunities to meet the labor market needs of employers and job seekers more effectively and more efficiently. It also offers mechanisms for doing so more equitably.

The New Economy is characterized by nearly instant access to information and knowledge. The Internet provides users almost everywhere with information 24 hours a day, seven days a week. As the vice president of analytical services for NetRatings recently observed, "The Web is now an integral part of the average person's daily life. People are conducting a wide range of their day-to-day activities online, such as banking, tax filing, sending invitations, shopping and corresponding with friends and family."[4]

Access to the Internet has grown dramatically in recent years. Responses to the December 1998 Current Population Survey (CPS) revealed that nearly half of all United States households had a computer in the house, while a third had Internet access from the home.[5] As of December 1998, more people reported using the Internet from the home (23.6 percent) than from work (12.0 percent) or from other locations (4.5 percent).[6] According to the January 2001 NetRatings monthly report, the rate of Internet use reached 60 percent in the United States, with more than 168 million people having Web access either in the home or in the workplace.[7] These numbers reflect overlap of Internet users who have access to the Internet from both work and home. Viewed separately, at-work Internet penetration accounted for 14 percent of all Web access, or 41 million workers, while home Internet access comprised 58 percent, or 162 million users.[8] Access on this scale was barely imagined by the general public a mere decade ago.

The Internet and online labor exchange that it facilitates can have a number of possible effects on labor markets in the United States and worldwide. First, *access* to labor market information and opportunities may be greatly expanded by the Internet. This is true for various groups—for example, minorities and women, those living in rural areas—as well as for employers. Second, the availability of online services may expand the *use* of labor exchange services generally. More job seekers and employers may conduct market searches because it is now possible to do so more easily and more quickly. Third, the Internet may broaden market *scope*, allowing both job seekers and employers who were once constrained to scanning markets locally to do so on a national or even international scale. A larger share of the nation's workforce may be exposed to competitive pressures from global markets as a result.[9] Fourth, the use of online labor exchange may also increase the *effectiveness* and the *efficiency* of searches. Both job seekers and employers can more quickly search more opportunities and at lower cost than with more traditional means. This helps employers, who need to find and hire workers with the right skills in a timely fashion, to be successful. Some experts theorize that increased use of online services could actually yield "choosier" workers, higher reservation wages (the wage at which a worker will accept a job), and longer unemployment duration.[10] Fifth, the use of such services may also promote *equity* of access and of outcomes, particularly for minority job seekers, and for small to medium enterprises that lack the resources to maintain a complete human resources department. The Internet does not care about the color of a job seeker's skin or the size of an organization's wallet. Finally, the introduction of online labor exchange may alter the mix of job search techniques used by job seekers, either displacing or adding to more traditional means. While there is evidence on some of these effects, much of it is preliminary. For others, very little is known as yet.

This chapter examines more traditional and newer online job search methods and what is known about their effectiveness. It also reviews some of the major automated labor exchange sites. Finally, it offers conclusions and provides policy recommendations regarding online labor exchange and related efforts.

Traditional Methods of Job Search

Labor exchange ultimately encompasses the interactions of employers attempting to find and hire the right workers and job seekers trying to identify and secure what they view as the best jobs given their education, training, and work experience. Job search patterns thus vary with the needs and desires of these two sets of customers in the labor market, as well as with the means available to them to conduct their searches.

Before the Internet explosion, job seekers were limited to traditional methods of searching for a job, such as referrals from private agencies or public employment agency services, school placement offices, and help-wanted ads in newspapers. Other traditional search methods included contacting an employer directly, contacting friends or relatives, sending out resumes or filling out applications, checking union hiring halls or professional registers, or using other active search methods. In response to the open-ended question, "How do you usually hear or learn about companies that are looking for people to hire?" the most common resources for finding jobs in the mid-1960s were friends and relatives (55 percent), newspapers (53 percent), and the employment services (34 percent), as indicated in Table 4.1.[11] The relative rankings of these job search methods were about the same for males and females.

Table 4.1
Usual Sources of Information about Job Openings for Blue-Collar Workers, 1966

Source	Percentage Using These Sources		
	All	Male	Female
Friends and relatives	55	53	60
Newspapers	53	54	48
Employment service	34	31	49
Other workers	15	17	7
Unions	8	10	---
Companies	9	10	6
Radio	5	6	---
Private agencies	3	3	3
Other	3	3	2
Number of cases	309	248	61

Source: Harold L. Sheppard and A. Harvey Belitsky, *The Job Hunt: Job-Seeking Behavior of Unemployed Workers in a Local Economy* (Baltimore: The Johns Hopkins University Press, 1966), p. 44.

When researchers asked respondents specifically whether or not they used each of several techniques, the results for the most popular techniques did not change significantly. Job seekers ranked newspaper ads (88 percent), employment services (84 percent), and friends and relatives (77 percent) as the most popular techniques of finding a job (see Table 4.2).

Table 4.2
Percentage of Blue-Collar Workers Using Selected Job-Finding Techniques, 1966

Job-Finding Technique	Percentage Using these Sources		
	All	Male	Female
Newspaper ads	88	88	87
Out-of-town papers	11	13	2
Employment Service	84	84	84
Friends and relatives	77	81	62
Company hiring gate	72	76	56
Government agencies (as employers)	27	31	11
Unions	20	24	5
Religious, welfare organizations, etc.	18	21	8
Private employment agencies	17	19	7
Number of cases	300	239	61

Source: Harold L. Sheppard and A. Harvey Belitsky, *The Job Hunt: Job-Seeking Behavior of Unemployed Workers in a Local Economy* (Baltimore: Johns Hopkins University Press, 1966), p. 62.

Job search methods varied by type of work. Blue-collar job seekers reported that the best sources for finding jobs were direct application to a company (33 percent) and the state employment service (31 percent). Interestingly, they reported that friends and relatives (26 percent), newspaper ads (17 percent), and private employment agencies (42 percent) were some of the *worst* ways to find employment (see Table 4.3).[12]

Table 4.3
Blue-Collar Workers' Evaluations of Job-Finding Sources and Techniques, 1966

Job-Finding Technique	Best Way (%)			Worst Way (%)		
	All	Male	Female	All	Male	Female
Direct application to company	33	34	29	11	11	10
State Employment Service	31	26	47	15	15	18
Friends and relatives	11	13	5	26	25	34
Newspaper ads	8	9	5	17	18	15
Unions	8	10	2	26	26	29
Private employment agencies	4	4	6	42	47	31
Religious, welfare organizations, etc.	1	---	5	37	39	36
Others; don't know	4	3	---	8	8	8
Number of cases	304	242	62	304	242	62

Source: Harold L. Sheppard and A. Harvey Belitsky, *The Job Hunt: Job-Seeking Behavior of Unemployed Workers in a Local Economy* (Baltimore: Johns Hopkins University Press, 1966), p. 62.

46

Research on trends in job search methods used from 1970 through 1992 indicates a significant increase in the percentages of job seekers using newspaper and other advertisements and fewer job seekers using public employment agencies.[13]

Newspaper classified ads were among the most popular search techniques for finding a job, but how effective were they? According to a 1975 study, although large proportions of employers used newspaper want ads, fewer employers actually hired workers through classified advertising. While almost half of the employers surveyed in San Francisco and just under 60 percent of Salt Lake City employers contacted had used wants ads to recruit workers, the percentage reporting *successful* hiring with wants ads was only 24 percent and 15 percent, respectively.[14] Use of newspaper want ads varied by size of employer and type of position filled. Large employers were heavier users of want ads and other formal channels of recruitment because they had more openings than smaller employers.[15] Large employers also were more likely to have the personnel and resources to sort through the numerous applications they obtained through widely broadcasting the availability of their job openings. Employers reported that they were most successful in hiring clerical, sales, and service workers through want ads, and least successful in hiring managerial and administrative positions.[16] As a result, newspaper want ads proved more efficient for job seekers that were looking for clerical, sales, and service jobs. Not surprisingly, the advent of the computer and the Internet has changed this picture markedly.

A study investigating the effectiveness of job search methods used in 1991 found that while contacting prospective employers directly was the most often used method, the most successful method was registering with a private employment agency. However, there was little difference between the most and least successful job search methods.[17]

Job Search Methods: Internet and Traditional

Whether Internet-based job search substitutes for or complements more traditional means of job search remains to be seen. In recent surveys (1998), the percentage of individuals conducting an Internet job search (15 percent) exceeded the proportion of unemployed job seekers using most of the nine traditional search methods, including using private employment agencies, contacting school employment centers, and using union registers or professional organizations.[18] Internet job search was on a par with placing or answering ads and contacting friends or relatives. Traditional search methods that exceeded rates of Internet job search included contacting the employer directly, contacting a public employment agency, sending out resumes, or filling out applications. However, some of these traditional job search techniques, such as contacting employers directly, sending out resumes, or filling out applications, may be combined with use of the Internet.

Seeking jobs through friends and relatives, want ads in newspapers, and employment services appears to have diminished in use with the rise of Internet-based services (see Table 4.4). Contacting an employer directly (65.1 percent) and sending out resumes/filling out applications (47.6 percent) remained the two most popular methods of job searching in 1999.

Table 4.4
Percentage Using Traditional Job Search Methods, 1994-99

Traditional Search Method	Year					
	1994	1995	1996	1997	1998	1999
Contacted employer directly	67.4	65.1	64.7	67.3	64.5	65.1
Contacted public employment agency	20.4	20.1	18.9	19.1	20.4	15.9
Contacted private employment agency	7.2	7.1	7.5	6.6	6.6	7.0
Contacted friends or relatives	15.7	18.0	16.6	14.6	13.5	13.4
Contacted school employment center	2.3	1.9	2.3	2.7	2.3	1.6
Sent out resumes/filled out applications	40.2	46.9	48.3	46.6	48.3	47.6
Checked union/professional registers	2.7	2.4	2.5	1.7	1.5	1.9
Placed or answered ads	16.7	17.7	17.3	16.3	14.5	12.5
Used other active search methods	3.5	2.9	3.9	4.6	4.4	5.7
Searched Internet						
All adults	---	14	23	36	42	54
Unemployed job seekers					15	
Civilian unemployment rate	5.1	5.2	5.0	4.4	4.0	3.7

Source: Peter Kuhn and Mikal Skuterud, "Job Search Methods: Internet versus Traditional," *Monthly Labor Review*, vol. 123, no. 10 (October 2000), p. 10.

In December 1998, 14.9 percent of unemployed workers surveyed searched for a job at home and 6.5 percent searched for a job outside the home. While Internet job search is most common among the unemployed, it also is substantially used by the employed. Employed workers search the Internet for other job opportunities from home (10.6 percent) or outside the home (4.4 percent) (see Table 4.5). According to the Pew Internet Project, among individuals who use the Internet, 33 percent use it to look for work.[19] Of those seeking employment, 70 percent of Internet users looked for a job on two or more consecutive days.[20] Recent evidence indicates that more than half of those seeking assistance from the employment service now do so online.[21]

Table 4.5
Internet Job Search Rates (percent) by Location of Access Site, December 1998

Internet Job Search Site:	Total	Employed		Unemployed	
		At Work	Absent	On Layoff	Job Seeker
Home	4.0	5.2	5.4	2.9	11.0
Outside the home	1.8	2.3	2.1	1.9	4.6
Any source	5.5	7.1	7.0	4.8	15.0

Source: Peter Kuhn and Mikal Skuterud, "Job Search Methods: Internet versus Traditional," *Monthly Labor Review*, vol. 123, no. 10 (October 2000), p. 4.

Leading analysts Kuhn and Skuterud (2000, p. 9) have reached the following conclusions:

- The Internet is *complementing*, rather than substituting for or replacing, more traditional job search techniques.

- Those using the Internet for job search may well be a "selected sample of persons who choose to look for work more intensely than other job seekers," as suggested by the fact that Internet users reported using more search techniques on average (2.15) than non-Internet users (1.69).

- The Internet may be one of several factors that have nearly doubled job search activity among those already employed in recent years.

- It is unlikely that the Internet has had large effects on job search trends *yet*—most of the anticipated change is still on the horizon.

The advent of the Internet and the rapid expansion of online job search vehicles in the mid-1990s also are associated with other effects that have important implications for equity and effectiveness in labor markets. Concerns have been raised over a persistent "digital divide" in access to technology that affects minorities, women, and other groups. While there is clearly a divide in terms of technology access by minorities, once access is taken into account, the picture changes markedly. In fact, Figure 4.1 clearly illustrates that

the gap [in the use of online job search] is completely explained by differential access to technology: when data are restricted to computer owners, black job seekers are *more likely* than white job seekers to search online; when data are restricted to persons with Internet access at home, 64 percent of black job seekers regularly look for work on the Internet, compared with only 48 percent of whites. In short, there is absolutely no indication that given access to technology, blacks or Hispanics are less inclined than whites to use the Internet for job search (Kuhn and Skuterud, 2000, p. 10, emphasis added).

Figure 4.1
Internet Job Search Rates with and without Computer and Internet Access for Unemployed Job Seekers, by Racial/Ethnic Group, December 1998

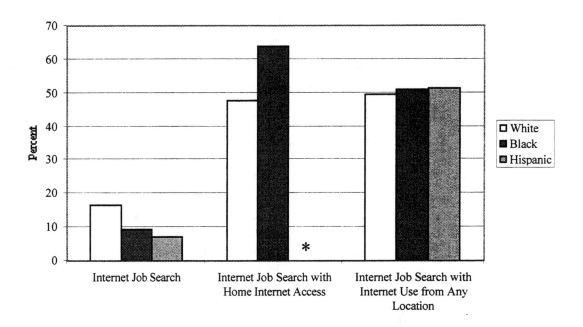

Source: Peter Kuhn and Mikal Skuterud, "Job Search Methods: Internet versus Traditional," *Monthly Labor Review*, vol. 123, no. 10 (October 2000), Table 5, p. 7.

*Data not shown where base less than 75,000.

There are few differences between men and women, regardless of access (Figure 4.2). It should be pointed out that the available evidence does *not* demonstrate that online job search has been more successful in terms of securing jobs than other methods for these or other groups. The U.S. Department of Labor is currently funding an evaluation of labor exchange services that may offer more definitive answers to this question in a few years.

Figure 4.2
Internet Job Search Rates with and without Computer and Internet Access for Unemployed Job Seekers, by Gender, December 1998

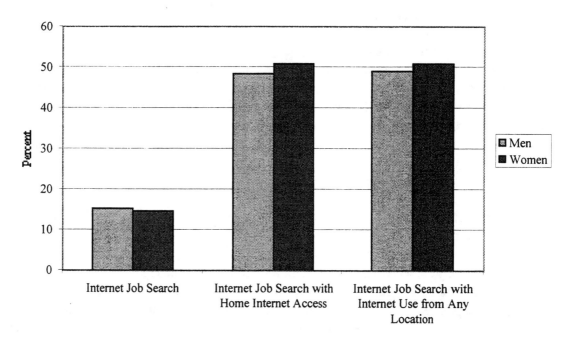

Source: Peter Kuhn and Mikal Skuterud, "Job Search Methods: Internet versus Traditional," *Monthly Labor Review*, vol. 123, no. 10 (October 2000), Table 5, p. 7.

These early survey findings suggest a number of clear and productive avenues for policy makers. One would be to expand existing efforts and/or launch new ones to make computer and Internet access universal, with special attention to the needs of minority populations. Certainly, expanding access to the Internet and various job search tools in one-stop centers, schools, libraries, community centers, churches, and other venues would also be very useful. Another would be to promote increased home-based access to technology among lagging groups. Access to technology is clearly the overarching issue. Policy makers at the federal, state, and local levels can tackle access in many different ways.

Automated Labor Exchange Sites

Automated labor exchange sites provide job seekers with important new tools to search for employment opportunities. These websites feature computerized databases and require only an Internet connection, a Web browser, and interest on the part of the individual job seeker. Applied Service Provider software allows job seekers to go directly to a company's website that has been digitally retrofitted to accept and prescreen applications, without having to rely on third-party job matching sources, including public and private employment agencies. Internet job websites or automated labor exchange

51

sites are convenient for both employers and prospective employees. Job seekers can search for information and available job openings on their own, in private. Automated labor exchange sites encompass the following categories: commercial sites, company sites, Web engine sites, newspaper sites, niche sites, and government-sponsored sites. Each category is described in detail below, along with specific examples.

General Commercial Websites

Commercial websites are among the most numerous automated labor exchange sites on the Internet. The market for labor exchange services is one of constant change. New websites come into existence frequently, while others are discontinued or are merged with larger, more stable websites. In fall 2000, our research team reviewed 20 different websites, half of which were commercial sites. Six months later, of the ten commercial websites, one had been discontinued and two had merged with other, larger websites. Among the major commercial sites reviewed were Monster.com, FlipDog.com, HotJobs.com, and Headhunter.net.

Monster.com, based in Maynard, Massachusetts, and Indianapolis, Indiana, is the flagship product of the Interactive Division of TMP Worldwide, Inc. It was launched in January 1999 as a result of the merger of the Monster Board (www.monster.com) and Online Career Center (www.occ.com), which were founded in 1994 and 1993, respectively. Monster.com is a global online network for careers, connecting companies with individuals seeking jobs. Monster.com claims to offer innovative technology and services designed to give consumers and businesses greater control over the recruiting process. Its network consists of sites with information on available jobs and applicants in the United States, Canada, the United Kingdom, the Netherlands, Belgium, Australia, France, Germany, Singapore, New Zealand, Hong Kong, Ireland, and Spain. Monster.com is part of a career network that job seekers can use to expand their career options and gain direct access to jobs and information for various companies. In addition, it provides interactive, personal tools to make the process more effective and convenient. Monster.com features include resume management, a personal job search agent, a career network, chat and message boards, privacy options, advice on job seeking and career management, and free newsletters. Monster.com offers employers various recruiting services, including real-time job postings, complete company profiles, and services for searching, screening, and routing resumes. In June 2001, the U.S. Department of Labor entered into a data-sharing agreement with Monster.com that aimed to provide improved real-time labor market information for customers.

FlipDog.com, based in Provo, Utah, began operations in April 2000. The company provides access to a large collection of job postings on employer websites. Using Internet technology, they collect job postings from large and small companies, and both public and private organizations. Their website uses technology from WhizBang Labs that crawls the Web and links to job openings found on employer websites. The job seeker is provided with a comprehensive directory of jobs found on the Web. The key features of FlipDog.com include resume management, a personal job search agent, advice on job seeking and career management, and a resource center.

HotJobs.com is a recruiting company that develops hiring products and services and provides them to employers for a fee. HotJobs.com was incorporated in February 1997. By 2001, it had established 12 offices across the English-speaking world, including regional offices in major markets of the United States, Canada, Australia, and the United Kingdom. The company's services include resume building and hiring management software, strategic consulting services, and career expos. Hotjobs.com also sponsors the "AgencyExchange," a marketplace that provides a direct business-to-business exchange between corporate hiring managers and staffing agencies. In June 2001, TMP Worldwide, the owners of Monster.com, announced an intention to acquire HotJobs.com.[22]

Headhunter.net was founded in 1996. Headquartered in Norcross, Georgia, the company has locations in 17 cities across the United States. Headhunter.net features include tailored job-posting packages for employers, complete job search privacy, a cache of easy-to-use tools, and various career-building services. Their site offers job applicants the option of saving searches for future reference, email alerts, and multiple resumes and cover letters, as well as numerous ways to search for a job.

Other commercial websites have similar attributes. Each of the four websites profiled offers free resume building and posting for job seekers who register and set up an account. An individual generally is not required to establish an account with the website to perform a job search. To search for a job, an individual can enter a number of restricting categories, including keywords describing the job, location (e.g., city, state, metro area, or country), employer, job field, job type (internship, summer, full or part time), salary range, school degree, and the date the job was posted.

Job posting is generally not free for employers. Commercial websites offer numerous pricing and posting strategies for employers, ranging from single job postings to membership arrangements that include multiple job postings.

According to a recent report from Jupiter Media Metrix, a firm that specializes in tracking website traffic,

> Traffic to career sites increased 32.2 percent, from 14.1 million unique visitors in February 2001 to 18.6 million unique visitors in July 2001. Meanwhile, total minutes spent at career sites grew 24.2 percent, from 327 million minutes in February 2001 to 406 million in July 2001. Younger users dominated career sites, with people aged 18 to 44 comprising 71 percent of all visitors to career sites in July 2001. The top career destinations were: Hotjobs.com, with 6.3 million unique visitors; Monster.com, with 6.2 million unique visitors and Jobsonline.com, with 5.0 million unique visitors.[23]

The planned acquisition of Hotjobs.com by Monster.com, announced in June 2001, will make the combined site the industry leader by far.

Company Websites

The websites of individual firms provide job seekers with detailed information on working for that particular company. Reviewing a business's website provides an excellent resource for job seekers and allows them to make informed decisions on whether to work for that employer or not. Major company websites selected for review in this chapter include Texas Instruments, Wal-Mart, USAA, and Xerox.

The Texas Instruments (TI) website (http://www.ti.com) opens with highlights of selected jobs and gives the reader the option to link to information technology job searches in Europe, Japan, Korea, China, and Taiwan. Further into the TI website, one can search for a job by key word or location. The website links to a page for submitting resumes. TI provides information on the benefits of working for the company, and efforts are made to sell the advantages of working for the company to prospective employees. Given the variety of locations within the company worldwide, a link is provided to help with relocation. This link takes the user directly to the appropriate city's website and provides information to the job seeker on the current openings with TI in each locality. Also, college students are provided a schedule of upcoming campus visits by TI personnel, as well as listings of available internships and co-op assignments, in which students attend school and work during alternating semesters.

The Wal-Mart website (http://www.Wal-Mart.com) offers a career section that allows job seekers to view jobs online as well as to review the benefits of working for the company. The site is organized to promote the company as "family oriented." The site offers a job engine that is separated into nine categories: business development, creative, customer service, engineering, finance and administration, marketing, merchandising, operations, and logistics; and production. Within each of these categories are lists of possible jobs at Wal-Mart along with appropriate online links to send in a resume. Some of the jobs listed provide details about qualifications and responsibilities. The site provides a description of the benefits of working for Wal-Mart (e.g., corporate culture, incentive bonus plan, health benefits, profit sharing, stock options), as well as highlighting some of the success stories of the company's employees.

USAA, a large insurance company, describes its mission and company activities on its website (http://www.usaa.com) to help job applicants learn more about the company. Information is provided about the advantages of working for USAA, including benefits, training, services, and facilities. The USAA website describes its hiring process and provides information on living in its headquarters city, San Antonio. The site lists current job openings, phone numbers of regional offices, and job lines.

The Xerox website (http://www.xerox.com) provides job seekers with information on the advantages of working at Xerox and promotes Xerox as a great place to work. Xerox attracts potential employees by promoting the diversity of the company and the advantages of its benefit packages. Xerox offers special scholarships to qualified candidates along with information on special work programs. Within the Xerox website, a job seeker can search for a job by location, job function, job title, job description, or job type. Xerox also posts job openings with independent companies that are authorized to sell Xerox products, along with links to sites for submitting a resume to these companies.

To date, most companies use their website to list those jobs that require higher levels of education, skill, and experience—especially in the arena of information technology. Thus, job postings on company sites tend to cater more to upper level, higher skilled employees. Since computer skills are required to hunt for a job online, companies tend to post jobs that require greater familiarity and comfort with information technology. Companies still rely on more traditional methods of recruiting to identify and attract applicants for jobs not requiring computer skills.

Web Engine Sites

Web engines are automated labor exchange sites that connect to major search engines, such as AltaVista.com, Lycos.com, and Yahoo.com. They are often connected to commercial search sites as well. Searches for employment on one of these Web engine sites amount to indirect searches on major commercial sites. For example, AltaVista.com searches 12 commercial sites, including Jobs.com, Dice.com, CollegeJournal.com, and BrassRing.com. AltaVista.com searches each of these commercial sites and then lists jobs that match individually specified criteria. On AltaVista.com, individuals can search for a job by title or key word, city, and state. Job seekers have fewer search options on these Web engines than on commercial sites, perhaps because they are less focused on connecting companies with job seekers. Instead, they are more generalized websites offering an array of search and informational services.

Lycos.com differs from AltaVista in that its site has more job search options. A job seeker can search for management positions and positions with startup companies, or specify a salary range or job type (full time, part time, intern, or summer). Lycos.com is connected to Headhunter.net, where its job searches are ultimately performed.

The Yahoo.com site is easier to navigate than the other sites because its screen is not cluttered with an abundance of links and text. As of early 2001, job categories were placed down the left side of the page to allow the user to browse. The standard search options for title/key word, city, or state options were centered at the top of the page. On the right were a number of additional links for developing a career, and estimating a salary, as well as tools for constructing a resume and researching a company or a community. On the lower portion of the page, there were links to supplemental employment information, such as news articles and special listings of certain jobs.

These Web engine sites have much in common with one another and with the more specialized commercial sites offering job-matching services. Overall, Web engine search sites offer fewer special amenities and career development programs than their commercial counterparts. However, they promote a multitude of commercial sites that are only a link away. If a job seeker cannot find a job using the Web engine site, then he or she can either click on a listed commercial job search site or perform a Web search using that particular Web engine.

Newspaper Community Websites

Local newspapers are using the Internet now to expand their readership. For example, the local newspapers in Austin, San Antonio, and Houston—*Austin American-Statesmen*, *San Antonio Express News*, and the *Houston Chronicle*—sponsor online versions of their papers. Each of these sites provides the same classified ads one could find in print. Cox Interactive Media and City360.com own all of these papers. Cox Interactive Media has realized the growing importance of the Internet and has taken steps to capitalize on new opportunities to increase revenues. People are now using the Internet to search for jobs, while the use of more traditional means may be on the decline. However, not only do these newspaper sites offer an electronic version of the classified ads, but they also help with resume building and a website set up for searching based on the Headhunter.net database. The 360.com sites offer a special option that allows users to learn more about the city in which they may work. This option could be extremely valuable and convenient for a person who knows little about a city and is considering relocating. Newspaper sites commonly feature guides to finding available apartments, restaurants, and local entertainment.

Specialized or Niche Sites

Niche websites offer automated labor exchange services catering to specific groups of workers for particular occupations and industries. Several specialized or niche sites on the Internet involve computer technology and health care. The niche websites selected for review here are PeopleSoft Services Procurement, Dice.com, and NurseAmerica.net.

PeopleSoft Services Procurement (http://www/peoplesoft.com), formerly SkillsVillage.com, provides employers with a blended model of applications and outsourced business services across the entire skill procurement life cycle: finding, hiring, and managing. PeopleSoft acquired SkillsVillage in June 2001. Procurement software allows companies to deploy available contract workers quickly and efficiently through a private network of suppliers. This is intended to provide companies with the ability to control the quality, cost, and efficiencies associated with finding, hiring, and managing their contract workers and staffing suppliers. The software provides individual job seekers with brief abstracts and direct links to company websites in information technology (IT) and human resource information systems (HRIS). They also offer links to available education and training courses for technology-oriented careers.

Dice.com is a more traditional automated labor exchange site. Founded in 1990 as a bulletin board service for IT consultants, Dice.com has experienced continuous growth throughout its history by providing information on jobs and careers to IT professionals. EarthWeb, a provider of career development and technical expertise for IT professionals, acquired Dice.com in February 1999. Dice.com provides online career management services to IT professionals nationwide. Dice.com offers job seekers opportunities to search job listings by region. Through its Custom Search Network, jobs listed on

Dice.com are simultaneously available on sites such as Dilbert.com and GirlGeeks.com. The Dice.com advanced search engine allows job seekers to search by key word, job title, skills, state or area code, and metropolitan area. Another tool includes software to help job seekers make more informed decisions about relocation. Job seekers can calculate moving costs, compare salaries in different areas of the country, create a custom relocation timeline, and receive free reports on schools and city amenities. Job seekers can also prepare for certification exams as part of the job search process by purchasing certification test preparation materials online. Dice.com's employer services are available to companies and recruiters seeking skilled IT professionals.

NurseAmerica.net is an online resource for hospitals looking for supplemental nursing staff and for nurses seeking part-time work. NurseAmerica.net allows hospitals and nurses to negotiate work arrangements and salaries directly. Hospitals pay a fee based on a percentage of the nurse's pay, which is similar to how staffing agencies work. The goal of NurseAmerica.net is to eliminate a hospital's dependence on outside recruiting firms and supplemental staffing agencies. Hospitals and medical facilities can list openings by date, geographic location, specialty, skill level, and salary. Nurses create personal profiles that are matched with employer needs. The results of the match are displayed and nurses can then accept or decline opportunities as they see fit.

Niche sites vary more than the other four categories of automated labor exchange sites, perhaps because of the differences among specialty occupations such as nurses and IT workers, as well as differences in the specific needs of their employers.

Government-Sponsored Websites

Government-sponsored websites list employment opportunities available in government agencies as well as in the private sector. Both the federal and Texas state websites give primary emphasis to employment applications. Downloading, completing, and submitting an employment application is generally the first step in obtaining any government job. As in the private sector, an application or resume has become a key job-finding technique. People still fill out application forms and create resumes as an integral part of the job-seeking process.

The Texas Workforce Commission is linked to the Governor's Job Bank and also has links to other government labor exchange websites as well as commercial, Web engine, and niche sites. Government websites primarily list job vacancies by government agency, but do not limit themselves to this type of directory. A person can search for jobs by occupation, pay scale, or location. With the Governor's Job Bank for Texas, an individual must download a software reader in order to read the current jobs available. The person only needs to download the offline reader (i.e., Adobe Acrobat) once. After that, he or she can access available jobs as they are updated each day. However, the time it takes to download the initial software reader could be better spent searching for a job on another website. This design feature interferes with the ideal situation of providing immediate information on job openings.

America's Job Bank (www.ajb.dni.us) is a partnership between the U.S. Department of Labor (DOL) and the public Employment Service (ES), a federal-state partnership providing labor exchange services to employers and job seekers through a network of 1,800 offices throughout the United States. Many ES offices are now co-located with one-stop centers. Employers register job listings through their home state, and state ES staff review applications. Validation and approval typically take about three days. Once the employer posts a job, it will remain on the list for 45 days. Job seekers can search the job bank using various inquiry strategies. They do not need to register to search for jobs, but do need to register to post a resume. America's Job Bank also offers assistance with preparing resumes and cover letters, guides to job trends, profiles of employers and states, and career exploration materials. A posted resume remains listed for 60 days. Resume fields include information on skills, abilities, job objective, and a note field that allows a job seeker to add any other information.

Remarkably, on none of the private or governmental websites reviewed in our research was "learning opportunities" treated as a major category or primary field for job matching. Given all the rhetorical emphasis on lifelong or continuous learning and on the increased responsibility that individuals bear for maintaining their own job security through improving their skills for the demands of the New Economy, one might expect a greater emphasis on learning. Since continuous learning is considered so important for workers and since workplaces are learning environments, shouldn't job seekers have the chance to specify what they want to learn on jobs they choose? Likewise, shouldn't employers who offer fertile learning environments be able to advertise their availability in job postings? Simply by listing learning opportunities as a category should call greater attention to this important issue for both employers and job seekers.

America's Job Bank now reports being visited by more than 10 million job seekers and employers weekly. America's Job Bank is one component of a broader online DOL initiative, America's Career Kit, which includes postings for all types of jobs. The other components currently include America's Career InfoNet (www.acinet.org), which provides job seekers and employers with access to national and state occupational and economic trend data, and America's Learning eXchange (www.alx.org), which provides searchable databases on training offerings, courses, seminars, and so on. A fourth component, America's Service Locator, provides customers a website for locating support services related to employment and training, such as child care and transportation services. Consumers can get help with job searches, resume building, and career exploration, among other services, all of which can be accessed without charge from WIA-supported one-stop centers. In June 2001, DOL and Monster.com entered into a data-sharing agreement through which the two entities will generate real-time indices of labor market information, based on standard definitions found in the Occupational Information Network (O*NET) and the Standard Occupational Classification (SOC) job classification system.

Governmental websites for labor exchange are becoming common worldwide. A survey conducted by the World Association of Public Employment Services (WAPES) with the International Labour Organization in May 2000 identified 19 countries operating

Internet-based job banks.[24] These countries were primarily, but not exclusively, developed countries. In addition to the United States, the countries included Austria, Belgium, Canada, Denmark, Finland, France, Germany, Greece, Iceland, Ireland, Netherlands, Norway, Philippines, Slovakia, Slovenia, Sweden, and Tunisia. Australia, though not covered in the survey, also has been very proactive in the provision of online labor exchange services. The percentages of the workforce accessing such services varied widely, even in similarly situated neighboring countries; for example, approximately 10 percent of Swedish workers access its online ES services each month, compared with only 3.5 percent of Norwegian workers. In all of these countries, the rate of online job bank usage was rising rapidly, by as much as 100 percent annually in some (e.g., Belgium).[25]

Conclusions and Recommendations

There is no question that online labor exchange is the wave of the future. Employers and job seekers alike increasingly will turn to online solutions to the problems involved in effectively and efficiently meeting the needs of employers and job seekers. This is not to say that online exchange is the solution for everyone and every situation. Yet, the forces pushing and pulling employers and job seekers online to avail themselves of job matching and related services are sufficiently strong that traditional job search methods will be both competing with and complementing Web-based approaches into the foreseeable future.

However, the rapidly growing number and continued evolution in labor exchange websites can easily overwhelm job seekers—and many small employers as well—with the variety of options available to them. To use online labor exchange effectively, a job seeker first must have *access*, including a computer, the Internet, and browser software. Where that access occurs is another issue. In addition, they must possess the requisite knowledge and skill to use computers and navigate the Internet, including helpful, user-friendly tools and information that they can understand and use. Workers without such access, knowledge, skills, and experience require greater assistance and training from Texas workforce professionals.

Hands-on personal tutoring may be the best approach for potential job seekers uneasy about using the Internet and computers. Simple and effective online tutorials can also help. The Internet requires a sense of familiarity that is best learned from repeated, hands-on practice. Labor exchange websites must be easy to use for those less skilled in using the Internet, but they must also offer more advanced tools for job seekers who are more skilled at using the Internet.

Several recommendations follow from this examination of online labor exchange.

Recommendation 4-1: Policy makers at all levels—federal, state, and local—in partnership with each other as well as with leading information technology firms, should expand and intensify efforts to make access to computers and the Internet truly universal. Modern labor markets demand universal access, and policy makers must respond to this imperative. Policy makers should devote special attention to the needs of minority populations, focusing specifically on promoting home-based access. Such access would potentially allow minority groups to redress persistent labor market inequities evident in employment/population ratios and unemployment rates. Expanding access to the Internet and various job search tools in one-stop centers, schools, libraries, community centers, churches, and other venues would also be very beneficial. Effective access to technology is a critical issue.

Policy makers at all levels can address access issues in many different ways that need not be detailed here. Chapter 2 discusses access issues in some detail and offers a number of potential remedies for rural Texas. Excellent examples of efforts to promote universal access in urban areas include the provision of laptop computers to all public school children in the Dallas and Houston Independent School Districts, two of the state's largest ISDs, which serve high concentrations of minority families. Also, Austin's FreeNet and Community Technology Center initiatives serve minority communities disproportionately. In this era of the knowledge economy, access should be viewed as something approaching a right. It has become far more than merely an opportunity. Access to technology must be viewed as a public good with which the private sector can assist.

Recommendation 4-2: Public and private sponsors of Internet-based labor exchange should give greater attention to "opportunities for learning" as a primary field in the job-matching process. Addressing learning explicitly would have the effect of raising the profile of learning opportunities and skill development as important factors in decision making in job matching—both for employers and for job seekers.

Recommendation 4-3: Workforce policy makers and practitioners at all levels should devote serious attention to reinventing and continuously improving labor exchange processes over the next few years in light of the new and expanding role played by online automated services. A policy of continuous improvement is the only way to maintain pace with the dynamic developments and possibilities offered by information technology.

Recommendation 4-4: To close the gap between less and more technologically proficient job seekers, the U.S. Department of Labor, in collaboration with state workforce agencies, local workforce boards, and other actors, should develop, refine, and offer training on both the use of computers and the effective use of online labor exchange services. The availability and growing use of online labor exchange services has begun to have noticeable effects on the ways employers and job seekers conduct the job search and matching process. Many workers—especially those with high levels of education and skill and those in specialized fields and occupations—may only require limited assistance, if any at all, from traditional ES or one-stop centers. Their needs may be addressed exclusively and very effectively through online exchange services, many of which may be operated in the private domain. Adequate safeguards will be needed to protect against fraud, inaccurate and misleading information about jobs, and other problems.[26] Other groups of job seekers—especially those with lower literacy and education levels and less facility and skill at using computers and the Internet—may well need greater human assistance, whether through one-stops, ES offices, libraries, community centers, labor hiring halls, or other venues, if their job searches are to be successful. In effect, policy makers and program administrators will need to consider approaching the mix of traditional and online labor exchange approaches with some form of triaging in mind, for employers as well as workers. At this point, it is not clear whether the advent and spread of online job matching will reduce the level of resources required to support effective public labor exchange in the future.

Recommendation 4-5: The U.S. Department of Labor, in collaboration with state workforce agencies, local workforce boards, and other actors in the public and private sectors, should continually assess their existing labor market information and labor exchange systems to ensure that they are appropriate, useful, and understandable to employers and job seekers with varying levels of education and skill. Readily understandable LMI is absolutely critical to an effective labor exchange in more market-oriented approaches to workforce service delivery. If such information cannot be accessed, used, and understood by major segments of the workforce, then markets cannot perform effectively, efficiently, or equitably. Equity may be the most important of these concerns. Again, adequate safeguards are necessary to protect consumers against fraud, inaccurate and misleading information, and other problems.

The status of online labor exchange sites worldwide remains in considerable flux, a situation that is exacerbated by the recent economic upheaval and resulting turmoil in economies and stock markets. There will likely be little stability among online labor exchange companies any time soon. Smaller, less robust providers will be acquired by or merged with larger, more viable ones. Relationships between existing private and public labor exchange actors, including the ES and one-stop centers, are expected to be uncertain for some time. Policy makers, especially those at the federal and state levels, must continue to monitor these developments and respond accordingly.

Notes

[1] International Labour Organization (ILO), *World Employment Report 2001: Life at Work in the Information Economy* (Geneva, 2001).

[2] Peter Kuhn and Mikal Skuterud, "Job Search Methods: Internet versus Traditional," *Monthly Labor Review* (October 2000), pp. 3-11.

[3] For a current list of the sites, see http://www.internetpost.com/Internetpost/AlphaList.html. Accessed: March 15, 2001.

[4] Nielsen/NetRatings information provided by Allen Weiner, Vice President of Analytical Services, NetRatings. Online. Available: http://www.NetRatings.com. Accessed: February 22, 2001.

[5] Ibid.

[6] Ibid.

[7] Kuhn and Skuterud, "Job Search Methods," pp. 3-11.

[8] Ibid.

[9] For a discussion of this issue, see Robert D. Atkinson and Randolph D. Court, *The New Economy Index: Understanding America's Economic Transformation* (Washington, D.C.: The Progressive Policy Institute, Technology, Innovation and the New Economy Project, 1998). Online. Available: www.neweconomyindex.org/.

[10] Alan Krueger, "Net Job Searches Change the Market and the Economy," *International Herald Tribune*, vol. 24 (July 2000), p. 8, reported in ILO, *World Employment Report 2001*, p. 249.

[11] Harold L. Sheppard and A. Harvey Belitsky, *The Job Hunt: Job-Seeking Behavior of Unemployed Workers in a Local Economy* (Baltimore: Johns Hopkins University Press, 1966), pp. 44-45.

[12] Ibid, p. 62.

[13] Michelle Harrison Ports, "Trends in Job Search Methods, 1970-92," *Monthly Labor Review*, vol. 116, no. 10 (October 1993), p. 65.

[14] John Walsh, Miriam Johnson, and Marged Sugarman, *Help Wanted: Case Studies of Classified Ads* (Salt Lake City: Olympus Publishing, 1975), p. 23.

[15] Ibid., pp. 22, 24-25, 28.

[16] Ibid.

[17] Steven M. Bortnick and Michaelle Harrison Ports, "Job Search Methods and Results: Tracking the Unemployed, 1991," *Monthly Labor Review*, vol. 115, no. 12 (December 1992), pp. 29-35.

[18] Kuhn and Skuterud, "Job Search Methods."

[19] Class presentation by Dr. John Horrigan of the Pew Internet Project, March 8, 2001.

[20] Ibid.

[21] ILO, *World Employment Report 2001*, p. 250.

[22] HotJobs.com. "TMP Worldwide, HotJobs Reiterate Dual Positioning: Reinforces Value, Differentiation Can Unleash Untapped Market" July 17, 2001 (press release). Online. Available: http://www.hotjobs.com/htdocs/about/news/071701.html/. Accessed: August 6, 2001.

[23] Jupiter Media Metrix, "Jupiter Media Metrix Announces US Top 50 Web and Digital Media Properties for July 2001." Online. Available: www.jmm.com/xp/press/2001/pr_081301.xml. Accessed: September 15, 2001.

[24] ILO, *World Employment Report 2001*, p. 250.

[25] For more on this effort and related issues, see Christopher T. King and Burt S. Barnow, "Information and Communications Technology and Workforce Service Delivery: A Comparative Look," in *Global Restructuring, Training and the Social Dialogue*, ed. Torkel Alfthan, Christopher T. King, and Gyorgy Sziraczki (Geneva: International Labour Organization, 2001).

[26] This issue is discussed in ILO, *World Employment Report 2001,* pp. 249ff.

Chapter 5. Improving the Operations of One-Stop Career Centers through Information Technology

Introduction

According to a longtime observer, one-stop centers have only two choices. They can either become "agile, entrepreneurial and highly responsive to markets," or they can become "completely irrelevant and die."[1] In order to serve all targeted populations, one-stop centers must stay technologically and structurally modern.

One-stop centers in Texas are commonly referred to as "workforce centers." These centers offer customers access to several job-related services at a single site. Over the past few years, Texas workforce centers have progressed in their ability to provide a broad menu of resources and media, creating centers that are more accessible and customer friendly. While the modernization of the Texas workforce system has been a success in many ways and services are available for both businesses and job seekers, the current reality is that not everyone has the skills and resources necessary to take advantage of the services offered at workforce centers. The people who currently can most effectively use the centers have access to transportation to reach local centers, are reasonably literate, and are comfortable using computers. For the most part, center customers probably already have the necessary tools to retain and succeed in a job and do not require the additional services available for customers facing barriers to employment. Unfortunately, if the goal of a workforce center is to help individuals who require extensive services or training to obtain or retain a job, the center may not be as effective or as equitable as its mission aspires.

The Evolution of Workforce Programs to Integration through One-Stop Centers

The roots of workforce programs today trace back to the New Deal in the 1930s as well as a series of federal employment and training laws passed beginning in the 1960s. Public employment and other safety net programs became a major focus of federal legislation in the 1930s, aimed at countering labor market problems brought by the Great Depression. In 1933, the Wagner-Peyser Act established the public employment service, a national program of labor exchanges operating through partnerships between the U.S. Department of Labor and state agencies. The Social Security Act of 1937 established the unemployment insurance system. Until the mid-1990s, the Texas Employment Commission (TEC) administered the employment service and unemployment insurance for the state.

Beginning in the 1960s, a series of employment and training programs surfaced in federal legislation, including the Manpower Development and Training Act (MDTA) of 1962, the Comprehensive Employment and Training Act (CETA) of 1968, and the Job Training Employment Act (JTPA) of 1973. The Workforce Investment Act (WIA) of 1998 was the first national legislation to coordinate and integrate labor exchange services with employment and training programs. Although WIA funding was more flexible than previous legislation, it carried restrictions and regulations outlining expected service levels and eligibility requirements for enrollment. It offered a system of checks and balances that decentralized the decision-making process by empowering governor-certified local workforce boards.

Coordination and consolidation of programs among separate agencies with different goals and agendas can be extremely difficult, not to mention the problems of separate federal agencies agreeing on issues. Some observers believe that coordination is complicated in Texas, which has a state government of "boards" and "commissions" rather than the more traditional "cabinet" form, in which the governor has the power to plan and direct the resources of state government.[2] Others argue that compared with other states, Texas has the significant advantage of facilitative state legislation.[3] No matter what its institutional environment, each state must find its way to implement the "one-stop" concept and the move to local control.

Beginning in the 1990s, through a series of studies, testimony, and reflections on experience, the Texas Legislature concluded that centralized, top-down, government-controlled job training programs were not most effectively meeting the needs of business and industry, nor were they being provided for the diverse communities across the state. The legislature began to consider other ways of administering an equitable and effective workforce system. In 1993, Senate Bill 642, the Workforce and Economic Competitiveness Act, created the Texas Council on Workforce and Economic Competitiveness (TCWEC). TCWEC was established to act as a workforce advisory committee, evaluating state workforce services and making policy recommendations to the governor.[4] Working with TCWEC, in 1995 the Texas Legislature passed House Bill 1863. In many ways, this legislation is considered a precursor to the national legislation passed in the Workforce Development Act of 1998. Sponsored by Senator Ellis and Representatives Oliveira and Coleman, the Texas legislation created the Texas Workforce Commission (TWC), integrated 28 workforce-related programs, and established a system of local workforce development boards throughout the state.[5]

The mission of the Texas Workforce Commission is to "promote and support a workforce system that offers individuals, employers, and communities the opportunity to achieve and sustain economic prosperity."[6] The TWC supports the local workforce development boards (LWDBs) by facilitating the flow of workforce resources and by providing technical assistance. For example, "HireTexas," the state's online employment site, is administered by TWC. LWDBs make use of the "HireTexas" program in specific service delivery.[7] The TWC also acts in an oversight capacity and advises the LWDBs of identified opportunities for improvement. The U.S. Department of Labor, in a 1997 study, suggested that a good one-stop system not only has clear guidelines to follow but also has the freedom to function as is best for the community.[8] Like other states, Texas is striving to find the appropriate balance between state and local concerns in its workforce system.

The Texas workforce system encourages local control.[9] Following procedures outlined in the legislation, the governor identified 28 local workforce areas. Local elected officials then appointed community and business representatives to local workforce development boards in each of these areas, based on nominations received from local chambers of commerce and others. The 28 boards provide a means of local control, developing and managing their own programs and funding. The local boards were empowered to create customized programs based on the specific needs of the local economy.

The board members are business and community volunteers, many of whom are local business owners or executives. Local boards hire staff to implement board decisions. The boards are charged with the task of initiating and overseeing the operations of the local workforce system. Services are provided through contracts competitively procured with public or private agencies. For example, the three centers in Austin are operated under a contract with ACS State and Local Solutions (formerly entitled the Lockheed Martin Corporation). Services in Central Texas are administered contracts with Mr. Jerry Haisler, the center's director, who manages a variety of subcontractors. In the year 2000, the 28 Texas workforce boards opened 33 additional workforce centers for a total of 129 centers in the state.[10] The quality of the centers and service opportunities vary, although all are funded by state taxpayer monies and federal grants.

While workforce centers offer a variety of assessment and referral services, most centers are used primarily by people who are seeking jobs.[11] The centers commonly include areas reserved for self-service, computer-aided job search assistance, career counseling, and other staff assistance. While each workforce center is distinct, some practices have been standardized through the state's full-service certification system. Ideally, upon arrival at a site, the customer is greeted by a receptionist, who asks relevant questions and directs the customer to the most appropriate service area. If the customer chooses to register in the state database, he or she is provided a form to complete, using series of codes and key words to describe current job needs and desired occupation. The state registration form is returned to the staff member, who explains the matching and referral process and encourages the customer to begin the job search process using the computer resources to search the existing job databases and review the center's Web-based resources and listings.

Posters and notices around many centers offer information regarding workforce training programs in various industries, job fairs, and computer courses. Available brochures may advertise programs offering help with transportation, child care, application for public assistance, and other social services. If a customer needs assistance, center staff are available to help to create a resume, to find a specific job listing, or accomplish other tasks necessary to facilitate the process of finding employment. Most centers have representatives on staff to help customers to access public assistance, veteran's benefits, or other local or state resources.

The Killeen Workforce Center, sponsored by the Central Texas Workforce System, is a nationally known one-stop center praised for its innovative design and excellent customer service. The Killeen Workforce Center has won several awards for its accomplishments in providing transportation, dropout prevention, and integrated service delivery.[12] The center in Killeen is also technologically innovative, in part due to a contractor whose funding and freedom from the state allows the center to test new technological innovations.[13] A variety of subcontractors, including the Central Texas Council of Governments and the Hill Country Community Action Agency, under the direction of Jerry Haisler, deliver center services in the Central Texas Workforce Area.

The 28 local workforce development boards deal with the issue of geographic coverage in different ways.[14] While some LWD areas have one full-service center along with a complement of satellite centers, other areas may offer two or three full-service locations without satellites. The Central Texas Workforce Board has made it a priority to place workforce center services strategically so that no customer has to drive more than 15 miles for workforce services.[15] The board's area covers seven counties and in 2001 contained three centers offering full services (Killeen, Temple, and Belton). In addition, the board had four satellite centers operating in Cameron, Copperas Cove, Rockdale, and Lampasas, as well as six kiosks offering computer access in rural locations. The satellite and kiosk centers offer varying degrees of workforce services. Satellite centers are smaller facilities, generally scaled-down versions of the larger full-service centers. The kiosks serve less densely populated rural areas through the local workforce website: www.workforcelink.com. The kiosks are located in public spaces, such as libraries, with TWC trained employees available on-site for support. Including kiosks and satellites, the Central Texas Workforce System provided services to more than 9,000 people a month from July 2000 through July 2001.[16]

The Central Texas Workforce Board has assured that its centers are technologically modern and up-to-date. The three full-service centers are all on the same email system, operated by a wide-area network, which improves communication between the centers, employees, and partners and expands services provided by the centers. There is computer training and assistance available for businesses, employees, and job seekers. If a job seeker does not have the computer skills to work alone, staff are available to offer assistance, or the customer can enroll in classes offering basic computer use. The Killeen center has an advantage in that many of its customers already have computer skills, due to their association with the military at Fort Hood, the local army base adjacent to Killeen.[17]

The Central Texas Workforce System has an Internet-based Alternative Service Delivery Platform, a database system that helps with both systems management and customer relations. The platform allows employers to list jobs online without leaving their office, a feature which is especially helpful for remote rural businesses as well as those located in congested urban areas. Through this system, employers and job seekers can post jobs and resumes, check the status of their services remotely, and see what activity there has been in their file or job application at any time. Along with the shared email system, this platform promotes the sharing of information throughout the workforce system. Therefore, no matter whom employers or job seekers contact, they will always obtain the same information because all information is logged onto the same database. The system contains firewalls separating staff and customer files to assure privacy. During October

2000 alone, the Central Texas Workforce System had 18,000 unique customers visit its website.[18] As evidenced by the large number of people served, the Central Texas Workforce Board recognizes the significant potential for offering online workforce service opportunities.

Groups Inadequately Served by the Texas Workforce Center System

The existing Texas workforce system successfully matches many job seekers with employment. The ideal of "one-stop service" is that all of a customer's business can be completed in a single contact, be it face-to-face, via phone, fax, Internet, or other means.[19] An important goal of a workforce center is to eliminate the need for customers to hunt around, call back several times, or repeatedly explain their situation. Service is to be convenient, accessible, and personalized.

However, not every citizen benefits from the existing Texas workforce system. Several unemployed individuals needing help are inadvertently excluded or underserved due to various barriers and other problems. As a result, the Texas workforce system is less effective and equitable. Information technology applications can help some of these groups, such as those who are profiled in the following sections.

Individuals with Transportation Problems and/or Other Accessibility Issues

A large obstacle in achieving the workforce center's mission is customers' inability to physically get to the center. The problem is exacerbated when a customer is referred to job training. Since little training occurs at the one-stop center location, customers must find transportation to yet another site when they enroll in a program focused on teaching job skills.[20] Individuals without transportation have difficulties accessing the system. Although most Centers are purposefully located close to bus stops in cities with public transportation, that does not cover everyone. Many areas in Texas have no public transportation.

The workforce center in Killeen offers transportation to such customers. Under special funding from the state, Killeen is piloting new and better services for other centers.[21] While the Killeen center can afford to offer transportation, it is definitely unusual. Most workforce centers are unable to offer transportation services.

Local workforce boards have the responsibility to ensure that services are accessible to individuals with disabilities.[22] Just being able to get in the door may not be the biggest obstacle. Disabilities range from mobility impairment to problems with sight and hearing. Some services themselves are impossible for disabled persons to use. Some Texas workforce boards are making strides to solve these issues. The capital area board installed a Braille printer. The Workforce Center of North Texas has special computers on site for the disabled.[23] But most workforce centers in Texas lack services geared for the disabled, a weakness of the Texas workforce system noted by the Texas House of Representatives Committee on Economic Development in its Interim Report to the 77th Legislature.[24]

Individuals with Low Levels of Literacy

When customers enter a Texas workforce center, they typically are guided toward a computer database or binder full of job openings to review. This procedure is completely ineffective for those who cannot read. As Comptroller Carole Keeton Rylander documented in her *E-Texas Report*, Texas ranked 47th among the 50 states in literacy.[25] Almost 25 percent of the adult population in Texas cannot read basic signs or maps, or complete job applications or deposit slips.[26]

Some workforce centers offer literacy classes, but not all centers can afford this. Even customers with low reading skills might be intimidated by the centers and feel too uncomfortable to access services. If they ask the right questions of the right people, they can be referred to literacy classes and related training to help them in their endeavors. But the likelihood of someone getting this far is fairly slim. One can hope that every person would have the inclination to inquire about literacy classes or options for those who do not read at an average level, but that may be presuming too much. Workforce centers may offer the tools, but they often fail to offer adequate instruction to assist customers in using them.[27]

Individuals Inexperienced with Computer Technology

Many aspiring job applicants do not feel comfortable with computer technology. Some have no experience using a computer. Yet workforce centers use computers more than any other avenue to help people find employment. This presents problems for those who are intimidated or do not have the skills to use computers. Some centers offer training classes designed to help people become more familiar with and less intimidated by computers. Or an employee may take the time to show people simple skills such as Internet searching or perhaps just how to use a computer mouse. However, during busy times, providing such individual attention is not always possible. In a crowded center, staff may never notice a patron who walks in, sees that there are computers everywhere, and walks out. Such visitors may never be approached by a workforce center employee to inform them about opportunities for instruction in literacy or the use of computers.

Individuals Unfamiliar with Work Environments

Some job seekers may not know how to deal with a working environment. Perhaps they lack the "soft skills" required for a serious work environment. Soft skills are those skills necessary not just for one specific job but for all jobs. They include how to speak to one's boss or how to dress appropriately for work. Many people have never learned how to effectively solve an issue with a co-worker or a boss simply by talking. Soft skills can also include the ability to find day care, to arrive at work on time, or simply to ask for help when necessary.[28] Many do not consider these skills important, but without them individuals are less marketable and less likely to be successful in their career paths.[29] According to a recent report by the EnterTech Project, employers repeatedly noted they are willing and able to teach job-related tasks, but it is much harder to teach a person to be a "good worker." [30]

Some center managers argue that short-term soft skills training is often more effective than long-term occupational skills training. The lack of soft skills can often lead to returning to the center without employment. Most centers offer various training classes intended to teach customers soft skills such as dressing appropriately, accepting supervision, coping with co-workers, and getting organized. However, due to financial restrictions and staffing constraints, the number and breadth of classes is simply inadequate to serve the population.[31]

Job Applicants Lacking Child Care

Another potential barrier facing many unemployed persons who may want to use a workforce center is lack of child care. Many single mothers and fathers lack child-care arrangements to leave home for even a short time. Workforce centers generally offer play areas for customers' children, but most offer only unsupervised care.

According to an interim report prepared for the 77th Texas Legislature by the House Committee on Economic Development, the biggest concerns for Local Workforce Development Boards are performance measures, funding, and child care.[32] Many boards have extensive waiting lists for child care. These lists will continue to grow as more parents move from welfare to work. Another shortcoming in child care is the limited hours of operation. Child care is usually not available outside the standard 8 A.M. to 5 P.M. workday. Many persons utilizing the one-stop center do so at nontraditional hours because of their work schedules.[33]

Although several workforce centers have a TANF employee on site to help people with services, an alarming number of workforce center employees are unaware of the services the state can provide welfare-to-work recipients. Several of the workforce center employees we interviewed, when asked about TANF and food stamps, were unsure how to help and referred us to an 800 number to call. A person walking into a workforce center eligible for other services thus may not be provided with all the information needed.

Using Information Technology to Enhance Texas Workforce Centers

Many individuals previously described could be reached with improved information technologies. Aimed at providing better customer service within the workforce system, the following recommendations address information technology enhancements that are currently available.

PDAs/ Scanners

Certain workforce centers currently employ computer devices that improve efficiency and accuracy within the system. Some workforce centers, such as the Killeen center, provide their employees with PDAs (personal digital assistants, such as palm pilots or handsprings). These allow the worker to travel to a meeting with a potential employer and enter information as it is received, thus improving the efficacy of the job bank system. The Texas Department of Human Services has also considered the possibility of using scanners to immediately enter data provided by a customer regarding his or her needs or applications.[34] This scan technology would be implemented both by the DHS and local workforce centers, thereby better linking the two systems. A worker will be able to scan in a customer's documents so that job seekers do not have to carry such papers as birth certificates and social security cards to each office. Through a scanner, a job seeker can import a resume, a proof of citizenship, or other important documents. Perhaps eventually a type of push technology will be in place, one that alerts the workforce center staff if a desired job has come into the system or when a customer is due for Medicaid renewal. In line with a recommendation made in Chapter 6 of this report, workforce center employees can be supported with easily accessed information and training on the Internet.

Workforce centers should use the best technology possible to provide front-line employees with real-time information that enables one-stop processes that meet customer needs. In the business world, companies utilize technology to maintain a competitive edge.[35] Texas workforce centers should do the same.

Overcoming Computer Literacy Problems with Touch Screen Technology

Many people are nervous and apprehensive about using computers. Most centers have "dumb terminals" available for those uncomfortable with computers. Such terminals allow customers to examine an entire database of jobs using only two keys. However, both the terminology and the technology of these terminals are inadequate. Admittedly, in order to completely close the digital divide, the goal is to train every customer to be computer proficient. Nevertheless, if a customer feels uneasy on the first visit to the workforce center and does not return, then the system may not have a second chance to serve that individual. It is imperative, therefore, to have appropriate terminals available for these customers.

Touch screens may prove highly effective in serving customers who are less comfortable with the computers. While more expensive than the conventional computers, touch screen technology has already been created and utilized in a variety of public places, from malls to sports arenas. Touch screens allow those who are uncomfortable with a keyboard to avoid initial stress, as well as offering potential access to individuals who are completely computer illiterate.

One of the least efficient practices of the current workforce centers is the initial intake process, in which the customer completes a form that is then entered into the system by another person. More efficient procedures can be implemented. For example, the staff member greeting the customer could input the customer's information directly into the database on the spot. In the same interchange, the staff member could direct the customer to services appropriate the individual's needs.

Soft Skills Training Programs

Lack of soft skills can cost an employee a job or the opportunity for a job. In addition to hard skills, such as typing and computer proficiency, employees must have the ability to work well with others, to manage their emotions, and to deal with stressful working situations. Computer-based programs are available to teach "soft skills." ACS State and Local Solutions (formerly entitled the Lockheed Martin Corporation), a contractor that operates several workforce centers throughout Texas, has developed software for soft skills training.[36] The program, entitled "Opening the Doors to Work," offers a flexible open-entry, open-exit format which allows customers to learn on their own schedule and pace.[37] Soft skills are probably best taught by mixing instruction using information technology with human interaction. By implementing a combined package of computer work (using video, interactive media, and skills testing) with a human facilitator, this program could go a long way toward bringing soft skills to the larger clientele. The EnterTech Project also seeks to combine hard and soft skills into a comprehensive training package. While many workforce centers currently offer some form of soft skills training, the number and variability of these classes are inadequate.

Online or Virtual One-Stops

With the spread of personal computers and improved special needs online access, it now appears that the best technology option may be to create an excellent online workforce center to be used by new and returning customers alike. One of the greatest advantages to an online one-stop is that it ameliorates the transportation and child-care issues. Many workforce centers are in hard-to-reach locations, effectively eliminating a portion of the potential clients who simply have no means by which to arrive at the center. The option to register online could permit a job seeker or employer to obtain service without having to physically travel to the workforce center. The online site would provide many of the services already offered at the physical locations, such as job registry, job matching, job bank access, online help with resumes, access to social services, and perhaps job training. This would require the creation of a more user-friendly online guide to access training, as well as the creation and implementation of more Web-based training. Soft skills may be the hardest set of skills to teach over the Internet, but the teaching of soft skills can be highly effective using basic software mixed with interactive media, such as chat rooms and video/audio programs. Programs such as the EnterTech Project are already working to create systems to teach soft skills in an equitable and effective way, and eventually such instruction may be delivered over the Internet.

A new gap will open as we attempt to access and educate both computer illiterate customers and those who do not have access to the Internet. While there is still a gaping digital divide in our society, created by socioeconomic and educational inequities, the trend is toward broader computer literacy. Texas must continue and expand the excellent work being accomplished in community centers, public housing, churches, community colleges, and schools to bring computer accessibility to everyone.

Much work remains to make online workforce systems effective and user friendly. Even the North Central Texas Workforce Development online site, which is lauded as an excellent site, is still quite general in its services, offering a listing of jobs statewide and nationally. This means that a user must go through the job application process for each of the online job banks, of which there are 56. This can be tedious and frustrating for users, especially for those unfamiliar with computers.

Compatibility remains a key problem. Bill Grossenbacher, director of Career Centers for ACS State and Local Solutions, noted that the most difficult aspect of implementing online or virtual job matching in one-stop centers is matching the program with the state's already existing hardware and software. To help resolve these problems in Texas, all commercial programs considered for use in creating a virtual one-stop center must be compatible with The Workforce Information System of Texas (TWIST) system. Most existing commercial programs are not compatible. While the TWC is working on a solution to this issue, this is major problem that impedes efforts to improve online job matching.[38]

Recommendations and Conclusions

Recommendation 5-1: Texas workforce centers should strive to stay technologically modern and up-to-date.

Recommendation 5-2: Literacy training and employability skills or "soft skills" training should be widely available.

Recommendation 5-3: The Texas workforce system should establish online or virtual workforce centers to provide services over the Internet.

Recommendation 5-4: Problems of incompatibilities between local, state, and federal systems must be overcome.

Information technology offers the promise of enhancing the services of workforce centers in several ways. Through the use of personal digital assistants, staff can post job openings immediately as they receive them from employers. Scanners could be used to input data, developing electronic records that can be shared across agencies, and avoiding a laborious process of duplicating entry. An online or virtual system can provide services and training to individuals who are unable to travel to a workforce center due to disabilities or lack of transportation or child care.

Advanced technology could improve the image of workforce centers, making them more visible in the community. The centers could be advertised on the World Wide Web. More high-skilled individuals may be attracted to use the workforce centers from remote or home access, especially if the workforce centers can obtain more postings for high-skilled job openings. This group would likely benefit from more advanced information technologies in workforce centers. Highly skilled individuals would be able to take advantage of the self-service features of the system.

A 1997 paper envisioned a future virtual workforce center, accessible through kiosk and satellite offices placed in a variety of public areas, including grocery stores and malls.[39] Tools and features such as touch screens, scanners, and PDAs are already in use in many Texas centers, and most LWDBs are in the process of improving their online sites.

Information technology can resolve some of the problems and challenges of the workforce center system in Texas. However, not every problem can be solved by technology alone. Some call for human intervention. Most solutions involve a combination of the application of technological tools and human resources. For example, illiterate persons trying to obtain employment will not be better served by having a faster modem. What may help these people more is to have adult literacy programs available online in the centers, along with the assistance of instructors or tutors who can guide them and help to make the process easier. Customers who are uncomfortable using computer keyboards may be better served by one-on-one, hands-on training, using touch screen computers. Such an approach can ease them into using a computer and help them to become familiar with the equipment.

Many of the problems with the workforce centers stem from the fact that there is not enough money for them to operate at their full potential. Most of the gaps in the system could be better handled with additional employees. The Federal Benchmarking Consortium concluded in its study that enabled employees provide the key to good one-stop service.[40] The consortium encouraged business to invest more time and money in hiring the right, qualified persons for the job, to train them fully, and to constantly keep them skilled in current technology. If workforce centers could hire additional qualified employees, more services of better quality could be offered to customers. Ample staff could be available to help individuals unable to read, those unfamiliar with computers, and other underserved groups. Knowledgeable staff can provide invaluable support to customers with accessibility requirements, as well as information about TANF and welfare-to-work programs. While some tasks can effectively be undertaken with computers, other tasks can only be achieved through human interaction. In the end, combinations of technology and human interaction are needed.

As its mission, the Texas Workforce Commission aims to "promote and support a workforce system that offers individuals, employers, and communities the opportunity to achieve and sustain economic prosperity."[41] To fulfill this mission, it is imperative that Texas ascertain which groups are not being served and implement solutions to close the gaps in service.

The need to improve the Texas workforce system is at hand. Although Texas was initially exempted from the federal standards mandated by the federal Welfare Investment Act of 1998, the grandfather clause will soon run out for participants in the Temporary Assistance to Families (TANF) program.[42] Beginning April 1, 2002, Texas expects to be prohibited from accepting as many work waivers, forcing more people to actively seek employment as a requirement to receive state aid. Serving the anticipated increased numbers of job seekers effectively will demand creative approaches involving more efficient uses of information technology and additional staff resources.

Notes

[1] Corporation for a Skilled Workforce, *Reinventing One-Stop Systems to Flourish in the Internet Environment,* comment by Larry Good, 2000 (pamphlet).

[2] Interview by Piper Stege and Jema Turk with Bill Grossenbacher, Director of Career Centers, ACS State and Local Solutions (formerly Lockheed Martin Corporation), Austin, Texas, May 23, 2001.

[3] Telephone interview by Robert W. Glover with Linda Angel, Strategic Planning, Manager, Excellence, Marketing, Creativity and Capital (EMC2), Central Texas Workforce System, Killeen, Texas. October 16, 2001.

[4] Robert McPherson, *Designing a Local Workforce Services Delivery System*, vol. 4 (Austin: Ray Marshall Center for the Study of Human Resources, The University of Texas at Austin, February 1997), p. v.

[5] Interview by Piper Stege and Jema Turk with David Duncan, Director of Governmental Relations, Texas Workforce Commission (TWC), Austin, Texas, March 31, 2001.

[6] TWC, *How Texas Works: 2000 Annual Report* (Austin, Texas, 2000), inside cover page.

[7] Ibid., p. 20.

[8] U.S. Department of Labor (DOL), "Final Report: Creating Workforce Development Systems That Work" (Washington, D.C., November 1, 1997), p. ES-2.

[9] Ibid., pp. 2-29.

[10] TWC, *How Texas Works: 2000 Annual Report*, p. 48.

[11] Interview by Piper Stege and Jema Turk with Mike Stratton, Manager, North Austin Workforce Center, Rundberg Road, Austin, Texas, October 7, 2000.

[12] TWC, *How Texas Works: 2000 Annual Report*, pp. 24-25.

[13] Interview by Piper Stege and Jema Turk with Gerry Fluharty, Special Initiatives/Products Specialist, Killeen One-Stop Center, Killeen, Texas, November 2, 2000.

[14] U.S. Department of Labor (DOL), "Final Report," pp. 2-18.

[15] TWC, *How Texas Works: 2000 Annual Report*, p. 24.

[16] Angel interview.

[17] Ibid.

[18] Fluharty interview.

[19] Federal Benchmarking Consortium, *Best Practices in One-Stop Customer Service: Serving the American Public Study Report* (Washington, D.C.: U.S. Government Printing Office, November 1997).

[20] U.S. Congress, House, *Workforce Investment Act*, H.R. 1385, 105th Congress, 2nd Session (1998).

[21] Ibid.

[22] Texas House of Representatives, Economic Development Committee, *Interim Report to the 77th Texas Legislature,* November 2000.

[23] Ibid.

[24] Ibid.

[25] Texas Comptroller of Public Accounts, *e-Texas Report: Recommendations.* Online. Available: http://www.e-texas.org/recommend/. Accessed: March 1, 2001.

[26] Ibid.

[27] Interview by Piper Stege and Jema Turk with David Groening, Private Consultant and Project Manager, Austin, Texas, April 12, 2001.

[28] Texas Comptroller, *e-Texas Recommendations.*

[29] EnterTech, *Knowledge, Skills and Abilities Required for Entry-level Jobs in the Technology Industry and the Related Supply and Service Industries.* Online. Available: http://www.utexas.edu/depts/ic2/et/ksa/ksa.html. Accessed: April 2, 2001.

[30] Ibid.

[31] Fluharty interview.

[32] Ibid.

[33] Ibid.

[34] Interview by Piper Stege and Jema Turk with Michael Lucas and Doug Smith, Committee Clerks, Texas House of Representatives Human Services Committee, Austin, Texas, October 23, 2000.

[35] Federal Benchmarking Consortium, *Best Practices in One-Stop Customer Service.*

[36] Interview by Piper Stege and Jema Turk with Steve Minnich, Vice President of ACS State and Local Solutions (formerly Lockheed Martin Corporation), Austin, Texas, October 15, 2000.

[37] Grossenbacher interview.

[38] Grossenbacher interview.

[39] McPherson, *Designing a Local Workforce Services Delivery System*, p. 57.

[40] Federal Benchmarking Consortium, *Best Practices in One-Stop Customer Service*.

[41] TWC, *How Texas Works: 2000 Annual Report*, inside cover.

[42] Duncan interview.

Chapter 6. Using Information Technology to Support and Train Case Managers in the Workforce System

Background

Texas was one of the first states to take action on reforming its workforce development system. The Texas Legislature recognized that there was a lack of coordination among workforce programs, and as a result, from 1989 to 1991, several studies were conducted.[1] These reports resulted in the initial conception of the Texas Workforce Commission (TWC).[2] During the 74th session of the Texas State Legislature in 1995, H.B. 1863 was passed, establishing TWC and the network of 28 local workforce development boards (LWDBs). The legislation consolidated numerous welfare and workforce programs within the new TWC, including the employment component of Aid to Families with Dependent Children (AFDC) and all programs operated under the Job Training Partnership Act (JTPA). The comprehensive reforms in the workforce system created by this legislation put Texas at the forefront three years before the federal government took action on workforce issues. TWC was responsible for allocating funds to the 28 local workforce boards. Each board, in turn, was held accountable for contracting for the delivery of workforce services in the area.[3] In addition, one of the features unique to the reform in Texas was providing LWDBs with child-care money and responsibility for carrying out this service. The added functions presented serious challenges for case managers unfamiliar with child-care issues.

On the federal level, the major reforms to the welfare and workforce systems came with the passage of the Personal Responsibility and Work Opportunity Reconciliation Act of 1996, which ended AFDC, replacing it with the Temporary Assistance to Needy Families (TANF) program; the Balanced Budget Act of 1997, which created welfare-to-work programs; the Workforce Investment Act (WIA) of 1998, which replaced JTPA with WIA programs; and the Perkins Act of 1998, which reformed secondary and postsecondary education programs.[4]

Through time, a common theme in both state and federal legislation has been an increased emphasis on local control. Decision making devolved from federal to state and local decision makers and privatization increased.[5] The philosophy was that local boards would drive the plans for the development of programs and staff according to the needs of each community.

Reform in the workforce development system did not occur overnight or without substantial turf battles among agencies. There was an "ongoing feud between the Department of Human Services and the TWC about who controls policy for welfare-related changes—despite the presumed consolidation of [education] and training [programs] in TWC."[6] Central to both the welfare and workforce delivery systems is the case manager.

Throughout history, the role of the case manager has evolved considerably—from the days of the 19th century systems of poor relief, to the settlement movement, to the medical almoners of the 1880s:

> Over time, social workers have acquired a special responsibility for people whose particular needs fall outside the aegis of other professions and agencies . . . personal social services meet a wide spectrum of needs arising from the more routine contingencies of living. Inevitably personal social services are primarily concerned with reacting to a crisis as it occurs, but today much effort is being invested in preventive work and in the enhancement of welfare in the wider community.[7]

Depending on the context, the term *case manager* has many different meanings. In this chapter, *case manager* is defined as the primary contact in a face-to-face interaction with individuals needing welfare, workforce development, or other social services. The case manager oversees the process of providing those services to that individual. As the term *case manager* is used in this chapter, it implies a person who is employed as a caseworker or career specialist. These terms are used interchangeably.

As the primary contact for any individual walking through the door of a workforce center, the case manager facilitates access to a wide range of services. In general, those needing the services of a workforce center are unemployed and/or lower skilled workers. Their needs often extend far beyond simply finding a job. The case manager must have a thorough understanding of the laws, rules, and regulations relating to welfare and workforce services. Also, the case manager must be able to work effectively with a variety of individuals, situations, and cultures. Today's case manager often wears multiple hats; he or she is the counselor, friend, and resource for one client, and authority, teacher, and trainer for another. Thus, case managers are required to provide assistance in an empathetic manner, while also being assertive in enforcing the requirements of programs. In today's changing economy, the ability to learn a skill set, once relegated to the business school discipline (e.g., computer-based technology, strategic planning, and goal setting) is also becoming increasingly important for the case manager.[8]

Compliance with the various rules and regulations can produce a paper chase for the case manager. The proverbial red tape of the welfare and workforce development systems often makes it difficult for the case manager to wear the hat of his or her choice. Caseworkers typically choose their profession to fulfill a desire to help others by matching them with jobs, increasing a client's economic independence, and ultimately ensuring that the needs of individual clients are met. The daily routine of filling out forms and pushing paper for increasing caseloads ends up superseding the more gratifying components of the job. Those who find it increasingly difficult to fulfill their initial aspirations often experience serious burnout.[9]

While caseloads vary greatly on the national level and throughout Texas, they are very high overall. The Central Texas Workforce Center in Killeen operates with a total of nine case managers who are specifically involved in providing services to customers in various programs: TANF, food stamps, WIA, ES (employment services), or welfare-to-work. Presently, each case manager at the Killeen Workforce Center has a caseload of approximately 60 clients. According to knowledgeable observers, caseloads of 40 to 50 clients or more impede the case manager's ability to manage the details of client planning, including identification and removal of employment barriers, successful goal-setting processes, and client tracking.[10]

While current caseloads may limit a case manager's ability to carry out his or her duties in an effective manner, an increase in workload will exacerbate this problem. Due to the time limits in welfare legislation, a large number of women were forced to leave Texas' welfare rolls, resulting in a 45 percent reduction in TANF recipients.[11] Despite initial declines, however, caseloads are expected to significantly increase in coming years. According to Ben Lopez, a program specialist at the Killeen Workforce Center, "Once the waiver for Texas welfare reform laws expires in March of 2002, there is an expectation that caseloads will dramatically increase by 50 percent or more."[12] Recent changes in the economy will also have an impact on caseloads. A slowdown of the economy in late 2000 and continuing into 2002 has reduced the number of available jobs in the state. A job deficit further affects caseloads and a case manager's ability to get clients into sustainable jobs. For example, a high-skilled worker, such as a software developer, will have a less difficult time finding comparable employment elsewhere. In contrast, a worker with minimal skills and multiple barriers will struggle to gain employment, and he or she will require assistance. In fact, earlier work predicted such a scenario:

> If as a nation we fail to improve the academic and occupational competencies of welfare recipients now—during a period when the economy is robust, state and federal treasuries are relatively full, and time limits have yet to expire for most welfare recipients—the problems of doing so will be even more difficult later on when the economy takes a serious downturn.[13]

Faced with ever-changing legislation, the demands of complex bureaucratic systems, changing responsibilities, and increased caseloads, the case manager faces an increasingly difficult situation. The function of today's case manager is central to the workforce development system. Operating within various contexts, caseworkers are confronted with the challenge of assisting and supporting a hard-to-serve population that faces multiple barriers to employment. Additionally, the case manager is responsible for staying current on federal and state regulations. This chapter examines the challenges of placing recipients into long-term employment rather than in the first available job. In discussing the role of the case manager, the most important question to consider is, how can the welfare and workforce systems invest in case managers to produce positive outcomes for individuals seeking help? In addressing this question, the chapter discusses current problems resulting from recent reforms and subsequent service fragmentation, proposes technological solutions, and offers other recommendations.

The Key Role of the Case Manager

The ability to acquire the necessary skills, do a job well, and hold onto it can make a significant difference in one's life. The typical case handled by the caseworker is one in which the client has little, or no, work experience, is living in poverty, has children, and, other than government assistance and possibly some support from the absent father, has no reliable means of taking care of them. Thus, the case manager's role is crucial to the assistance of moving this household from a state of immobility and dependence to a state of progression and self-sufficiency.

Studies reveal that adults receiving TANF not only require a tremendous amount of assistance but also need considerable encouragement. In fact, in the 1998 fiscal year, almost half of the adult Texas population receiving TANF had no work history.[14] The findings of a study on the impact of welfare time limits in Texas indicate that two-thirds of the women forced to exit the welfare system completed high school or acquired a GED, yet over half were functioning well below their educational attainment levels.[15] This situation poses a serious challenge to assisting this population in its transition from welfare to sustainable work. A 1996 study conducted by the Urban Institute compared adults who were receiving assistance by educational status and found that welfare recipients who had dropped out of high school were least likely to participate in skill-building activities.[16] Due to high job turnover rates, such adults are further isolated by their inability to escape the welfare cycle. Jobs for which they are qualified are commonly low wage, providing minimal benefits. Such employment is unstable and offers little security, making it very difficult for these women to remain employed.[17]

This population has not only had limited access to education, training, and employment but has also endured more hardship than most people ever experience. Issues that many people take for granted—literacy, reliable transportation, child care, shelter, and the ability to pay rent—create crises for this group and become additional barriers to training and jobs. Although these might seem to be non-work-related problems, they are certainly related to success in obtaining and sustaining employment. Indeed, a national study conducted by Mathematica Policy Research revealed that of the 1,200-plus welfare recipients involved in employment retention programs, approximately 70 percent of those who found jobs "reported problems outside of work that made it difficult to hold onto their jobs."[18] Child care, finances and budgeting, family problems, and transportation were cited as most problematic in retaining a job.[19] An EnterTech study cites additional barriers, providing further insight into the breadth of the problem. In the EnterTech study, instructors with experience teaching welfare populations report attitudinal weaknesses (e.g., lack of self-awareness and self-confidence, fear of success, a diminished sense of responsibility; sexual, physical, and emotional abuse; and lack of sleep) as prominent hindrances among their students.[20] These typical obstacles prevent many individuals from obtaining and maintaining employment. As a result of these numerous issues, it is often very difficult for such individuals to be hired into well-paid positions or to keep well-paid jobs once they obtain one:[21]

Both welfare and workforce development providers indicate that more of their current caseload is hard-to-serve, that is, they face multiple barriers to employment and, once employed, require additional supports to remain employed. Typical barriers include substance abuse and mental health problems, low basic and family life skills, and little to no work experience.[22]

Moreover, with growing caseloads, the responsibilities of the case manager are likely to expand well beyond the delivery of the welfare check. Adequate and effective provision of services will become increasingly important:

> This population requires intensive services to help them become job-ready. More intensive services might result from the agency being able to combine resources to serve a client. For example, welfare and workforce development agencies may be able to use resources from their respective programs to provide a more comprehensive package of support services for a client.[23]

Current Problems

The intent behind enactment of the legislative measures in Texas was to streamline and enhance the workforce and welfare systems. However, attempts to integrate these two systems were met with challenges from the conflicting ideologies and lack of cross-training on legislative reforms and regulations affecting both systems. Assisting hard-to-serve populations means not only providing the training necessary to gain entry into the workforce but also providing the tools necessary to maintain a job. This challenge involves the shifting of steadfast ideologies. Since workforce centers are the main entities coordinating the welfare and workforce development systems at the front line, the polarity of their respective guiding philosophies needs to be addressed. Due to the work participation and caseload reduction goals of welfare-to-work, as well as time limits for cash assistance, the TANF approach emphasizes getting clients into a job quickly.[24] These welfare reforms, consequently, will have a negative effect on workforce development. The "work-first" philosophy generally dictates that individuals be placed in the first job available, which generally means low wages, few benefits, and minimal or no advancement opportunities. According to national statistics, the outcome is that almost half of those who leave the TANF rolls return within a year.[25] This situation creates problems both for individuals needing employment and for prospective employers, who may not be able to afford to invest time or money into training individuals with very low skills.[26]

A convoluted process of diversions often characterizes the work-first approach. The procedures make it difficult for individuals to find, let alone, sustain employment. This process, taking weeks to a month to unfold, essentially shuffles individuals back and forth between welfare and workforce systems. In Texas, prior to the acceptance of an application for public assistance, a client is first sent to a resource room at the Department of Human Services (DHS) to seek shelter, food, and employment assistance. At this point, regardless of whether one's application is accepted or not, it may be held while the client is diverted to the workforce agency for a self-directed job search.

Finally, the processing of the application does not actually begin until a client is able to demonstrate that he or she has made a genuine effort to find employment.[27]

While TANF is guided by the work-first approach, the workforce development philosophy focuses more on investing in and building human capital. This approach emphasizes the importance of training clients for higher wage jobs with advancement potential.[28]

> One employment and training worker suggested that clients should use the time available on TANF to take advantage of WtW [welfare-to-work] and other programs so that when they do get a job, it will be a better job and they will have the skills for continued employment and advancement, thus reducing the chance of ever needing welfare again.[29]

With the implementation of WIA, there has been conflict between the philosophies of the welfare and workforce systems. Influenced by the incentives and political urgencies accompanying welfare reform legislation, WIA now largely embraces a work-first approach.[30]

Case Managers Need Information Support

For TANF clients receiving additional benefits through the welfare-to-work program, a number of activities and services are available. To meet the aforementioned challenge of job obtainment and retention, TANF recipients should be encouraged to access services available at each phase of the continuum, as shown in Table 6.1. Case managers should receive training in these areas to make sure their clients are utilizing the range of services available to them. Further, this additional information can help the case manager support the client throughout the process, from initial entry to exit from the system.

Table 6.1
Services for TANF Clients Required to Participate in Work Activities

Case Management
Pre-employment Services

Assessment
    Job readiness training
    Family life skills
    GED/ABE
    Basic skills training
    Job-specific skills training

Employment Services

Job search/job club/job placement
    Resource room (job bank)
    Labor market information
    Job development
    Work experience

Post-employment Services
Retention services   Advancement services (may include additional skills training)

Source: Nancy Pindus, Robin Koralek, Karin Martinson, and John Trutko, *Coordination and Integration of Welfare and Workforce Development System*s, Chapter 2: "Coordination and Service Delivery." Online. Available: http://aspe.hhs.gov/hsp/coord00/index.htm. Accessed: February 13, 2001

Case Managers Need Training

A second challenge relates to the lack of initial training for the case manager on the impacts of workforce and welfare policies. The one-stop workforce centers were allocated funds that were tied to needs-based formulas, thus creating specific types of case managers. As a result, some case managers focused solely on providing WIA-related services (e.g., adult, youth, dislocated worker), TANF choices, welfare-to-work, food stamps, or child care. Therefore, a case manager may be proficient in one aspect of the system (e.g., workforce), but may not have been exposed to the service offerings available under the new legislation (e.g., benefits for welfare recipients). Since the legislation did not include a cross-training component for the case manager, the availability of a wider range of employment and training services for welfare recipients may not be fully realized by the case manager under the current structure.

In Texas, the training for TANF and WIA legislation and policy is primarily conducted at the local level through local workforce development boards. The TWC provides technical assistance to boards requesting help, as well as offering information on final rules for TANF and WIA. Workforce development notices, outlining the TANF customer's eligibility for WIA, are distributed statewide by the TWC via electronic means. Based on information provided, each LWDB decides whether to enroll a TANF recipient in WIA or not. Each LWDB must become familiar with applicable federal and state regulations and ensure that contractors are abiding by the regulations. Field monitors from the TWC visit each LWDB area to ensure that regulations are followed. In some Texas workforce areas, cross-training of WIA and TANF workforce specialists is conducted to provide TANF recipients with additional services.[31] Given the general lack of integration among training services, information technology can support the case manager by making information on both welfare and workforce systems readily available. Though there have been attempts to integrate the two systems, to date these have not been as successful as intended.

Current Technology Uses

A number of technologically oriented approaches have been developed and implemented on both the local and state levels to assist with the coordination of services between the welfare and workforce systems.

The Workforce Information System of Texas (TWIST) is a state-supported system that relies on local data input provided by case managers and others. Using the state's existing technology, TWIST attempts to integrate statewide data so that case managers can share information about clients in real time. The client's complete profile, along with a database of job opportunities, is available online, thus eliminating the duplication of effort in entering client information at each point of contact. The database tracks the client as he or she moves within the system.

From both a management and staff perspective, TWIST provides some innovative and efficient ways to deliver services. The former executive director of the Texas Workforce Commission said, "TWIST is our answer to finding a way to use technology as a means to place Texans in jobs and provide them with the training they need to keep those jobs. Ultimately, it is about improving the quality of life for Texans." A TWIST program manager further commented that "as state employees, we need to find ways to do more with fewer resources. TWIST is an integrated approach that enables users to spend less time managing information and more time helping their clients."[32] The system includes information on TANF, employment services, the Food Stamp Employment and Training Program, JOBS, JTPA, child care, unemployment insurance (UI), supplemental security income, food stamps, and child support.[33]

One drawback of the TWIST program is that the system is not accessible to anyone outside of the TWC network, including social service entities and housing agencies.[34] Also, for some case managers within the system, there is still a sharp learning curve with respect to this software, and thus they often do not use the system to its fullest capabilities.[35] Other drawbacks include problems with timeliness, completeness, and accuracy of the data.

In 1999, the Texas Legislature created the Texas Integrated Enrollment Redesign System (TIERS). The primary goal of TIERS was to improve access to social service programs administered by the DHS by creating an integrated system for determining eligibility requirements for its programs.[36]

One of the challenges posed to TWIST and TIERS is that there are contradictory program requirements and separate funding provisions for federal and state policies. While the two systems are beneficial to their respective agencies, the fact that they are separate exacerbates the fragmentation of the system. As a GAO study concluded: "The variety and complexity of eligibility requirements for different federal programs have presented a major challenge for the State's plan to design an integrated system intended to improve the efficient completion of eligibility processes."[37]

In addition to statewide technology initiatives, local workforce boards have adopted technology systems specifically designed to meet the needs of each community. For example, each workforce specialist at the Killeen Workforce Center has a desktop computer with Internet access. The Business Services Unit at the Central Texas Workforce Board facilitates sharing of information to network users on job orders placed into the system. The information sharing is accomplished by keying in specific job order information, which is then sent via email distribution to designated users within the network. A specialist working with a customer can see a job order and its specific qualifications in real time and then print the order for a customer referral. The same specialist may view any job order placed in the system by accessing the workforce center's website at www.workforcelink.com. The website maintains a data bank of available jobs for job seekers and allows a local business to place job orders as well. The specialists can use the website to encourage customers to enter their resumes online. Businesses that place job orders on the website can search the center's resume database for potential interviewees. This technology, called "Taking Care of Business," was developed by a staff member of the Central Texas Workforce Center in Killeen, Texas.[38]

Customers on public assistance receiving center services via the Choices/FS E&T/welfare-to-work programs are also eligible to receive formal assessment. As part of the assessment process, a career interest inventory entitled "Career Compass" asks customers to answer several questions online to determine types of careers in which they might be interested.[39]

Finally, another technology used by the workforce specialists is an information and referral database called Paladin. This software allows staff to seek potential community resources for a customer's unmet needs. A specialist can search for resources by city and type of resource and then make the necessary referral.[40]

While there have been attempts to integrate systems and to make information more readily accessible to the case manager, seamless delivery of services to the client has not been fully realized. The goal of the TWC is to create a system that is less programmatic for the case manager and more focused on a comprehensive approach to service delivery via trained case managers. State and federal regulations have resulted in the creation of 28 LWDBs that are all on different levels in terms of delivery of services. The staff hired by the workforce boards and their contractors represent a wide variety of skills sets. The different skill levels have resulted in workforce boards offering differing levels and quality of workforce services and information technology systems.

The shortcomings of the technology in these systems have been especially challenging for the case manager because of the limited coordination between the automated workforce and welfare systems. In the new welfare environment, case managers are accountable for results (placements) as well as being expected to use the system to find out what services the clients are eligible to receive. According to the GAO report cited earlier,

> With respect to information needs for case management, the major shortcoming—which exists to varying degrees across the states—is an inability to obtain data on individual TANF recipients from some of the agencies serving them, including job assistance agencies. This situation makes it difficult for TANF case managers to arrange needed services; ensure that the services are provided; and respond quickly when problems arise, such as when a recipient does not attend a scheduled work activity.[41]

Computer access by case managers to information regarding food stamps, TANF work activities, child support enforcement, Medicaid eligibility determination, and transportation subsidies for TANF is often limited. A GAO study concluded that "case managers in most localities do not have desktop access to data from automated systems for welfare-to-work grants, the JTPA, job listings, child welfare programs, vocational rehabilitation, and subsidized housing."[42]

Furthermore, interviews conducted with over 400 case managers indicate the limitations of training opportunities, the lack of coordination between agencies, and the challenges faced by welfare and workforce reform. Daniel O'Shea, a research associate from the Ray Marshall Center for the Study of Human Resources of the LBJ School of Public Affairs at The University of Texas at Austin summed up the shortcomings as follows:

> Case mangers often complain that the technology is too slow and they don't receive adequate training. A further challenge is that even though the services are all in one place, there are different reporting requirements for each program. Finally, every time regulations change, reporting measures change.[43]

How Can Information Technology Help Support and Train Case Management and Workforce Staff?

Improved communication among the technology systems and databases within the workforce and welfare systems is needed to help deliver services to clients in Texas effectively, efficiently, and equitably. Information technology solutions should be designed to better support and train case managers. Technology applications that allow the case manager to instantaneously access information could support their understanding of the complex set of regulations and procedures for federal and state requirements.

Further, software could enable the case manager to track clients in the workforce and welfare system to ensure they are meeting requirements and not getting "lost" in the system. Information technology could enable the case manager to identify services for which a client is eligible and to tap into those resources. Technology such as online database services could provide the case managers with a real-time list of available support services (e.g., child care or transportation) for their clients.

Technology can enhance the case manager's ability to deliver services, thus functioning as a complement, not as a substitute, for the case manager. The end result of technology solutions should be that clients are leaving the system to enter higher paid positions with growth and advancement potential. A report prepared for the U.S. Department of Health and Human Services further supports this balance of technology and human interaction:

> It appears that the ability to access many referral services and take a more holistic approach to addressing barriers to work is especially important for the hard-to-serve client. Looking ahead, however, the increased reliance on technology may not meet the needs of those clients who require more personal attention. However, technology may free up time for providers so that they can devote more attention to the hard-to-serve. Location, access, and referral mechanisms need to be considered from both vantage points—maximizing the effective use of technology and facilitating the progress of the hard-to-serve.[44]

Others agree that using e-learning tools to train case managers provides high-quality instruction at a low marginal cost.[45]

Given these observations, the following recommendations seek to facilitate the learning process for case managers in the welfare and workforce systems and to support their role in providing information about available services to the client. These alternatives seek out solutions that would help the case manager, while not being too burdensome by requiring substantial additional training. Further, the technology solutions suggested are complementary components to enhance the services provided by the case manager.

Combining technology with the human aspect of case management ensures that services are provided in a more efficient, effective, and equitable manner. The delivery of services can become a more enriching experience both for the client and the case manager through technology solutions that can help case managers stay current on the latest guidelines and requirements of federal and state programs.

Recommendation 6-1: Local workforce boards and other agencies that provide case management services (including DHS and TWC) should use a mix of push and pull technology to keep abreast of current trends in Texas relating to best practices and examples of workforce and welfare services. Push technology is when a server initiates contact with the client when new information is available and ready to be transmitted. The specifically tailored content is delivered to the end user via an intelligent software client that uses the Internet to send the information.[46] A person using push technology allows data to be sent automatically to his or her computer at regular intervals, such as news updates every hour, or when triggered by an event, such as when a Web page is updated.[47] Push technology has been touted as an alternative to the way the World Wide Web currently operates, where users go online to search for information.[48] *Pull technology* is when the end user asks the server to send any new information to the desktop. A person is using pull technology when he or she surfs the World Wide Web to seek out and download information to his or her computer. The technology could also help deliver updates of state and federal regulatory requirements to the case manager via the desktop.

The benefits of push and pull technology are that no additional skills or training are required to use them. Given the time constraints of case managers, having to constantly learn and be trained on new technology systems was reported as a concern and as something that took time away that could be spent helping the client.[49] In order to operate effectively, case manager simply would need a computer with an Internet connection.

The current implementation of push and pull technology can be seen in a variety of sectors, including the music industry (e.g., RealNetworks, Gigabeat, Music Buddha, MoodLogic), news and information organizations (e.g., the PointCast Network, IBM New Ticker, AirMedia Live Internet Broadcast, Berkley Systems' AfterDark Online, My Yahoo! News Ticker), book stores (e.g., Amazon), and online recruiters (e.g., CareerSite). Push and pull technology is also being utilized in the medical industry. Indianapolis-based Guidant Corporation, a medical technology company, is using BackWeb Technologies (a provider of push communication infrastructure for e-business) to "streamline the distribution of sales and training materials to its national network of 1,000 medical device sales representatives. Guidant will use BackWeb for its educational program, delivering computer-based training and modules with media-rich content to each end user's desktop through the company's Intranet infrastructure."[50]

Recommendation 6-2: Reconfigure the EnterTech software module or use the EnterTech approach to develop training for case managers in all aspects of the workforce and welfare system. With additional time and resources, the EnterTech Project could develop an "EnterCaseManager" program based on the EnterTech Model. This would involve adapting and modifying the software to include the tools necessary to enhance the services delivered by the case manager.

The model could be adapted to include competencies and skills required for the case manager. As a further enhancement, a "question-and-answer" component could be developed. An "Ask EnterCaseManager" feature would allow case managers to ask questions regarding state and federal regulations and/or requirements, to which the software would respond by producing a list of answers, similar to the Q&A feature of the Microsoft Office Suite.

Recommendation 6-3: Texas should implement computer-based case management systems to improve the delivery of services. Texas can learn from the experiences with computer-based management systems used in other places. According to the deputy director of the Workforce Development Program at the National Center on Education and the Economy, a few localities have made progress in applying computer technologies and database systems to support case management. Examples of computer-based case management systems in use include the following:[51]

- METSys, which is installed in a few hundred sites around the United States, is a database system that stores very detailed information, such as intake, assessments, service plans, contact notes, strategies, and so on. It is a fairly robust database designed to make a case manager's job easier. Unlike most systems, which are relatively reactive, METSys is more proactive. As a form of push technology, it is equipped with a function that operates as a tickler/reminder. When the system is turned on, a note can flash on the screen to remind the recipient of appointments or other important information. The system was developed by private vendors.

- The U.S Department of Labor has been developing a system called the One-Stop Operating System (OSOS). While this system tracks clients in one-stop career centers, it falls short of what a real case management system needs to do. The design of information systems has been largely controlled by technical staff that place a high premium on management information systems and accountability reporting, with almost no attention to the needs of frontline service staff and the challenges they face in managing large caseloads.[52]

- Community-based organizations (CBOs) are taking a more active role in the delivery of workforce services due to the devolution of federal programs to the local levels. Gradually, more local and state governments are providing workforce and welfare services. An example of a CBO using technology to enhance the delivery of its services is the Cleveland Housing Network, Inc., which uses Internet-based technology to share data resources (e.g., on access to affordable housing) for community revitalization in Cleveland.

METSys, OSOS, and the Cleveland Housing Network, Inc., are current examples of systems that help train and support the case managers using technology. While this is not an exhaustive list, it offers a starting point to illustrate how information technology can be used to deliver case management services in a more efficient, effective, and equitable manner.

Conclusion

Since the implementation of workforce and welfare reform in Texas in 1996, the role of the case manager has become more complex. The intent of reforms in welfare and workforce programs sought to achieve an integrated system, but the messages conveyed were widely divergent. The underlying philosophy in workforce was to invest in people through skills training and career advancement. In contrast, welfare reform (TANF) favored a work-first approach by imposing strict guidelines on welfare recipients that pressured them to take the first available job. As a result, many TANF recipients have not been able to take advantage of education and training opportunities offered by the workforce centers. To ameliorate this disconnect, it is imperative that Texas invest in case managers. Implementing technology-based solutions to train and support case managers can assist them in the efficient, equitable, and effective delivery of workforce and welfare services. Providing information technology tools to train and support case managers will help to better serve targeted populations and to encourage the development of a seamless system.

Notes

[1] W. Norton Grubb et al., eds., *Toward Order from Chaos: State Efforts to Reform Workforce Development Systems* (Berkeley: National Center for Research in Vocational Education, January 1999), p. 14.

[2] Ibid. p. 9.

[3] Telephone Interview by Tina Ghabel with Louis Macias, Director of Workforce Administration, Texas Workforce Commission (TWC), Austin, Texas, March 15, 2001.

[4] Allison Moy, Papers on "Welfare-to-Work" and "Workforce Investment Act," *2001 Practitioner's Guide to Federal Resources for Community Economic Development.* Report prepared by the National Congress for Community Economic Development (Washington, D.C., February 2001), pp. 171–177.

[5] Christopher T. King, "Federalism and Workforce Policy Reform," *Publius: The Journal of Federalism,* vol. 29, no. 2 (Spring 1999); and Richard P. Nathan and Thomas L. Gais, *Implementing the Personal Responsibility Act of 1996: A First Look* (Albany: The Rockefeller Institute of Government, State University of New York, 1999).

[6] Grubb et al., *Toward Order from Chaos,* p. 50.

[7] "Social Service." *Encyclopedia Britannica.* Online. Available: http://members.eb.com/bol/topic?eu=117546&sctn=2. Accessed: March 11, 2001.

[8] Telephone Interview by Tanya Cruz with Deborah Morris, Assistant Deputy Commissioner, Planning, Evaluation and Project Management, Texas Department of Human Services, Austin, Texas, March 14, 2001.

[9] Interview by Tanya Cruz and Tina Ghabel with Crystal Bearley, Career Specialist, Capital of Texas Workforce Center, Austin, Texas, February 27, 2001.

[10] Morris Interview. Also, email from John Dorrer, Deputy Director, Workorce Development Program, National Center on Education and the Economy, "Case Manager Issues," to Tina Ghabel, March 12, 2001.

[11] Texas Department of Human Services, *Management Information Focus Report,* Austin, Texas, April 2000.

[12] Email from Ben Lopez, Program Specialist, Central Texas Workforce Center, Killeen, Texas, "Ensuring Adherence to TANF Regulations at the Killeen Center," to Tina Ghabel, February 28, 2001.

[13] Grubb et al., *Toward Order from Chaos,* p. 88.

[14] Texas Department of Human Services, *Selected Characteristics of Adults Receiving TANF in FY 1998 by Number of Months of Total AFDC/TANF Receipt, Program Budget and Statistics,* as cited in Texas Department of Human Services, *Employment Retention and Advancement Project Case Management,* Austin, Texas.

[15] Leslie O. Lawson and Christopher T. King, *The Reality of Welfare-to-Work: Employment Opportunities for Women Affected by Welfare Time Limits in Texas.* Prepared for the Urban Institute (Washington, D.C., September 1997).

[16] Stephen H. Bell, *The Prevalence of Education and Training Activities among Welfare and Food Stamp Recipients,* New Federalism, National Survey of America's Families, the Urban Institute (Washington, D.C., October 2000).

[17] Lawson and King, *The Reality of Welfare-to-Work.*

[18] Anu Rangarajan, *Keeping Welfare Recipients Employed: A Guide for States Designing Job Retention Services.* Doc. No. PR98-20 (Princeton: Mathematica Policy Research, Inc., June 1998), p. 11.

[19] Ibid.

[20] EnterTech, *Target Learner Characteristics Report.* Online. Available: http://www.utexas.edu/depts/ic2/et/learner/intro.html. Accessed: April 5, 2001.

[21] Bell, *The Prevalence of Education and Training Activities among Welfare and Food Stamp Recipients.*

[22] Nancy Pindus, Robin Koralek, Karin Martinson, and John Trutko, *Coordination and Integration of Welfare and Workforce Development System*s, Chapter 2: "Coordination and Service Delivery." Online. Available: http://aspe.hhs.gov/hsp/coord00/index.htm. Accessed: February 13, 2001.

[23] Ibid.

[24] Pindus et al., *Coordination and Integration of Welfare and Workforce Development Systems*, Chapter 4: "Challenges to Coordination."

[25] U.S. Congress, House Committee on Ways and Means, Subcommittee on Human Resources, "Time on Welfare and Welfare Dependency." Testimony by LaDonna Pavetti, Research Associate, the Urban Institute, Washington, D.C., March 23, 1996. Online. Available: http://www.urban.org/welfare/pavtes.htm. Accessed: February 2, 2001.

[26] Grubb et al., *Toward Order from Chaos,* p. 88.

[27] Ibid.

[28] Pindus et al., *Coordination and Integration of Welfare and Workforce Development Systems,* Chapter 4.

[29] Pavetti, "Time on Welfare and Welfare Dependency," p. 2.

[30] King, "Federalism and Workforce Policy Reform," p. 65.

[31] Information on training related to TANF and WIA legislation in Texas was provided through email from Ben Lopez, Program Specialist, Central Texas Workforce Center, Killeen, Texas, "TANF and WIA Legislation," to Tina Ghabel, February 28, 2001.

[32] Explanation of TWIST System in Texas. Online. Available: http://www.sybase.com/detail/1,3693,204205,00.html. Accessed: March 6, 2001.

[33] United States General Accounting Office, Health, Education, and Human Services Division, *Welfare Reform: Improving State Automated Systems Requires Coordinated Federal Effort* (April 2000), GAO/HEHS-00-48, p. 49.

[34] Macias interview.

[35] Ibid.

[36] GAO, *Welfare Reform: Improving State Automated Systems Requires Coordinated Federal Effort*, p. 49.

[37] Ibid., p. 56.

[38] Information related to technologies utilized in the one-stop center in Killeen was provided by Ben Lopez, Program Specialist, Central Texas Workforce Center, Killeen Texas. Mr. Lopez is in charge of ensuring adherence to TANF regulations at the Killeen Center. The Taking Care of Business (TCOB) technology was developed by Gerry Fluharty, Special Initiatives/Products Specialist, Central Texas Workforce Center, Killeen, Texas, February 28, 2001.

[39] Ibid.

[40] Ibid.

[41] GAO, *Welfare Reform: Improving State Automated Systems Requires Coordinated Federal Effort*, p. 9.

[42] Ibid., p. 34.

[43] Interview by Tanya Cruz and Tina Ghabel with Daniel O'Shea, Research Associate, Ray Marshall Center for the Study of Human Resources, LBJ School of Public Affairs, The University of Texas at Austin, March 28, 2001.

[44] Pindus et al., *The Coordination and Integration of Welfare and Workforce Development System*, Chapter 5.

[45] Telephone Interview by Tanya Cruz with John Dorrer, Deputy Director, Workforce Development Program, National Center on Education and the Economy, Washington, D.C., March 16, 2001.

[46] David Lidsky, "Online Content: The Web Delivers News, Sports, Weather, and Even Software Come to Your Desktop," *PC Magazine Online*. Online. Available: ZDNet http://www.zdnet.com/pcmag/feastures/push/_open.htm. Accessed: March 6, 2001.

[47] About the Human Internet Guide for Beginners. Definition of Pull Technology. Online: Available: http://www.learnthenet.com/english/glossary/pull.htm. Accessed: July 3, 2002.

[48] About the Human Internet Guide for Beginners. Definition of Push Technology. Online: Available: http://www.learnthenet.com/english/glossary/push.htm. Accessed: July 3, 2002.

[49] Bearley interview.

[50] Gregg Shai Gardner, "Silicon Wadi," *The Jerusalem Post* (December 24, 2000), Economics Section, p. 9. Online. Available: Lexis-Nexis Academic Universe, http://web.lexis-nexis.com/universe/. Accessed: March 6, 2001.

[51] Dorrer interview.

[52] Dorrer interview.

Chapter 7. Preparing Students for the New Economy

In this new economy—a knowledge economy—skills matter more than in the past. Skills are what allow people to navigate change successfully. And for workers to be highly productive, they must have the education and training necessary to keep them in tune with the onward march of technology. As America moves further into this age of information and global competition, it becomes increasing important that we make critical investments in our "human capital"—that is, in the knowledge, education and skills of our workers. Today, tomorrow, and far into the future, a highly skilled workforce is and will be our competitive advantage.[1]

Robert Reich, former U.S. secretary of labor

To be successful in today's economy, students are expected to be fluent in technology, whether or not they pursue a technology-based career. As the economy demands that workers engage in continuous learning throughout their working lives, skills to transition between work and education will serve students well. Schools in the Austin, Texas, area are attempting to infuse technology into the entire curriculum, culminating in sophisticated high-tech training at the high school level, to develop and train qualified workers for the Austin area. All of these efforts are essential to the application of technology to deliver a workforce that is well prepared to work in the economy of today and tomorrow.

Technology can also help to solve existing issues that face schools, such as lack of student engagement and poor rates of school completion. Some programs, such as Tech Prep, are proven to help students stay in school by making clear connections between high school, community college, and the many technical careers that are increasingly available.

The labor market for information technology (IT) workers in the United States has generated considerable controversy and attracted the attention of various researchers, national commissions, and industry associations.[2]

Austin's Answer: Grow Your Own Workforce

Since the 1980s, high-technology firms in Central Texas have dramatically increased the demand for highly skilled workers. In response, according to the director of the Capital Area Tech-Prep Consortium, "The focus for Austin has been to grow your own. Austin has been primed since the eighties to find ways to connect education to the workplace. We've had a boost of career and technology in the high schools, and have implemented standardized course models."[3] There is proof of this "boost" in the Austin area today.

Through intermediary organizations, Austin high-tech firms have focused on integration of technology into instructional processes and the curriculum.

The focus on technology and skills training and the support of the high-tech industry in Austin are reflected in the existence of several intermediary organizations, and in model school-to-career programs focused on technology in the outlying school districts in Del Valle, Georgetown, Leander, and Round Rock.

Through the commitment of school boards, superintendents, industry, and intermediary groups, some districts have launched promising pilot high-tech course sequences in their high schools and are introducing technology to many students at the elementary and middle school levels.[4] However, issues such as the lack of accepted skill standards and inadequate career knowledge and preparation at the secondary level make it difficult to integrate K-12 education to help students transition successfully into the labor market or postsecondary education. The fact is that most students will work immediately after high school, whether full time or part time, while they pursue postsecondary education. To be successful in the labor market, they are likely to need some postsecondary education and training. The role of high schools is, first, to keep students engaged in school, and second, to help them focus and prepare their transition into postsecondary education and/or training.

Some of the solutions lie in educating school leadership about the importance of technology and instituting skill standards that make it easier to communicate effectively with industry. In addition, it is imperative to ensure that the high school curriculum is adequately preparing students for New Economy jobs. This can be facilitated through the articulation agreements with community colleges, as exemplified by many of the Tech-Prep programs that have been established via the enactment of the Perkins Act in 1990.[5] In addition, an industry-led set of standards helps districts focus their training for students. Providing a trained workforce of teachers who are prepared to not only integrate technology through all grade levels but also to teach information technology (IT) coursework is a critical element to preparing students for today's economy. It is also an important element of developing a highly skilled workforce through the existing education system.

ARIES Alliance and IT Skill Standards

Training must be sufficiently infused with technology in order to give students an edge, even in an environment that is not typically considered technical, such as manufacturing. Today, even the most basic manufacturing operations are often performed in a technological context. Software companies and computer manufacturers are not the only economic actors that are concerned about the shortage of workers with IT skills. The shortage affects virtually every manufacturing and service industry, as these segments of the economy increasingly employ technology in their operations. Large multinational corporations report that their economic survival is keyed to the sharpness of their "technological edge," and this, in turn, places similar demands on the myriad of large and small local and regional suppliers, vendors, and organizations providing services to these corporations.[6] According to the education director of the Computer Science

2000/National Science Foundation Project, technology should be transparent. The level of knowledge and skill of the whole population has to increase, and people need to be able to do things such as installing RAM and software.[7] The ARIES Alliance, a nonprofit organization affiliated with the Capital Area Tech-Prep Consortium, was formed to "create, through an industry/education alliance, a competency-based education system to solve the workforce shortage problem for information technology companies."[8] ARIES is working to do so in the Austin area through a variety of initiatives.

One of the ways that the ARIES Alliance is addressing technology education for the new workforce is through improving the high school curriculum. ARIES is sponsoring a pilot program in the Round Rock and Georgetown school districts to help prepare students for high-technology industries.

In addition, standards are an important aspect of integrating technology into education. First, they help to ensure that the hardware and software infused into schools is well used. Second, they provide clear guidelines as to how technology should fit into the school's curriculum. Third, standards help administrators plan and utilize staff training time most effectively.[9]

According to the National Workforce Center for Emerging Technologies (NWCET), industry-based standards will help students to be successful in the technology- and information-based economy.[10] Located at Bellevue Community College near Seattle, Washington, NWCET has been designated by the National Science Foundation (NSF) as an advanced technology center for the information technology industry.[11] With NSF funding, NWCET developed a series of skill standards in the information technology industry that are becoming widely adopted for use nationwide.

The NWCET standards are divided into eight occupational clusters within information technology. These are described in Table 7.1, with a sample of the skills that are required for each category. Problem management, task management, and problem solving are considered skills that should be present across all of the categories.

Table 7.1
Summary of NWCET Skill Standards for Information Technology

Skill Standard	Description	Sample of Skills Required
Database development and administration	Uses simple to complex designs which can require high-level programming languages. Database design includes live links between websites and databases, and questions of security and integrity can affect design strategies.	Understand database structure, apply tests and diagnose problems, identify and acquire missing information, communicate with users on specifications, and research, identify database trends, and develop analysis and recommendations.
Digital media	Creates presentation for products. Importance placed on continually updating skills and ability to manage projects. Need to be able to work with sound, video, and computer-generated animation source files.	Develop first prototype and application skeleton, acquire media, coordinate with other developers, and lead project reviews with team and customers.
Enterprise systems analysis and integration	Primary goal is to use technology to help business gain a competitive advantage. Make decisions about technology systems, without necessarily being involved in technical details of implementation. People in this field will often start with a technical background.	Develop and conduct interview process with users; analyze, summarize, and document findings; gain understanding of business trends as they affect technology; acquire technology and business knowledge and skills; and act as leader in technology throughout organization.
Network design and implementation	Can work either on the design of new or maintenance of existing networks. Also can work with one vendor technology or select technology for a broader environment. Need to acquire knowledge in network hardware and peripherals, network operating systems, and application software.	Perform system backups and routine monitoring, identify and solve problems, work with system installation, upgrade and implementation of audits, attend training to learn new technologies, install and test network active equipment, assess benefits and risks of implementation, research network solutions, and plan for user training.
Programming/software engineering	May work on creating general office to highly specialized software; some will define customer requirements and be functional analysts, while others will write code. Need to be able to communicate technical information to nontechnical users.	Develop functional design document for product, test code within project specifications, interface with systems engineering team; finalize proposal outline, budget, and scope of work; organize testing procedures and schedules; and interface between technical documentation team and marketing groups.
Technical support	Key to success is to develop both	Identify resources and solutions

100

	technical and good customer relationship skills. Eventually understand issues such as organizational design that affect technology decisions. Organizational skills and attention to detail are important.	to problems, research equipment for specific use, test and troubleshoot technical systems, compare technology based on use/cost and make recommendations, and survey and analyze current system use and develop implementation plans for new systems and system expansions.
Technical writing	Design screens, Web pages online, technical help, or training manuals. Will either work on a team and specialize, or take on wider responsibilities. Often constrained by technical restraints and publication standards.	Write training manuals, interview users and assess manual's effectiveness, develop overall concept, navigational structure and visual concept for website, and research and develop content and production schedule.
Web development and administration	Difficulty is in balancing creativity with what the medium allows. Web developers start by maintaining websites and move into creating new sites. Eventually can be asked to analyze website effectiveness from user perspective. May eventually choose to focus on specific Web technologies.	Develop concepts for Web design and organization, design, build, and test Web pages and links; update and maintain websites, build databases and websites and test for functionality; track tasks, milestones, and budgets; develop set of standards that is approved by entire team; and deliver presentations to upper management.

Source: Northwest Center on Emerging Technologies. *Building a Foundation for Tomorrow* (Bellevue, Wash., 1999).

Applications of Skill Standards in Central Texas

In cooperation with the Capital Area Tech-Prep Consortium and the ARIES Alliance, students in the Round Rock and Georgetown will have a chance to learn skills based on the standards developed by the NWCET. The school districts in Round Rock and Georgetown plan to pilot a four-year sequence of courses for students to prepare them for careers in IT. With the "Computer Science 2000" curriculum, students will have the opportunity to sample all of the IT courses during their ninth-grade year in an introduction to information technology course, and then choose among a selection of IT pathways. These pathways mirror the NWCET categories listed in Table 7.1. Round Rock ISD was chosen as a pilot site because it has a strong integrated program for technology, a technology coordinator on each campus, and leadership committed to technology. Three classes of ninth-grade students in three of four area high schools signed up for the course beginning in August 2001.

Future plans for expansion include Georgetown High School and Crockett High School in Austin. These schools were chosen because of the commitment of their principals and the involvement of teachers in writing the initial introduction to IT curriculum. The

101

entire Austin Independent School District (AISD) hopes to be involved with this program in the school year 2002-2003. AISD is the largest district in the region, with nearly 80,000 students and 12 high schools.[12]

The ARIES Alliance and the Capital Area Tech-Prep Consortium are part of a project recently awarded to Austin Community College from the National Science Foundation (NSF). The project will work with the Texas Skill Standards Board (TSSB) to implement and tailor the NWCET standards for the state of Texas. According to their revised project plan, "with such high-quality, nationally developed standards we will achieve local buy-in, greatly streamline the process for Texans, and assure that we will have nationally portable skill standards."[13] The project has developed a four-step process that will facilitate the integration of these skill standards; a panel of subject matter experts will

1. review the NWCET standards,

2. perform a broad review of the results of the panel,

3. reconvene the original panel to review broad survey, and

4. develop worker-oriented information using experts, a supervisor, job analyst, and a representative of the ARIES Alliance and the TSSB staff.[14]

When the ARIES Alliance submits these standards to the board, they are likely to be accepted because they are based on existing nationally recognized NWCET standards.[15]

The competency-based "Computer Science 2000" curriculum was designed in collaboration with the A+ and Net+ sequence, and with a task force, including teachers, students, community members, and industry working together for over a year. The task force examined several programs and chose a vendor-neutral program that is based on standards and certifications that will allow students to work for a variety of companies. Many high schools, such as Del Valle, have chosen to implement Cisco labs. However, the administrators of Round Rock schools object to what they perceive as the proprietary nature of the instruction offered in Cisco labs. According to the assistant director for School-to-Career at Round Rock ISD, "They [Cisco] are selling billions of dollars of goods to the district, and students are only trained to work with Cisco."[16] According to the director of the Capital Area Tech-Prep Consortium, Cisco labs reach only a small proportion of students.[17] As a proprietary system, Cisco trains students to use Cisco equipment and products with the intention to prepare students to work with Cisco's service provider customers.[18] Although Cisco labs can provide students lucrative opportunities in networking careers, in the view of Rock Round educators, Cisco certification can also be limiting to students.

Instead, Round Rock has chosen to use an A+ lab, which is less expensive to implement than Cisco and leads to an A+ certification that can be used industrywide. CompTIA, a national professional association, is the developer and sponsor of the A+ certification. CompTIA offers vendor-neutral certification in a variety of areas, including A+, which qualifies students as entry-level computer techs, to I-NET+, which gives students base-level Internet technology, to Linux +, which involves vendor-neutral Linux knowledge.[19] Students will then take a series of certification tests, offered online by CompTIA, to show their qualifications to work in a variety of areas. Affirming its value, the Texas Education Agency (TEA) purchased the CompTIA software in early 2001 so that all school districts in Texas can have access to it free of charge.

Assured Experiences for Students in Round Rock

The Round Rock school district has made technology a priority and approved bond funding specifically targeted to staying current with information technology. Round Rock is attempting to "marble" its curriculum with technology to prepare students for the high-tech world that faces them, whether or not they choose to pursue a career in information technology.

The approach adopted in Round Rock will help support students as they prepare for their careers. "It is that technology has empowered people with managerial discretion to work with suppliers, clients, and customers in complex, often world-wide networks of people and institutions. If the old economy was a layer cake of structure and hierarchy, the new one is marbled throughout with technology."[20] In order to function effectively in the New Economy, students need to have integrated technology into their education early on so they will have the opportunity to practice using technology and also begin to think of new ways to integrate technology into their life and work.

The effort begins in kindergarten. The IT preparation sequence, along with the "Round Rock Assured Experiences" in K-8, help prepare students for the IT industry and the New Economy. In Round Rock, students have a powerful start because they are introduced to technology in kindergarten, not the ninth grade. As the assistant director of School-to-Career in the Round Rock Independent School District described:

> We make it an assured experience by bringing in the technology experience in kindergarten. In elementary school, students use technology as needed for projects. For example, if students need to use a spreadsheet, they use Excel. For presentations, kindergartners are using PowerPoint.™ In one elementary school classroom that I visited recently, third graders were tracking their stock quotes by using charts.

Through assured experiences woven into its curriculum, Round Rock recognizes that students will need to have a new set of skills to compete in the 21st century. Technology is fully integrated into the curriculum for kindergartners through eighth graders. The curriculum matches the Round Rock ISD requirements for technology skills and understandings with the assured experiences. For example, in the second grade, Round Rock standards say that students should be able to create, save, and retrieve a document, and gather, organize, and enter data into a teacher-created spreadsheet. Assured Experiences also requires that students develop a PowerPoint presentation on the solar system.[21]

Integrating technology into the curriculum for all students becomes even more complicated at the high school level. Many high school students are already interested in preparing for technology careers. Floyd Bevers, transition coordinator at Del Valle High School, reported that when students choose between industry "strands," or areas of interest, technology is chosen most often.

One of the potential stumbling blocks, according to the assistant director of school-to-career programs in Round Rock, is confusion regarding which classes count as technical credit at the secondary and postsecondary level. For example, according to the Texas Education Agency, computer science courses are considered academic in high school, but are labeled technical at the community college level by the Texas Higher Education Coordinating Board.

Another challenge is to find qualified teachers. Given the current teacher shortage, and the need for qualified workers in the technology field, it is not a surprise that qualified teachers who can integrate technology into their coursework and teach courses that train students for the many IT opportunities are difficult to recruit and retain. In the Austin area particularly, where the demand for skilled high-tech employees has been brisk, local school districts have encountered grave difficulties in recruiting and retaining teachers who are sufficiently fluent in technology to teach courses such as network administration. In many cases, people who have those skills work in the industry, where they generally earn significantly more money than teachers. One solution is to train existing teachers in technology. Del Valle High School is fortunate to have such a teacher in Jim Roe, who teaches in the Cisco lab at Del Valle.

The Round Rock school district also has offered training to teachers. With the help of a grant from the Capital Area Tech-Prep Consortium, teachers were provided with additional evening training in the Adobe Suite, led by an Austin Community College instructor. Even though participating teachers were not compensated for their time, their tuition was paid, and teachers were motivated to develop computer skills and share their skills with their students.[22]

High schools are having some success in training teachers and developing their faculty, but they rely heavily on collaboration with postsecondary education to deliver the technical training. Postsecondary institutions, especially community colleges, have developed programs and technologies, including distance learning, to extend their reach to students. Recent high school graduates, students in community colleges, and those who are engaged in continuous education can all benefit from these increased activities of community colleges.

The High-Tech Educator Network

In addition to vendor-specific training programs such as the Cisco Academy, the Capital Area Training Foundation (CATF), through the High Tech Educator Network, targets high school mathematics, science, and technology teachers to expose them to high technology and "provide them with real world connections for the classroom."[23]
Through monthly meetings, CATF aims to establish a dialogue between educators and

industry and eventually encourage the use of technology in the classroom and effect change in instructional delivery. Initially organized with the assistance of Congressman Lloyd Doggett, the Network involves a wide range of representatives from industry, educators from four school districts, the Dana Center at The University of Texas at Austin, and other educators. The program was designed to feature industry-led monthly seminars for educators and electronic collaboration throughout the school year, as well as teacher internships and industry-led workshops in mathematics, science, and technology during summers. During the industry-led seminars, speakers from the high-tech industry give educators an overview and provide information on occupational references for their curriculum. The Network's website, www.4empowerment.com, provides teachers with the opportunity to be part of a chat room to expose them to new curricula and provide them with new ways to communicate. The teacher internships, which are based on the Bell South Teacher Internship Model, aim to help teachers transfer their work experience to the classroom through "industry skill-standards-driven instructional units" by providing them with real-world data for their classrooms. Teachers receive information on career opportunities for their students, including opportunities to obtain appropriate postsecondary education.[24]

Technology can also be used to teach a variety of skills while recognizing that students enjoy technology and will be able to use it in a variety of settings. At Leander High School, technology is taught in a variety of ways. Some courses may not focus explicitly on technology, but provide the information in context. For example, in the drafting course, students are instructed in computer-aided drafting. Even though students may not go on to be drafters, the course teaches them how to use technology. According to the school's transition coordinator, Brig Mireles, "Drafting allows kids to do so many things, they can fit together and work as a unit, and learn animation, for example. They can go on from here to do any kind of animation. They are fearless when it comes to computers and software."[25]

Integrating technology into the K-12 curriculum, and especially into secondary education, can prove to be very powerful in keeping students engaged in school and helping them move into postsecondary education. Over the past decade, Tech-Prep has provided models that link secondary and postsecondary education through formal agreements between high schools and colleges that help make this process clearer and easier for students.

Tech-Prep

Tech-Prep programs require collaboration between postsecondary institutions and high schools, teacher preparation and training, public and private sector involvement, and a clear articulation of standards. Coalitions in the form of public/private partnerships, such as the Capital Tech-Prep Consortium and the Capital Area Training Foundation (CATF) in Austin, provide models for activities that intermediary organizations can engage in to bridge the connection from school to career.

Postsecondary institutions often have the resources and faculty to provide technical training. Although high schools can provide some training, many will rely on postsecondary institutions. Programs such as Tech-Prep become increasingly important to both high schools and community colleges as they are required to meet the increasing need for technical education.

According to Susan Goldberger and Richard Kazis, postsecondary institutions are in a better position than high schools to offer technical training:

> Occupation-specific training should be delivered primarily by postsecondary institutions, technical training centers, and their business and labor partners through a combination of classroom instruction and other job training. High schools can provide some of this training, but would focus on more generic and workforce preparation. Postsecondary institutions would serve as the backbone of the nation's technical training system.[26]

A recent evaluation of career academies, a school-to-career model found in over 1,500 high schools nationwide, presents evidence that many successful high school academy programs are "building closer relationships with local community colleges to promote the movement of students through technician certification programs as well as to encourage readiness for university study."[27] Such alliances, consistent with the career academy model, help students prepare for a variety of occupation and postsecondary choices after high school.

In Texas, Tech-Prep is defined as "a college preparatory program that combines rigorous academic coursework with a sequence of technical courses that lead to specific targeted careers."[28] It is federally funded through Title III of the Carl D. Perkins Vocational and Technical Act of 1990 and recently reauthorized through 2003 by Title II of the Perkins Act of 1998. The Tech-Prep program model includes college preparation, career counseling and guidance, Individualized Education Plans, rigorous curriculum, integrated academic and technical courses, and worksite training where appropriate. In order to create a seamless K-16 education system, secondary and postsecondary educators come together and develop articulated programs.

In *The Neglected Majority*, Dale Parnell, the originator of the Tech-Prep concept, proposed a pilot four-year "2+2" degree program integrating work in high school with community college. It was intended to run parallel with and not replace the current college prep-baccalaureate-degree program. These 2+2 programs would combine a common core of learning and technical education with a foundation of basic proficiency development in mathematics, science, communications, and technology—all in an applied setting. Parnell's idea eventually became the Tech Prep program.[29]

Tech-Prep has been producing positive results. According to Robert Franks, director of Tech-Prep programs at the Texas Higher Education Coordinating Board, for example, only 4 percent of the Tech-Prep students failed to complete their associate's degree at North Central Texas College. Tech-Prep is successful primarily because most students have already had a semester of college courses under their belt before leaving high school, according to Franks.[30]

According to Lewis Lemmond, a presenter at a recent Tech-Prep statewide conference, the results of a recent survey of high school students show that "what we consider to be strong programs, such as Tech-Prep and articulated programs, have quite a bit of bearing on whether students pursue postsecondary education."[31]

The success of Tech-Prep programs is confirmed by their growth. Since 1994, the number of state-approved Tech-Prep associate degree programs has tripled.[32] Figure 7.1 shows the growth in Tech-Prep associate degree programs in applied sciences approved for two-year colleges by the Texas Higher Education Coordinating Board.[33]

Students are increasingly interested in Tech-Prep programs. In the school year 1994-1995, 21 percent of high school career and technology students participating in coherent sequences were enrolled in Tech-Prep programs. By the 1999-2000 school year, over 33 percent of such students were enrolled in Tech-Prep programs (see Figure 7.2).

Figure 7.1
Number of State-Approved Tech-Prep Associate Degree Programs, 1996-2000

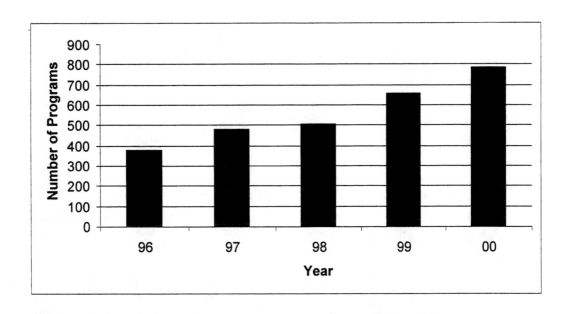

Source: Carrie H. Brown, *Tech-Prep Texas. Closing the Gaps: How Tech-Prep Programs Have Increased Participation and Success in Texas Schools, A Five Year Study* (Beaumont, Tex.: Region 5 Education Service Center, February 2001), p. 15.

Figure 7.2
Growth in High School Tech-Prep Program Enrollment, 1993-2000

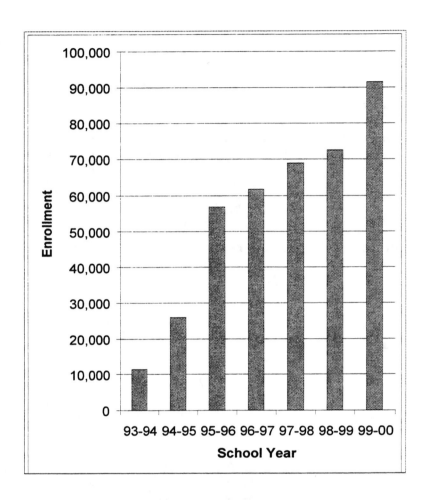

Source: Carrie H. Brown, *Tech-Prep Texas. Closing the Gaps: How Tech-Prep Programs Have Increased Participation and Success in Texas Schools, A Five Year Study* (Beaumont, Tex.: Region 5 Education Service Center, February 2001), p. 17.

One of the reasons that Tech-Prep programs are effective is that they link vocational and academic education. Programs are successful when core academic subjects are integrated in vocational and technical lab courses and teachers emphasize the relationship between education and the workplace.[34]

Applied learning can also help to improve high school completion rates by giving students compelling reasons to stay in school. According to Ron Garcia, the principal at South Grand Prairie High School Academies, the Emergency Medical Technician (EMT) program and their Cisco labs, along with Internet design, offer the incentives that keep some students in school.[35] The key, according to the state director of Tech-Prep programs, is to provide career counseling, establish realistic career and education goals, and show students exactly how to do it. "It's blinding-flash obvious. If they have a reason to get good grades, and a reason to complete the program, it makes it much more likely for them to do so."[36]

Conclusions and Recommendations

Many issues need to be addressed to prepare students to succeed in the New Economy workforce. These issues have become especially relevant in cities such as Austin, where local high-tech employers have become increasingly concerned with finding enough qualified job applicants to match their workforce needs. Likewise, educators are focused on ensuring that students have opportunities for employment and continuing education after high school. Linking high school with postsecondary education, as in Tech-Prep programs, has been shown to help keep students in high school and to enter higher education in larger proportions. The involvement of industry-based groups such as the ARIES Alliance shows the potential impact of industry-led groups. The implementation of the nationally recognized NWCET standards into Austin-area high schools, along with their likely recognition by the Texas Skill Standards Board, is another indication of the important role that intermediary groups can play in bridging the gap between industry and education. The approach of Round Rock ISD in providing students with "assured experiences" in computer technology offers an example of how schools can address the technology skills that their students will need in the modern workplace.

Several recommendations follow from our examination of approaches that Texas schools are using to prepare students for work in New Economy jobs:

Recommendation 7-1: School districts should introduce students earlier to information technology tools through integrating their use into school tasks as a regular part of the curriculum. Round Rock Independent School District has demonstrated how this can be accomplished effectively in its Assured Experiences approach. At the same time, the district introduces students to available career opportunities, informing them how such opportunities can be realistically pursued.

Recommendation 7-2: Texas schools should make use of vendor-neutral programs, designed to provide students with transferable knowledge and skills that do not limit learners to working for a particular company or with particular brands of equipment. In preparing students to be successful in information technology careers, vendor-neutral instruction can prepare students to pursue careers with different firms and to gain access to further training that will help them be more flexible in the job market.

Recommendation 7-3: Texas postsecondary institutions should establish additional written articulation agreements with secondary schools. Putting agreements and commitments into writing eliminates many of the difficult issues that high schools face in hiring teachers and providing the appropriate equipment for technical training. Through dual-credit and credit-in-escrow arrangements to collect college credit, high school students can gain a "jump start" on their postsecondary education. The experience of taking college courses also gives many students the confidence and encouragement to pursue training and education beyond high school.

Recommendation 7-4: Texas education and training entities should use nationally recognized skills standards, such as those provided by the National Workforce Center for Emerging Technologies, to increase cooperation and articulation between industry and schools. In collaboration with NWCET, the Capital Area Tech-Prep Consortium and ARIES are piloting the implementation of IT skill standards in schools in Round Rock and in Georgetown. This effort may provide a model for Austin-area schools and possibly for schools across Texas.

Notes

[1] Robert Reich, former U.S. Secretary of Labor, quoted in Northwest Center on Emerging Technologies, *Building a Foundation for Tomorrow* (Bellevue, Wash., 1999).

[2] For example, see Peter Freeman and William Aspray, *The Supply of Information Technology Workers in the United States* (Washington, D.C.: Computing Research Association, 1999); National Research Council, Committee on Workforce Needs in Information Technology, *Building a Workforce for the Information Economy* (Washington, D.C.: National Academy Press, 2001); and U.S. Department of Labor, Office of Policy, *A Nation of Opportunity: Building America's 21st Century Workforce*. Report prepared by the 21st Century Workforce Commission (Washington, D.C., June 2000); and Carol Ann Meares and John F. Sargent, Jr., *The Digital Work Force: Building Infotech Skills at the Speed of Innovation* (Washington, D.C.: U.S. Department of Commerce, Office of Technology Policy, June 1999).

[3] Interview by Susan Vermeer with Dale McCollough, Executive Director, Capital Area Tech-Prep Consortium, Austin, Texas, March 20, 2001.

[4] Interview by Susan Vermeer with Sharyl Kincaid, Assistant Director of School to Career, Round Rock, Texas, March 22, 2001.

[5] Carrie D Brown and Rob Franks, "Tech-Prep 101" (paper presented at the Texas State Tech-Prep Conference, Austin, Texas, March 19, 2001).

[6] Northwest Center on Emerging Technologies, *A Foundation for Tomorrow*.

[7] Interview by Susan Vermeer and Madge Vasquez with Mary Jo Sanna, Project Director, Computer Science 2000/National Science Foundation Project, Capital Area Tech-Prep Consortium, Austin, Texas., March 20, 2001.

[8] Ibid.

[9] Independent Schools Association of the Central States, *Technology Newsletter*. Online. Available: www.isacs.org/monograph/techletterNov2000.html. Accessed: May 5, 2001.

[10] Northwest Center on Emerging Technologies, *A Foundation for Tomorrow*.

[11] In 2001, the Center changed its name from the Northwest Center for Emerging Technologies to the National Workforce Center for Emerging Technologies.

[12] National Science Foundation Revised Project Plan for Proposal No. 0101726, "Computer Science 2000/ARIES Alliance," in response to Memo of April 25, 2001 from R. Corby Hovis. Obtained from Mary

Jo Sanna, Project Director, Computer Science 2000/National Science Foundation Project, Capital Area Tech-Prep Consortium, Austin, Texas, May 11, 2001.

[13] Ibid.

[14] Ibid.

[15] Interview by Susan Vermeer with Anne Dorsey, Assistant Director, Texas Skills Standards Board, Austin, Texas, May 9, 2001.

[16] Kincaid interview.

[17] McCollough interview.

[18] Cisco, *Training and Certification*. Online. Available: http://www.cisco.com/warp/public/10/wwtraining/. Accessed: April 12, 2001.

[19] CompTIA, *Certification*. Online. Available: http://www.comptia.com/certification/index.htm. Accessed: March 23, 2001.

[20] National Commission on the High School Senior, *The Lost Opportunity of Senior Year: Finding a Better Way* (Washington, D.C., January 2001).

[21] Kincaid interview.

[22] Ibid.

[23] Email from Jim McClure, Professional Development Coordinator, Capital Area Training Foundation, to Susan Vermeer, May 10, 2001.

[24] Ibid.

[25] Interview by Susan Vermeer with Brig Mireles, Transition Coordinator, Leander High School, Leander, Texas, March 19, 2001.

[26] Susan Goldberger and Richard Kazis, *Revitalizing High Schools: What the School-to-Career Movement Can Contribute* (Washington, D.C.: American Youth Policy Forum, Institute for Educational Leadership, Jobs for the Future, and National Association of Secondary School Principals, 1995), p. 25.

[27] N. Maxwell and V. Rubin, *High School Career Academies: A Pathway to Educational Reform in Urban School Districts* (Kalamazoo, Mich.: W. E. Upjohn Institute for Employment Research, 2000).

[28] Brown and Franks, "Tech-Prep 101."

[29] Dale Parnell, *The Neglected Majority* (Washington, D.C.: Community College Press, 1985).

[30] Interview by Susan Vermeer and Madge Vásquez with Fitz Husbands, Director, High Schools That Work and Tech-Prep, and Robert Franks, Director, Tech-Prep Programs, Texas Higher Education Coordinating Board, Austin, Texas, March 19, 2001.

[31] L. E. Lemmond, "Where Are Our Spring 2000 High School Graduates Today?" (paper presented to the Texas Tech-Prep Conference, Austin, Texas, March 19, 2001).

[32] Carrie Brown, *Tech-Prep Texas: Closing the Gaps. How Tech-Prep Programs Have Increased Participation and Success in Texas Schools: A Five-Year Study* (Beaumont, Tex.: Region 5 Education Service Center, February 2001).

[33] Ibid.

[34] Maxwell and Rubin, *High School Career Academies.*

[35] Interview by Susan Vermeer and Robert W. Glover with Ron Garcia, Principal, South Grand Prairie High School, Grand Prairie, Texas, February 19, 2001.

[36] Franks in Husbands and Franks interview.

Chapter 8. Postsecondary Education, Workforce Development, and Distance Learning

Introduction

The information technology boom over the past decade has brought great prosperity to our nation and to Texas. Public universities and community and technical colleges have played important roles in this economic age, providing research and development, technological innovations, and a ready supply of well-prepared workers. They have also served as engines for economic development. In Texas alone, institutions of postsecondary education have bolstered the economy by generating nearly $25 billion a year in revenues and spending multipliers.[1] For many firms and organizations, postsecondary education is the primary tool for ensuring the production of high-quality workers who can successfully compete in a global economy.

This chapter explores postsecondary education institutions in Texas and their use of technology to enhance workforce development. Special focus is placed on educational programs and activities in Central Texas and South Texas. This chapter is based upon secondary research via Internet searches, governmental reports, and public sector documents, as well as primary research through interviews with college administrators and other staff. The chapter features sections on (1) the importance of postsecondary institutions in preparing the workforce; (2) current problems and gaps within the system, and (3) technology solutions utilized by public universities and community and technical colleges for workforce development. It concludes with recommendations for enhancing the equity, efficiency, and effectiveness of technology-based workforce development services within public universities and community and technical colleges.

The Significance of Postsecondary Education in Preparing Our Workforce

Postsecondary education is crucial for all of us because it increases the productive capacity of individual citizens, contributes to economic growth, and secures a future of possibilities and prosperity. Industry relies on postsecondary education to provide the skills necessary for educating and training the current and future labor force. Nevertheless, at both the national and state levels, educational institutions are finding it challenging to adequately prepare our children, young people, and adults to work in the New Economy. Though the nation and major urban areas within our state have prospered tremendously from the current technological revolution, we still face skill shortages in many occupations. These shortages have caused American employers to look abroad for a workforce that can help sustain our economic progress. One indicator of this is the proliferation of H1-B visas for foreign workers to fill high-skilled technology occupations in the United States.

Challenges to Postsecondary Education in Texas

The Special Commission on 21st Century Colleges and Universities, commissioned by then–Lieutenant Governor Rick Perry, identified two pressing issues facing the Texas postsecondary education system today: the changing demographics in the state and the rapid development of a knowledge-based economy.[2] The current and projected demographic shift in the nation and in Texas is a major factor affecting postsecondary education. One of the fastest growing states in the nation, Texas will soon be a minority-majority state. By 2030, 37 percent of the population will be Anglo, 46 percent Latino, 9 percent African American, and 8 percent from other racial/ethnic groups (primarily Asian).[3] Although Texas is quickly gaining a foothold in the knowledge-based economy, the state is already in dire need of citizens with postsecondary levels of education and technological skills simply to keep up. The stark reality is that those racial/ethnic groups lagging behind in educational attainment are those that are growing fastest. Together, Latinos and African Americans already account for more than half of the school-aged population. In addition, almost half of all Texas students are considered economically disadvantaged.[4] The tenuous economic situation of students in Texas makes equity and access to postsecondary education critical challenges and requires policies and programs that address the issue of economic disparity as well as affordability of postsecondary education. Figure 8.1 provides a breakdown of students enrolled in community and technical colleges by racial/ethnic group for the 1998-1999 school year.

Figure 8.1
Number of Students Enrolled in Community and Technical Colleges, Academic Year 1998-1999, by Race/Ethnicity

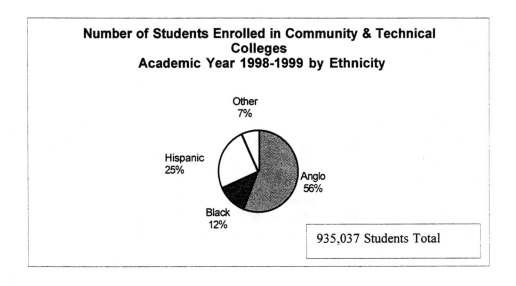

Source: Texas Public Community and Technical Colleges, *2000 Statewide Factbook*, CBM001 and CBM00A.

Over the past decade, the growth rate in U.S. jobs requiring a college degree has doubled.[5] This is of particular concern in view of the enrollment, retention, and graduation rates within community colleges and public universities in Texas. Statistics compiled by the Texas Higher Education Coordinating Board for 1998-1999 show that a total of 935,037 students were enrolled in Texas community colleges and technical colleges. Of this total, 41 percent were enrolled in academic programs, 32 percent in technical programs, and 27 percent in continuing education programs. Fifty-six percent of these students were Anglo, 12 percent African American, 25 percent Hispanic, 7 percent other,[6] and 4.9 percent international.[7]

The most startling statistics are those representing first-time-in-college students receiving remediation. Of the total 101, 246 students enrolled in Texas community colleges and technical colleges in the fall of 1998, 51 percent were enrolled in remedial courses.[8] This poses a serious challenge for postsecondary education, as students must spend extra time and resources on remedial courses before they can move on to academic courses required for graduation, let alone advanced courses. Nevertheless, some progress has been made over the past decade. In 1990, community and technical colleges graduated only 27,021 students. By 1999, the number of graduates had increased to 38,504. Figure 8.2 illustrates the degrees/certificates awarded by race/ethnicity from 1990 through 1999.

Figure 8.2
Community and Technical College Degrees/Certificates
Awarded by Race/Ethnicity,
1990-1999

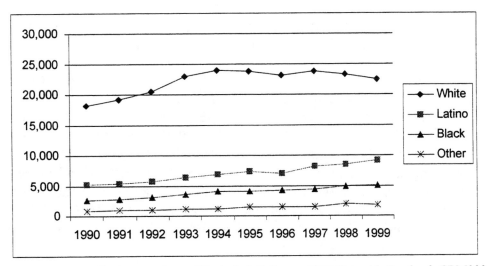

Source: Texas Public Community and Technical Colleges, *2000 Statewide Factbook*, CBM009.

As mission-driven institutions designed to serve the communities in which they are located, community colleges play a unique role in brokering access and equity in postsecondary education. Community colleges provide educational opportunities for students who may not have the financial resources to attend four-year institutions or who cannot attend school full time because of work commitments or family obligations. Community colleges serve students who choose to stay close to home rather than move away to attend college. These institutions specialize in the business of "homegrown human capital development." Community colleges have often taken up the task of remediation for entering college students. Strategies such as Tech-Prep, which links community college education with high school, provide tools that may reduce the need for remediation in the future by enhancing the preparation of students coming from high school to community college.

As defined in the 1990 Carl D. Perkins Vocational and Applied Technology Education Act, *Tech-Prep Education Program* refers to a combined secondary and postsecondary program which (1) leads to an associate degree or two-year certificate; (2) provides technical preparation in at least one field of engineering technology, applied science, mechanical, industrial, or practical art or trade, or agriculture, health or business; (3) builds student competence in mathematics, science, and communications (including applied academics) through a sequential course of study; and (4) leads to placement in employment.[9] Incoming Tech-Prep college students arrive with accumulated credits and are able to move through their associate's degree or vocational/technical program more efficiently. Tech-Prep students also tend to have higher postsecondary annual attendance rates and lower annual dropout rates than other students.[10]

The future role of community and technical colleges is especially important given recently announced goals for the state's postsecondary education systems. Texas needs to close the gaps in postsecondary education participation by enrolling approximately 500,000 additional students in postsecondary institutions by 2015. The Texas Higher Education Coordinating Board estimates that 60 percent of these students will begin their postsecondary education at community or technical colleges.[11]

Like community and technical colleges, public universities are also striving to increase enrollment, retention, and graduation rates at their institutions. In March 2001, the Texas Higher Education Coordinating Board (THECB) released a report on public universities in Texas. The study showed that during the fall of 1999, a total of 407,074 students were enrolled at public universities. As illustrated in the Figure 8.3, of this total, 59.7 percent were Anglo, 9.5 percent were black, 19.2 percent were Latino, and 6.6 percent were other. In terms of statewide college readiness statistics, 52.6 percent of entering freshmen passed the Texas Academic Skills Program (TASP) test, while 28.9 percent of incoming freshmen required remediation work.[12] The statewide average graduation and persistence rate was 63.5 percent.[13]

Figure 8.3
Public University Enrollment in Texas, by Race/Ethnicity, Fall 1999

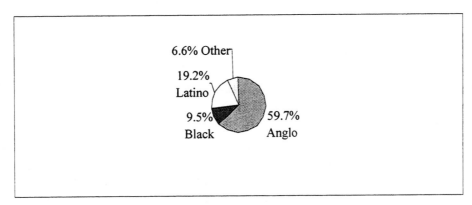

Source: THECB, *Report on the Performance of Texas Public Universities*, March 2001.

In addition to the demographic shift in population, postsecondary institutions must grapple with access issues faced by rural communities. Expanding educational services via distance learning technologies, such as Web-based courses and teleconferencing, offers viable solutions, but establishing the infrastructure is costly, requiring investments in facilities, technology networks, and instructors. Most postsecondary education institutions are finding it difficult to recruit and retain qualified faculty and staff. Providing sufficient resources and time for faculty to develop curricula and instruction are other gaps that must be addressed.

Given the projected demographic changes, and the rapid transformation of information technology, postsecondary institutions must be strategic in the programs they develop to prepare all students with the best education and skills for succeeding in the New Economy. This requires initiatives to recruit, retain, and graduate students who traditionally have not had access to postsecondary education. This is especially important for mathematics, science, and technology. It also includes maximizing and leveraging all of the resources, technology, and equipment currently available. As stated in the report *Moving Every Texan Forward*, "We must find ways to improve access quickly, provide flexible routes for lifetime learning, provide high quality workforce training, incorporate technology effectively, and maintain excellence throughout the system."[14]

Technology-Based Solutions for Workforce Development

Community and technical colleges and public universities use a variety of technological resources to provide students with vocational, academic, and professional training. Technology-based workforce resources at the university level include computerized career guidance software programs, which allow students to explore various career options, degree requirements, and company information. University and community college career centers also provide interview preparation and practice through videotaped

119

mock interviews, as well as electronic resume referrals to prospective employers and online job banks. Some campuses, such as Texas A&M Corpus Christi (TAMU-CC), have computer-assisted instruction and offer training using simulation technologies and touch-screen technology to deliver workforce services. For example, TAMU-CC sponsors Job Kiosk, an interactive computer touch screen that allows users to search and review various federal jobs.[15]

The Virtual College of Texas

One of the benefits of information and communication technology is its ability to transcend the barriers of time and distance. Distance education provides an opportunity for continued education and lifelong learning for those with access to a computer and the Internet. As a result, these technologies are increasingly becoming a standard tool for both community colleges and public universities. An example of a program that is utilizing information technology as a resource to educate students across Texas is a statewide Web-based network of community college courses known as the Virtual College of Texas (VCT).

Launched in 1998, VCT is a collaborative of 50 community college districts and three campuses of the Texas State Technical College System (TSTCS). VCT is sponsored through the Texas Association of Community Colleges (TACC) and administered by Austin Community College. The basic strategy behind the VCT is to share distance learning resources such as faculty, courses, student and administrative services, and telecommunications infrastructure, among its participating colleges. Through the VCT, students may take distance learning courses anywhere in Texas while receiving support services from a local college. The Southern Association of Colleges and Schools (SACS), which is the regional accreditation body for all Texas colleges and universities, accredits each participating college. To take a course from a remote (also known as the "provider") college, a student enrolls at a local community or technical (also known as the "host") college. The host college supports the student with services, including advising and counseling, financial aid, technical support, and access to learning resources. The host college receives the student's tuition, fees, and the state's reimbursement for the enrollment and is responsible for awarding course credit, maintaining the transcript records, and administering tests in a proctored environment.[16] An instructor at the provider college delivers the course to the host college's students, as well as to students enrolled at the same course at the provider's college. The instructor administers assignments, tests, grades, and all course activities.[17]

Administrative matters such as obtaining accreditation, providing student services, establishing comparable tuition rates, and transferring course credits are issues that most distance education programs face today. The VCT has worked out innovative solutions to many of these practical problems.

The VCT course instructional formats include Internet, telecourse, two-way video, and Web-based components that complement traditional teaching. Internet-based courses are the most widely used format within the VCT. Course offerings are diverse, ranging from U.S. Government to C++ Programming.[18] "Courses offered through VCT are easily transferable to Texas four-year, degree-granting institutions because most courses offered through VCT adhere to the same numbering system and basic course descriptions that apply to the courses of Texas four-year colleges. Courses may be transferred out of state, though transcripts may be scrutinized more closely because it is an inter-state transaction."[19]

The VCT project began with only 623 students in FY 1999 and has witnessed increasing enrollment since its inception. Enrollment rose by 46 percent to 909 students in FY 2000 and increased again by 78 percent to 1,620 students in FY 2001.[20] The three-year pilot project was scheduled to end in the summer of 2001. However, the TACC has recognized the program as a success, and consequently the VCT will continue as an on-going service to two-year districts/systems statewide.[21]

Other Distance Education Programs

The Electronic Campus of the Southern Regional Education Board (SREB) offers another "electronic marketplace" for courses, programs, and services. Initiated in the 2000-2001 academic year, this pilot project removes out-of-state tuition barriers by offering students access to certified degree programs via distance learning. This is especially beneficial for working adults or students in rural areas who cannot travel to attend a course or are interested in an academic program or course not offered at their local college or university. Participating institutions include hundreds of community and technical colleges and public universities. As of spring 2001, residents in 16 SREB states were eligible to participate in the program: Alabama, Arkansas, Delaware, Florida, Georgia, Kentucky, Louisiana, Maryland, Mississippi, Oklahoma, South Carolina, Tennessee, Texas, Kentucky, Virginia, and West Virginia. All of these states offered courses and programs in the Electronic Campus during the 2000-2001 academic year.[22]

Launched in 1998, the Western Governors University (WGU) is a project of the Western Governors' Association, offering competency-based degree and certificate programs. The university is also "virtual" in the sense that it does not have a physical campus. This "virtual university" offers courses created by 45 colleges, universities, and corporations across 22 states, Canada, and Guam. WGU offers five associate's degrees, two bachelor's degrees, two graduate certificates, one master's degree, and one undergraduate certificate. WGU provides "competency-based" education that allows students to rely on skills and knowledge gained through previous work, education, and life experiences. Rather than awarding degrees based on accumulated number of credits, WGU requires students to demonstrate their skills and knowledge (competencies) required for a particular degree or certificate program at the university. The competencies are determined by professionals in a particular field as deemed essential for mastery of that field. For these reasons, WGU does not accept transfer credits from other universities. The university requires all participants seeking to complete a WGU degree or certificate to demonstrate proficiency on the WGU assessments for that particular program.

Instructional delivery methods include email, the Internet, closed-circuit cable television, video- and audiotapes, videoconferencing, satellite broadcasts, and voicemail. WGU has a "distributed faculty," meaning they do not hire their own teaching faculty. Rather, classes are taught by the faculty of WGU's network of education providers. This list includes instructors at colleges, universities, nonprofit organizations, publishers, and private corporations.[23] The courses offered by the university are required to meet the WGU distance learning standards, based on the principles of good practice developed by the regional accrediting agencies for programs offered by accredited institutions.[24] On June 6, 2001, the Accrediting Commission of the Distance Education and Training Council (DETC) granted accreditation to WGU.[25] Tuition and fees paid by students go directly to WGU, which in turn, reimburses the institution at a previously set rate. The university also provides an online library, an online bookstore, and online and telephone advising services.[26]

According to the Texas Comptroller of Public Accounts *e-Texas Report*, WGU has not yet been particularly successful. As of the spring 2000 term, WGU had only 200 students enrolled in its degree programs, with another 150 students taking individual courses. As of summer 2001, WGU had graduated a total of only four students. When it began operations, WGU was projected to have 500 degree-seeking students by the year 2000, with another 3,000 students in certificate programs and 7,000 in corporate training programs.[27]

In spite of these "virtual" postsecondary options, only a very small fraction of Texas students in need are being served. In addition, to date, these colleges and universities are making available only partial offerings toward degrees and certificates. In view of student access issues on the one hand and the limited provider offerings and availability issues on the other, there is considerable room for improvement. Virtual college offerings are largely potential at this point.

Technology Training and Development

Academic and vocational programs geared toward technology training have become a priority among institutions of postsecondary education, as well as governmental agencies. Labor shortages in labor markets, such as semiconductor manufacturing and software development, are pressuring Texas institutions to increase their capacity to meet industry needs. Austin Community College hosts one of the innovative models in technology training. Six years ago, ACC, in collaboration with semiconductor firms in Austin, developed a two-year semiconductor manufacturing technology program. The academic program has been recognized as a promising model, enrolling an average of 240 students every semester. The industry goal is to have at least 500 students enrolled every semester.[28]

The University of Texas at Austin has served as a pioneer in technology training and development, especially through its technology incubator. The Austin Technology Incubator (ATI) has received support from The University of Texas, the City of Austin, and the Austin community. ATI works with a variety of investors, professional service providers, and outside industry experts to help support promising high-growth companies in a variety of technology-based industries.[29] Staff at Texas A&M-Corpus Christi are in the process of launching a similar science and technology business incubator. This initiative, the Incubator for Technology Enterprise in Corpus Christi (I-TECC), seeks to generate partnerships between TAMU-CC faculty, Del Mar College faculty, and incubator technology businesses.[30] Other technology-related programs include Texas State Technical College's unique E-commerce technology program[31] and Del Mar College's Cisco Regional Academy, which collaborates with area high schools and provides Cisco training and certification.[32] Midland College has a partnership with I/Tech Services, a Microsoft-certified technical education center, and offers Microsoft Certified Systems Engineer (MCSE) training on campus.[33]

Other successful technology education and training endeavors have been based on public-private partnerships, such as the Capital Area Training Foundation (CATF) and the previously mentioned semiconductor training program at Austin Community College. Recently a national partnership between IBM and the Hispanic Association of Colleges and Universities (HACU) was announced to help bridge the digital divide. The partnership includes a marketing program for HACU member institutions, faculty, and students, which offers IBM computer technology at a special rate. IBM will also be working closely with HACU to recruit Hispanics to pursue high-tech careers.[34]

Given the projected population growth in Texas and especially along the border, it is imperative to consider the resources and technologies available for postsecondary education in South Texas. The IC^2 Institute at The University of Texas at Austin has launched a binational initiative to "transform and diversify the economic and social conditions of the border region through 21st Century technologies for manufacturing, business, services and health care."[35] This project, known as the Cross-Border Institute for Regional Development (C-BIRD), seeks to establish a knowledge technology network along the Texas/Mexico border that will spur regional development through the creation of technology infrastructure, business recruitment, and jobs. Current project partners include CBIRD-The University of Texas at Brownsville/Texas Southmost College and CBIRD-Instituto Technologico de Estudios Superiores de Monterrey, Nuevo Leon, Mexico.[36] Texas A&M-Kingsville is also in the process of establishing a South Texas distance learning center. The center would serve as a hub site to disseminate distance learning programs throughout South Texas, facilitating access for rural and smaller communities. Project partners include the Coastal Bend Health Education Center, the Texas Workforce Commission, the Region 2 Education Service Center, and school districts in South Texas.[37]

Conclusion and Recommendations

Though a myriad of technological and educational resources exists within community colleges and public universities in Texas, there are still barriers and gaps within the postsecondary education system. There is a need for a seamless K-16 educational system that begins preparing people for careers early in the educational process. Well designed and implemented Tech-Prep programs and School-to-Career initiatives encourage students to continue their learning at the postsecondary level. Community colleges and public universities must be prepared to provide young people and adults with quality instruction and job skills that will enable them to successfully enter the marketplace.

The following recommendations include some strategies for enhancing the equitable and efficient use of technology within community colleges and public universities.

Recommendation 8-1: Postsecondary institutions should expand distance learning, using cable and broadcast television, satellite networks, Internet and Web-based courses, and interactive video technologies. Special focus should be placed on reaching underserved rural communities.

Recommendation 8-2: Federal and Texas state governments should increase funding for technology resources and facilities and for technology training of faculty and staff at postsecondary institutions.

Recommendation 8-3: Postsecondary institutions should provide incentives to recruit and retain qualified faculty and staff who teach technology courses. This includes restructuring incentives for faculty to develop and teach courses online.

Recommendation 8-4: Public universities and community colleges should engage with private industry in public/private partnerships to improve the linkages between industry needs and postsecondary curricula, so that Texas workers can be equipped with the appropriate education and training to work in the New Economy.

Recommendation 8-5: Texas public universities and community and technical colleges should secure additional funding for the recruitment and retention of Latino and African-American students, especially in mathematics, science, and technology. Also, these institutions should provide programmatic and financial support to help ensure that students graduate.

Notes

[1] Texas Comptroller of Public Accounts, *The Impact of the State Higher Education System on the Texas Economy* (December 2000). Online. Available: www.window.state.tx.us/specialrpt/highered/. Accessed: March 12, 2001.

[2] Office of the Governor, State of Texas, Special Commission on 21st Century Colleges and Universities, *Higher Education in the 21st Century… Moving Every Texan Forward*, released January 2, 2000.

[3] Ibid. p. 5.

[4] Texas Comptroller of Public Accounts, *e-Texas Report, Chapter 6: Education*. Online. Available: http://www.e-texas.org/recommend/ch06/ed06.html. Accessed: August 1, 2001.

[5] Ibid, p. 5.

[6] "Other" includes Asian, American Indian, and students reported with unknown ethnicity.

[7] Texas Higher Education Coordinating Board, *Texas Public Community and Technical Colleges, 2000 Statewide Factbook*. Online. Available: www.thecb.state.tx.us/CTC/ie/ctcsf/. Accessed: March 11, 2001.

[8] Ibid.

[9] Texas Higher Education Coordinating Board, the Texas Education Agency, and the Texas Department of Commerce, "TECH-PREP in Texas, Education that Works: Status Report: A Snap-Shot of the Impact of the Tech-Prep Initiative in the Governor's 24 Planning Regions," report prepared by Carrie Hughes Brown, Director of Tech-Prep/School-to-Work Initiative Management Project, Beaumont, Texas, April 1996, p. 2.

[10] Carrie H. Brown, *Closing the Gaps: How Tech-Prep Programs Have Increased Participation and Success in Texas Schools, A Five Year Study* (Beaumont, Tex.: Region 5 Education Service Center, February 2001), p. 20.

[11] Texas Higher Education Coordinating Board, *Closing the Gaps by 2015* (Austin, Tex., October 2000), p. 11.

[12] Texas Higher Education Coordinating Board, *Report on the Performance of Texas Public Universities* (Austin, Tex.: March 2001).

[13] This six-year persistence rate represents those undergraduates who entered a university as first-time, full-time undergraduates in fall 1993 who have graduated or who have not yet graduated but continued to be enrolled at the university in fall 1999.

[14] Texas Governor's Office, Special Commission on 21st Century Colleges and Universities, *Higher Education in the 21st Century . . . .Moving Every Texan Forward*, p. 6.

[15] Interview by Madge Vásquez with John Collis, Career Counselor, Texas A&M Corpus Christi, Corpus Christi, Texas, November 21, 2000.

[16] Virtual College of Texas. Online. Available: www.vct.org . Accessed: March 9, 2001.

[17] Virtual College of Texas, Operations Manual, p. 3. Online. Available: www.vct.org. Accessed: July 25, 2001.

[18] Ibid.

[19] Email to Tina Ghabel from Ron Thomson, Director of Operations, Virtual College of Texas, Austin Community College, "VCT Stats," August 1, 2001.

[20] Ibid.

[21] Ibid.

[22] Southern Regional Education Board, *Electronic Campus*. Online. Available: www.electroniccampus.org. Accessed: March 12, 2001.

[23] Western Governors University, *About WGU: Frequently Asked Questions*. Online. Available: http://www.wgu.edu/wgu/about/faqs.html. Accessed: August 1, 2001.

[24] Ibid.

[25] Western Governors University, "Western Governors University Earns Accreditation from the Distance Education and Training Council," June 13, 2001 (press release). Online. Available: http://www.wgu.edu/wgu/about/release58.html. Accessed: August 1, 2001.

[26] Western Governors University, *What We Are*. Online. Available: http://www.wgu.edu/wgu/about/whatwe.html. Accessed: August 1, 2001.

[27] Texas Comptroller of Public Accounts, *e-Texas Report*.

[28] Interview by Madge Vásquez with Alan Rasco, Vice-President Workforce Development, Austin Community College, Austin, Texas, December 8, 2000.

[29] The University of Texas at Austin, Austin Technology Incubator. Online. Available: www.ic2-ati.org. Accessed: March 12, 2001.

[30] Interview by Madge Vásquez with Paul McKimmy, Director of Workforce Development, Texas A&M Corpus Christi, Corpus Christi, Texas, January 8, 2001.

[31] Texas State Technical College, *About e-Commerce Technology Program.* Online. Available: www.set.tstc.edu/DeptInfo/AboutECT.htm. Accessed: March 9, 2001.

[32] Interview by Madge Vásquez with Anne Matula, Dean of Business, Del Mar College, Corpus Christi, Texas, January 8, 2001.

[33] Midland College, *The Midland Advanced Technology Center.* Online. Available: http://www.midland.cc.tx.us/~atc/index.html. Accessed: March 10, 2001.

[34] *Business Wire,* "IBM and Hispanic Association of Colleges and Universities Join Forces to Address the Digital Divide," March 5, 2001. Online. Available: Lexis-Nexis Academic Universe, http://web.lexis-nexis.com/universe/. Accessed: March 10, 2001.

[35] The University of Texas at Austin, IC^2 Institute, Cross-Border Institute for Regional Development. Online. Available: www.ic2.org/cbird.html. Accessed: March 10, 2001.

[36] Interview by Madge Vásquez with Abderrahmane Megateli, CBIRD Project Coordinator, IC^2Institute, The University of Texas at Austin, February 9, 2001.

[37] Interview by Madge Vásquez with Tadeo Reyna, Distance Learning Director, and Dana Fahnholz, Distance Learning Coordinator, Texas A&M Kingsville, Kingsville, Texas, January 10, 2001.

Chapter 9. What Can We Learn from Military Training?

Background

The United States military forces have been successful in training new recruits from all walks of life to achieve results quickly and efficiently. In addition to successfully training a heterogeneous pool of individuals, the military has been at the forefront in the development of software training standards and the use of technology for training and job matching. In short, the military has made strides in enhancing the equity, efficiency, and effectiveness of technology-based training.

The public and private sectors in the civilian world can learn much from both benefits and problems that the military has found in the use of technology for training. This chapter examines the advancements in training that the military has made, benefits and problems it has experienced, and the path that the military is moving toward concerning information technology. The chapter focuses on three arenas related to training in which the military has been active: (1) fostering the development of technical standards through collaborating with civilian organizations, (2) using technology in military training, and (3) using technology to match individuals leaving the military to find jobs in the civilian sector.

Development of Industry Technology Standards

To cut training costs, the U.S. Department of Defense (DoD) has been active in a collaboration to develop a distributed (distance) learning management system that is based on common industry technology standards. The Advanced Distributed Learning (ADL) initiative is a major collaboration among the military and other federal agencies, private sector technology suppliers, and the education and training community. Participating organizations are formulating voluntary guidelines to make learning software "accessible, interoperable, durable, reusable, adaptable, and affordable."[1] Before the ADL initiative began in 1997, the development of common industry standards had been difficult to achieve because vendors of training applications were developing computer-based materials on a company-by-company, proprietary basis, resulting in high development costs.[2] ADL provides the forum to use common standards to reduce development costs and leverage the power of computer, information, and communication technologies to provide tailored training to students anytime, anywhere. The flowchart depicted in Figure 9.1 describes the strategy of the ADL initiative.

Figure 9.1
The DoD Advanced Distributed Learning System

Classroom	Distance/Distributed Learning	Advanced Distributed Learning
Instructor-led technology insertion	Video teletraining Embedded training Computer conferencing Interactive television Electronic classrooms Interactive multimedia Computer-based training Audiographics Audiotapes/videotapes Correspondence courses, in addition to Legacy systems	Integrated networked systems Interoperable platform Reusable learning objects Widespread collaboration Global knowledge databases Intelligent knowledge repositories Virtual classrooms, in addition to Legacy systems

Right-time, right-place learning → Anytime-anywhere learning

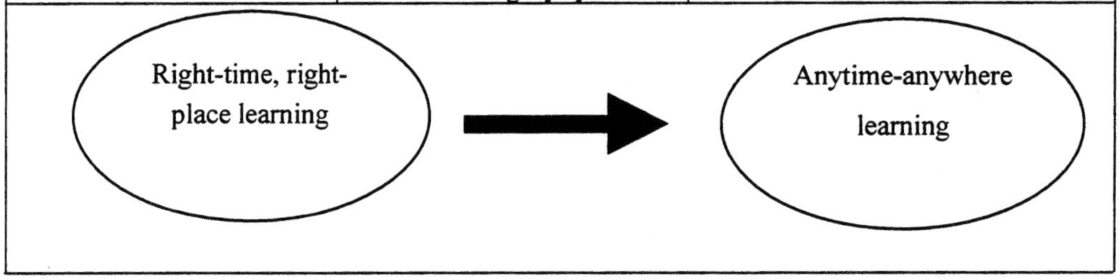

Source: Department of Defense, Office of the Under Secretary of Defense for Personnel and Readiness, *Strategic Plan for Advanced Distributed Learning, Report to the 106th Congress,* April 30, 1999, p. 10.

The figure shows how training and learning are changing. Previously, teaching/training consisted of face-to-face instruction between one teacher and several students at a particular time and location. Now, there are opportunities for more people to learn a subject through distributed or distance learning, where the teacher and students are in numerous geographic locations. As Figure 9.1 shows, ADL allows students to obtain training at their own time, location, and pace. ADL frees students from any geographic or scheduling restrictions that the teacher may impose, providing anytime, anywhere learning.

To achieve anytime, anywhere learning, ADL released a set of specifications and guidelines, the Sharable Courseware Object Reference Model (SCORM), in January 2000. Over a two-year period from 1997 to 1999, representatives from the military and industry hashed out SCORM. The guidelines built upon earlier collaboration in standards organizations, such as the Learning Technology Standards Committee of IEEE, the Instruction Management Project, and the Aviation Industry CBT Standards.[3] SCORM guidelines provide the foundation for how the DoD and the civilian sector will use technologies to operate in the learning environment of the future.

In 1999, ADL established the first series of ADL Cooperative Labs (Co-Labs) to test the SCORM standards and validate new ADL technologies. The ADL Co-Laboratory Network is comprised of independently supported entities, including a hub and two functionally defined nodes that serve distinct areas of operational responsibility. Co-Labs are located in Alexandria, Virginia; Orlando, Florida; and Madison, Wisconsin. These Co-Labs provide open testing environments for private industry, academia, and governments to collaborate on the development of learning standards and the demonstration and evaluation of learning technologies.[4]

Despite the fact that DoD had its own interests at heart in the development of industry standards, both vendors and users of training will greatly benefit from common industry standards. Vendors want to develop software that they can sell to a wide and open market. Common standards expand the potential market. If the software is compatible with systems used in both private and public sectors, the end user of learning software will likely be able to use software off the shelf without having to purchase additional hardware or other equipment. The user also wants to be able to purchase such software at reasonable rates and reuse the software to assist others in learning.

According to ADL studies,[5] the initiative has increased both efficiency and effectiveness. The use of ADL technology-based instruction has reduced costs by 30 to 60 percent and training time by 20 to 40 percent. In addition, organizations using ADL technology-based instruction have shown improvements in organizational efficiency and productivity. The studies show an increase in the effectiveness of instruction by 30 percent and an increase in student knowledge and performance by 10 to 30 percent. ADL claims to achieve these cost efficiencies by distributing instructional components inexpensively to physically remote locations.[6] Unfortunately, there has not been any independent validation of the ADL studies and claims, but ADL claims of time and cost savings indicate the need for further exploration.

On July 11, 2001, leaders of the ADL Co-Lab, the MIT Open Knowledge Initiative (OKI),[7] and the IMS Global Learning Consortium[8] announced their intention to cooperate to close the gap between innovative pedagogical technology and production learning resources. These groups will team up to accelerate the development and deployment of innovative and practical online learning tools, systems, and techniques.[9]

The Use of Technology in Military Training

Military training comes in a variety of forms to fulfill a variety of purposes. Training in the military can mean teaching troops to operate as a coordinated unit or instructing individuals for certification to conduct their occupational specialties within a branch. Military training is unique because it prepares recruits from civilian society to protect the nation as soldiers, pilots, sailors, and marines. In essence, a majority of military training

131

is "just-in-case" training in that these maneuvers and procedures may only be used if the nation goes to war. Nonetheless, the civilian sector can still apply the lessons that the military has learned in the use of technology for training.

The military trains both the individual and the team, viewing the training of the individual as a means to produce successful and competent teams.[10] The training of an individual is often considered an infrastructure cost because the individual fills a position such as clerk, mechanic, or technician within an organization.[11] The military focuses most of its training efforts on the team, since it is the work of the team that makes a mission a success or failure.

Types of Training

The military does not use technology in every aspect of training soldiers, pilots, sailors, and marines. Military trainers use three primary teaching models: (1) conventional instruction, (2) computer-based instruction (CBI), and (3) simulation.

Conventional instruction is the traditional method of training. Through lectures, discussions, and exercises, instructors convey information and serve as role models to students. Compared with more recent models of teaching, which use information technology, conventional instruction is seen as expensive because it requires funding for instructor salaries, facilities, and materials. Conventional instruction is further criticized for being insensitive to student needs by locking the student into a set time, pace, and geographic location.

As part of its instructional approach, the army emphasizes on-the-job training to develop the professional skills of its soldiers. As an example, when the field artillery branch of the army trains new soldiers with responsibility for equipment and weapon systems, recruits are assigned to a noncommissioned officer (NCO), a soldier with rank and experience who is responsible for their professional development. Depending on time and money, the NCO will take his or her soldiers out to a military training site and practice the usage of the equipment or weapon system.[12] This hands-on approach is prevalent in the military and is the foundation for effective training of new soldiers. It quickly familiarizes them with their responsibilities and duties, which in turn facilitates an effective combat team.

Conventional instruction can be replaced or enhanced by the use of computer-based instruction (CBI). The military was an early advocate of the use of CBI, which can encompass everything from the use of CD-ROMs to Internet-based instruction. The Army National Guard serves as an example of how the military has implemented CBI, through interactive CD-ROM and Internet-based programs to deliver part of their training. The National Guard uses the Internet in some of the Captain's Career Courses (CCCs). These courses have centralized student databases that allow instructors/administrators to provide immediate feedback as to how well an officer is progressing through the course. The technology can inform the instructor on how much time (literally, the number of minutes spent online) the officer has been working on the program during the month and how far he or she has progressed.[13] Internet-based instruction is not used in every CCC; the technical training aspects of some areas, such as field artillery, cannot be accomplished effectively through CBI. Loading a howitzer cannon with a high-explosive projectile cannot be simulated through a computer. At this point, technology has not advanced sufficiently to allow for this type of CBI training.[14]

In January 2001, the army began offering its soldiers free distance learning classes via the Internet. The idea came as a request from then-Army Secretary Louis Caldera to his deputies to develop a recruiting tool to entice people to choose the army over college.[15] The resulting plan, Army University Access Online (AUAO), provides soldiers with opportunities to earn college and university degrees while on active duty in exchange for a commitment to serve at least three years beyond their initial enrollment.[16] The army provides 100 percent funding for tuition, books, course fees, a laptop computer, a printer, an Internet account, and live, 24-hour technology support.[17]

Part of a collaboration between industry and government, the AUAO provides training through its eArmyU website, an electronic learning portal where soldiers can receive free, online education from 24 colleges and universities.[18] Members of the AUAO include providers of online degree programs, learning technology providers, project management consultants, infrastructure support, and the Council on Academic Management.[19] The army does not create the curriculum; rather, a consortium of colleges has organized the process to offer more than 87 programs. The initiative began with test sites at three army posts (Fort Benning in Georgia, Fort Campbell in Kentucky, and Ft. Hood in Texas). As of August 2001, over 4,300 soldiers had participated at the three sites.[20] The program is expected to increase its delivery of services to be available army-wide (to accommodate up to 80,000 students) in 2003.[21] The five-year, $453 million online program is expected to provide valuable insights relating to the delivery of online education programs to a large and varied audience. For this reason, the program is being monitored by many in the higher education field. The Alfred P. Sloan Foundation has provided a grant to set up a panel of education experts to monitor eArmyU.[22]

In addition to CD-ROM and Internet-based programs, the army utilizes video teleconferencing (VTC) in the advanced training of its soldiers. Within Texas, VTC sites are located in Dallas, Austin, San Angelo, Killeen, and Houston. Using videoconferencing, the instructor and the students can be in various geographical locations and still participate in an interactive class simultaneously among the sites.[23]

NCOs and enlisted soldiers in the army also use CBI for training and skills development as a means for gaining necessary points for promotion to the next rank.[24] At this point, CBI is mostly used for training an individual on a particular topic or skill. The military uses simulation, instead of CBI, to train teams.

Simulation is a popular training tool for the military because it allows individuals to practice their skills hands-on as a team while avoiding the use of expensive equipment,

133

ordinance, and supplies. Further, simulated training methods help prevent loss of life, save time and money, and protect the environment. Military technology simulation can be categorized into two types: live and virtual simulation.[25]

Live simulation is training using actual equipment in an environment that closely resembles actual conditions. An example of live simulation is when U.S. Army units go into the field to play out a potential scenario. Ft. Hood's 4th Infantry Division (ID) has the ability to conduct live simulation, as it is the only unit in the United States to have been converted totally to digital equipment. Fourth ID serves as the army's primary experimental unit for combat and communications equipment. New technologies are tested in the 4th ID before they are used in the army as a whole.[26] Equipment such as global positioning satellites (GPS) allows 4th ID soldiers to have situational vision, which provides soldiers with the most up-to-date and accurate information, such as locations of enemy units, locations of friendly forces, terrain features, and forecasted weather. Such information is then passed to the commander so he or she can make the best decisions to win the battle. The 4th ID routinely conducts live simulation training using new digital equipment.

The second type of simulation is virtual, which is much like a computer or video game. The trainees interact with a computer-generated representation of the actual equipment and circumstance. This type of simulation can be used to train for basic or advanced skills, and individual or collective units. Historically, virtual simulation has been employed for training aircraft pilots, but it is now being applied to training tasks where the equipment cannot actually be used due to limited resources or environmental constraints. Instead of having to physically send combat units into the field to conduct maneuvers, the entire simulation occurs digitally. An example of the virtual simulation is Warfighter, a massive training exercise that involves one of the ten army divisions every two years. Warfighter is a joint training event for the army, air force, navy, and marines that simulates a full-scale war in a variety of environments, weather, and other possible real-life situations, such as extensive loss of life or weapons.

The army is also experimenting with other forms of virtual simulation. In 1999, the army awarded a five-year contract to the Institute for Creative Technologies (ICT) at the University of Southern California to enlist the entertainment industry of Hollywood, in collaboration with computer scientists, to develop a Star Trek-style "holodeck" to train soldiers for battle simulations and to acquaint them with cultural aspects of new stations prior to assignment.[27]

Visual simulation is not the only simulation technology that the ICT is researching. ICT is engaged in research that will simulate human senses such as hearing, touch, smell, and orientation in a way that cannot easily be distinguished from reality. Incorporating these elements into the visual simulation creates an environment that will better train the service member.[28]

Benefits to Using Technology in Training

CBI and simulation technologies offer several advantages over conventional training: savings in time and costs, improved training through facilitating individualized instruction, and more accurate analysis after the training exercise is complete.

The use of CBI and simulation technologies reduces the time needed to conduct training. In the army, CBI courses can be accessed whenever the soldier has a free moment. If the army did not utilize CBI, the soldier would have to go through conventional training, which would take the soldier out of the work environment for a long period of time. CBI is also consistent with the army's preference for the on-the-job training. CBI provides supplemental individualized training while allowing more time on the job. Like CBI, simulation also cuts the time needed to conduct training. Experience in the military reveals that simulation can cut training time by about half because people learn more quickly by doing. Simulations allow for content to be delivered in the manner that the information will be used.[29]

Once initial investments in technology are made, the use of CBI and simulation also results in lower training costs. Traditional training includes the direct costs of travel, per diem, and lost productivity. The use of CBI and simulation can eliminate some costs entirely. For instance, soldiers are often told to refer to the Web rather than request hard-copy manuals from a physical location or central office. All unclassified training manuals and other publications are now on the Internet on the PERSCOM (Personnel Command, the army's equivalent of a human resources office) website. Troops are able to access training materials easily at any time. Since these documents are now online, printing and mailing costs for the army have diminished. The use of video teleconferencing (VTC), another form of CBI, also benefits the military by saving the travel and accommodations costs that would be required to bring all the students and the instructor to one place. VTC is also useful in live simulations as it allows soldiers to resolve technical field problems versus sending out technicians to every individual location for every problem.

The use of simulation technology has translated into savings for the military. The National Training Systems Association (NTSA) cites examples of these savings:

- Driving a tank costs $75 per mile; a tank driver simulator costs $2.50 per mile.

- Operating an Apache helicopter costs $3,101 per hour; a simulator costs $70 per hour.

- Flying an F-16 fighter costs an estimated $5,000 an hour; an F-16 simulator costs $500 per hour.[30]

The use of simulations for training has benefited the military by allowing individuals to train on equipment that would be expensive to actually use. Of course, it should be acknowledged that a full benefit-cost analysis should take into account the initial and continuing capital investments in the technology, including hardware and software.

Simulations also offer valuable training tools in helping identify critical moments in battle engagements. All interactions can be recorded and assessed after the training has been completed. Decision making in critical situations can be reviewed, honed, and improved through the use of constructive simulation models. The military has found that "simulation allows you to enter live training at a higher level of proficiency," and one can train to a higher standard.[31] The use of technology for training is certain to be further explored since it allows the military to train more effectively at reduced cost.

CBI and simulation have enhanced the equity, efficiency, and effectiveness of workforce services delivery in the military. Equity is addressed in the use of both CBI and simulations. The military does not make a distinction between low and high achievers, economic background, race, or gender. The military makes a decision on what a soldier's job will be on the basis of his or her proficiencies, interests, and the needs of the military at that time. Once this determination is made, each soldier, pilot, sailor, and marine must have a certain amount of training according to his or her job assignment, otherwise known as a Military Occupational Specialty (MOS). The service member's educational background does not play a role in the amount or the quality of training that he or she receives. Efficiency is improved because the military does not have to print and mail manuals to service members, pay for the travel and accommodations of service members to remote locations, or to use expensive expendable equipment. Lastly, effectiveness in technology-based training is enhanced—or example, decision-making abilities produced through simulation. Since all interactions are automatically recorded in simulations, decisions made by training participants at critical moments in the simulation can be later evaluated and assessed. The equity, efficiency, and effectiveness of technology-based training have been demonstrated by the benefits experienced by the military in using CBI and simulation.

Problems Encountered by the Military in Using Technology in Training

Despite the many benefits of technology for training, barriers do exist concerning both CBI and simulation. For example, the CBI utilized by the Army National Guard can take two to three years to complete because of the slow nature of the program. Soldiers in the Army National Guard unit are actually citizens with full-time jobs and therefore have to balance these commitments with the role of being a soldier on a part-time basis. The National Guard's distance learning program is designed to allow the soldier to complete the course at his or her own time and pace. While it is more convenient for the citizen/soldier to train from home, many drop out of the program because it takes so long to complete the training. Citizen/soldiers must work on the course at night and on weekends. Nothing is officially being done yet, but the army has asked for a reevaluation of the program. One of the original problems is that regular army officers developed the program. Though their intentions were good, they did not completely understand the time constraints that restrict citizen/soldiers. Further, the original program was developed with no input from the National Guard. For the distance learning phase of the course to be feasible, it needs to be cut down to one year.[32]

Simulation also faces challenges, namely the varying rates of modernization, ensuring the interoperability of systems, and the updating of facilities. For training technology to be effective, the military must ensure that all the CBI materials and virtual simulation sites are modernized at approximately the same rate. Typically, funding for air force simulator upgrades is not provided at the same time that an aircraft is updated. One airman stated, "Our simulators are consistently behind the aircraft in configuration."[33] If the simulator does not match the actual equipment, it is practically useless in that the individual will have to be consciously aware of the differences between the simulator and the actual equipment. The addition of only some of the required changes to the simulator results in a less-than-complete system that will affect the readiness of the troops.

Along with the problems associated with varying rates of modernization, communications, and interoperability of systems are two major issues. First, the army has two sets of communication systems that are incompatible. Therefore, training two or more units that are using different communications systems is nearly impossible. An example of the interoperability issue is Ft. Hood's 4th Infantry Division (ID). Fourth ID is the only division that is fully digitized, making it difficult to organize and coordinate exercises with other units that do not have the same technology. Currently, each branch of the military is attempting to make its systems interoperable. The next step will be to make all the branches interoperable so that more joint training among the services can occur.[34]

Second, failure to renovate facilities can become a barrier to the use of technology in training. Old buildings that house computer labs and virtual simulation sites often need to be remodeled to include air conditioning units to support the computers. Sometimes the budget for this is not available, thereby minimizing the use of such technology.

The problems described here can affect the efficiency and effectiveness of technology-based delivered training. Efficiency is lost when students drop out of the program because it takes too long to complete. Just like conventional training programs, technology-based programs must be designed with the user in mind. Ideally, users should assist in the design of the program and pilot the program to ensure that the program achieves its objectives. Effectiveness is also at risk. The fact that the military does not modernize its simulations and equipment at the same rate threatens the effectiveness of the training. If a student is trained on a simulator that does not match the actual equipment currently used in the field, the training will be inadequate. Lack of interoperability (having incompatible communication and operating systems) can also be a barrier to joint training exercises or reduce the effectiveness of training. Technology-based programs must be interoperable across a variety of platforms. Otherwise, the users may not be able to communicate and train with others. These barriers must be addressed by the military to ensure the efficiency and effectiveness of technology-based training.

Challenges and Opportunities in Transferring the Benefits of Military Training Practices to the Civilian Sector

Although the military has generally done well in using technology in training, transferring such experiences to the civilian sector presents unique challenges. The military is a controlled environment, where insubordination is not tolerated and repercussions can be harsh. Punishments for disobeying the rules and orders include withholding half of month's salary for a period of time, requiring the service member to perform extra duties after normal work hours, and placing the service member under house arrest. The military's command and control structure allows it to integrate and to enforce equity in its culture much more easily than the average civilian company. In general, the civilian sector cannot exercise the type of command and control in order to ensure equity. Until American society respects the talents and contributions that can be made by all people, equity in training will remain an issue.

Despite the difficulty in transferring the military's approach to ensuring equity in training, the civilian sector has opportunities to increase efficiency and effectiveness using the military's approaches. The military's on-the-job training (OJT) methods can be easily transferred to the civilian sector, and are already practiced by some large companies, including United Defense LP, General Dynamics Land Systems, and TRW.[35] A key to OJT in the military is to train on essential tasks, rather than on every element of the written job description or handbook. Another opportunity for improving job training in the civilian sector is through the use of CBI, which can enhance the efficiency in the civilian sector by placing a company's training manuals, schedules, and communication systems on the Internet. Like CBI, simulations will also increase efficiency. Simulations can save the civilian sector on the expense of using costly, irreplaceable equipment and of travel and accommodation costs. Careful planning and budgeting can assist in making these monetary savings happen. Likewise, the civilian sector can better enhance effectiveness through simulation. Federal agencies and local public safety organizations' use of simulation can enhance training effectiveness by allowing safe "just-in-case" training. For example, it is dangerous for the Federal Emergency Management Agency (FEMA) to practice a response to a chemical weapons attack using real chemical weapons. Computer-based simulations allow FEMA to practice moving personnel and assets in such a situation.[36] Even in training for less extreme jobs, simulation can improve job effectiveness. Simulation programs can be designed to allow the trainer and trainee to later evaluate decisions made in the simulation. Simulation evaluations can then be used to improve job performance and capabilities when the trainee faces the same situation in real life.

As demonstrated, the military has been very active in researching and utilizing technologies in training its troops. As the following section describes, the military has recently applied computer technology to job-matching efforts for those leaving military service. However, the army still relies on conventional practices to make job assignments to those entering the military.

The Army's Job-Matching Procedures

The army does not use technologies such as CBI or simulation to assign jobs to entering soldiers. Before soldiers enter the army, they take the Army Service Vocational Aptitude Battery (ASVAB) test to determine job allocations. This test is a standard Scantron test and does not use new technology delivery methods. A soldier submits his or her job preferences, and the army places the soldier in a job that the soldier would be most appropriate for, based on his or her ASVAB score, the needs of the army at the time, and the soldier's expressed preferences. The jobs that the soldiers are assigned to are called their MOS or Military Occupational Specialty. Afterward, job skills assessment is the responsibility of the individual soldier's unit commander, the training NCO, or the section chief. Assessment is done through school selection and training, as well as competition for promotion.

While the army does not employ advanced technology for making initial job assignments, it does use technology extensively to assist soldiers transitioning to the civilian sector. In 1990, the army contracted with Resources Consultants, Inc., to implement the Army Career and Alumni Program (ACAP). This federally funded program was established to assist soldiers leaving the service during the army's downsizing period. ACAPs are physical job assistance centers located at every army post.

ACAPs once conducted training using conventional instruction and one-on-one personal counseling, but are now rapidly moving toward using CBI for these services. The program requires soldiers to attend a pre-separation briefing for outprocessing. This briefing includes a description of the services ACAP provides. In recent years, the briefing has been presented to soldiers via computers. This has allowed soldiers to go through the briefing on a self-paced basis, finishing at a later date if necessary. In addition, ACAP formerly had a conventional three-day workshop that trained soldiers on the ins and outs of job searching—self-assessment, networking, resume writing, salary negotiation, and so on. Six interactive training modules focused on the various aspects of job assistance have replaced this three-day workshop. The modules include an electronic mock interview that is taped and can be viewed by the soldier for assessment. In addition to the modules, ACAP has computers available with Internet access that soldiers can use to conduct online job searches. The online job search site consists of international, national, state, military-related, and skill-related categories, which provides the soldier with a wide variety of links.[37] These automated modules empower soldiers to be in charge of their own job search.[38]

Because the training modules were implemented only recently, in August 2000, it is still too early to determine their job-matching effectiveness. Unfortunately, ACAPs do not keep statistics on job placements because they are not job placement offices. ACAPs measure their success in terms of the reductions in money that the federal government saves in paying unemployment compensation.[39] In addition, the ACAPs gather anecdotal success stories and conduct regular surveys of clients served to gauge the usefulness of ACAP services. Surveys assess client satisfaction under the following headings: automated pre-separation counseling, automated job search modules, other automated services, all services in general, general remarks, and suggestions regarding changes that can better serve the client. On a scale of 1 to 5, with 5 as the highest, the Ft. Leonard Wood ACAP in Missouri earned an overall score of 4.8. Soldiers express greater satisfaction with the use of CBI than conventional workshops because CBI allows them to go through the program at their own pace and on their own time. They also have professional help available in the center if they need assistance.[40]

It is unknown why the army has not incorporated the use of technology to assign career paths to incoming soldiers. The current method used may be sufficient for the job placement tasks of the military. However, the army has actively incorporated the use of the Internet and computer-based instructional modules to assist in the job placement of soldiers leaving the military. Technology has been utilized to reduce the personnel needed to assist soldiers and to leverage the resources available on the Internet.

The army's ACAPs are similar to the "one-stops" or workforce centers provided through the Texas local workforce development boards (LWDBs). Both are designed to be one-stop centers for job search assistance. Despite this overarching similarity, there are several differences between ACAPs and workforce centers in terms of management, clientele, and advertising. First, ACAPs are federally funded and managed worldwide by one vendor under a single contract. Each ACAP around the world provides the same services in the same format. By contrast, workforce centers are developed, managed, and customized to meet the needs of the local economy. Second, the client base of ACAPs and the workforce centers are different. Among the clients served by workforce centers are the illiterate, computer illiterate, and people unfamiliar with the work environment. Generally, ACAPs do not serve these groups because of the initial selection standards and training provided by the army. To enter the army, people must have a high school degree or GED. While in the army, soldiers are required to become familiar and comfortable with the use of computers. Soldiers also become intimately familiar with the responsibilities of holding a job in the army. Third, ACAPs do not have to advertise their services to attract clients. All soldiers leaving the army are *required* to attend an ACAP briefing. Workforce centers do not have this luxury; they must advertise their services to attract clients to their site. Workforce centers can learn from the army's ACAPs required courses for technology. Since workforce centers deal with a wide variety of people from different educational and socioeconomic backgrounds, it would be beneficial for those with remedial skills to be required to attend a program or series of classes geared to prepare them to effectively use the technology-based courses and tools.

Another program offered by the U.S. Department of Labor's Veterans' Employment and Training Service (VETS) assists service members and veterans with obtaining work in the civilian world. The Use Your Military Experience and Training (UMET) provides services for current and former military personnel to obtain licenses and certifications through its website.[41] The website's "Transitioning to Civilian Careers" section provides information to job seekers on licensure and certification requirements for civilian jobs. The other major section, "Hiring Qualified Veterans," provides information to help employers understand how military training and experience translate to the civilian sector.[42]

Recommendations

The following recommendations address how the civilian sector can best learn from and implement some of the successes of military training. It is important to note that not all military training can be transferred directly to civilian settings. The military's unique mission and environment differentiate it from the civilian sector. The mission of the military is to protect the United States from all enemies, foreign and domestic. The importance of protecting the U.S. ideals and way of life impacts how the military operates and trains. U.S. companies generally do not directly face the possibility of war and loss of life. Therefore, the civilian sector can train in a less intensive setting. The following recommendations listed represent first steps in applying the military's training experiences to the civilian sector:

Recommendation 9-1: The Texas workforce system should learn from the experience of the military in training and using technology. The federal government has made major investments in learning and training through the military services. At least some of this experience with using leading-edge technologies in training a heterogeneous population could be transferred to civilian applications. The emphasis that the U.S. military continues to place on OJT and on hands-on learning environments is both revealing and instructive. It contrasts with the experience of the workforce system. The use of OJT has declined in the national workforce system since passage of JTPA in the 1970s. However, as noted in this chapter, several defense contractors make effective use of the military's OJT training methodologies. The Army Career and Alumni Program (ACAP) system, which assists individuals who leave the military to find jobs in civilian life, may offer guidance to Texas workforce center operations. The military has apparently successfully replaced three-day conventional workshops with modular computer-based training. However, the ACAP experience reaffirms the need for on-site professional staff to assist and tutor job seekers in the ACAP centers. ACAP centers are located on every army base and, at a minimum, the Texas Workforce Commission should ensure that workforce centers are in communication with the ACAP system, learning from one another and collaborating on initiatives of joint interest.

Recommendation 9-2: The Texas workforce system should promote the use of ADL specifications and guidelines, Sharable Courseware Object Reference Model (SCORM). Backed by a collaboration of over 75 businesses, 26 universities, and 42 federal government agencies, including the U.S. Department of Labor, the adoption of SCORM specifications and guidelines is likely to occur in workforce programs. The Texas workforce system needs to recognize that this is the future in which it will be operating. Such standards make sense for both users and vendors. Vendors that design joint training programs between two or more organizations need to ensure that the training technology

141

is interoperable, meaning that software and hardware made by different vendors are able to share data.

Texas state agencies, including the Texas Workforce Commission, the Texas Higher Education Coordinating Board, and the Texas Education Agency, have roles to play in disseminating information about SCORM and promoting alignment with SCORM. Developers of programs such as EnterTech can monitor the status of SCORM and become involved by making contact through the ADL website, which is located at http://www.adlnet.org/collaborate/collaborate.cfm.

Recommendation 9-3: Training programs need to incorporate feedback from the population that the training aims to assist. The development of an effective training program is an interactive process that invites the collaboration of those it is designed to serve. This is an essential component to produce good pedagogy, as emphasized in chapter 3 of this report. Such a customer orientation goes beyond simply measuring "customer satisfaction." It is also not a one-time endeavor, but rather a process of continuous improvement. A negative example is the National Guard, which had part-time citizen/soldiers dropping out of CBI training programs because they took too long to complete. The full-time soldiers who developed the program had failed to recognize the time constraints faced by citizen/soldiers. When programs are planned and designed, the user should be side by side with the designer. For example, in the design of the army's Computerized Automatic Virtual Environment (CAVE), the user was side by side with the engineer in order to tell the engineer what features should be added or discarded.[43] Such a process leads to more effective training and better use of technology.

Recommendation 9-4: Public sector agencies should explore the applicability of simulation to train their employees. As the experience of the military illustrates, simulation through technology offers much potential as a training device. It is especially appropriate under circumstances in which high-cost equipment is placed at risk through the training or a trainee faces loss of life or limb. Agencies such as the Texas Department of Public Safety may encounter such circumstances and thus should investigate simulation training.

Entities that use simulation training should ensure that all simulators are current with the equipment actually used on the job. Public sector agencies should ensure that training budgets include sufficient funds for capital renovation and building maintenance for the facilities that will house the CBI or simulation hardware.

Conclusion

The American military has taken a leadership role in applying technology to training in at least three arenas: (1) in the development of common technical standards for training, (2) in the use of CBI and simulation technology to deliver training, and (3) in using information technology for job-matching activities. This chapter has analyzed how the military has used technology to enhance equity, efficiency, and effectiveness in its training practices. The military's success in training new recruits from all walks of life to conduct a variety of skilled jobs offers examples that could, with modification, be transferred to the civilian sector.

Notes

[1] Advanced Distributed Learning, *About ADL*. Online. Available: http://www.adlnet.org. Accessed: November 5, 2000.

[2] Herb Bethoney, "Spec Unites Learning Systems," *PC Week Labs, eWeek* (June 27, 1999). Online. Available: http://www.zdet.com/. Accessed: November 5, 2000.

[3] Advanced Distributed Learning Story, *About SCORM*. Online. Available: http://www.adlnet.org/ourstory/scorm.cfm. Accessed: April 8, 2001.

[4] Ibid.

[5] Advanced Distributed Learning, *About ADL*. Online. Available: http://www.adlnet.org. Accessed April 8, 2001.

[6] Ibid.

[7] The MIT Open Knowledge Initiative is a collaborative project with Stanford University, Dartmouth College, Harvard University, North Carolina State University, University of Michigan, University of Pennsylvania, and the University of Wisconsin.

[8] The IMS Global Learning Consortium develops open technical standards to support distributed learning that are available to the public without charge. IMS is a nonprofit organization supported by global members in more than 40 Contributing Members and over 200 Developer Network Subscribers.

[9] Advanced Distributed Learning Network (ADLNet), *MIT Open Knowledge Initiative, ADL Co-Laboratory, and IMS Cooperate to Advance Learning Technology*, July 11, 2001 (press release). Online. Available:http://www.adlnet.org/news_events/news/full_story.cfm?News_Id=89&News_Type=1&Filter=1,2,5. Accessed: August 2, 2001.

[10] J. D. Fletcher and Paul R. Chatelier, "Training in the Military," in *Training and Retraining: A Handbook for Business, Industry, Government, and the Military*, eds. Sigmund Tobias and J. D. Fletcher (New York: Macmillan, 2000), p. 276.

[11] Dexter Fletcher for the Under Secretary of Defense for Personnel and Readiness, Readiness and Training Directorate, *Development and Assessment of ADL Prototypes*, p. II-4.

[12] Interview by Vanessa C. Mitra with Captain Andre Sexton, Field Artillery, U.S. Army, Ft. Sill, Oklahoma, April 4, 2001.

[13] Interview by Vanessa C. Mitra with Captian Bruce Ferrell, Army National Guard Force Readiness Officer, Austin, Texas, November 13, 2000.

[14] Sexton interview.

[15] Brian Friel, "A College of One," *Government Executive Magazine* (August 1, 2001). Online. Available: http://www.govexec.com/features/0801/0801managetech2.htm. Accessed: August 3, 2001.

[16] Ibid.

[17] Army University Access Online (AUAO), *Resources: FAQ's*. Online. Available: http://eARMYU.com/public/public_resources_faqs.asp. Accessed: August 13, 2001.

[18] Army University Access Online (AUAO), *More About AUAO*. Online. Available: http://eARMYU.com/public/public_about-auao_more-about-auao.asp. Accessed: August 13, 2001.

[19] Army University Access Online (AUAO), *Partners*. Online. Available: http://eARMYU.com/public/public_about-auao_partners.asp. Accessed: August 13, 2001.

[20] Ibid.

[21] Gail Repsher Emery, "Army Project Boosts E-Learning Prospects," *Washington Technology*, vol. 16, no. 8 (July 16, 2001). Online. Available: http://www.washingtontechnology.com/news/16_8/federal/16859-1.html. Accessed: August 3, 2001.

[22] Friel, "A College of One." Online. Accessed: August 3, 2001.

[23] Email from Dr. Phyllis D. Robertson, Director, Warfighting Integration and Development Directorate, to Vanessa C. Mitra, Ft. Sill, Oklahoma, November 21, 2000.

[24] Sexton interview.

[25] Fletcher and Chatelier, *Training and Retraining*, p. 37.

[26] Sexton interview.

[27] Ted Shaffrey, "U.S. Army Hires 'Star Trek' Veteran to Create Soldier Simulation," *Westside Weekly* (February 18, 2001). Online. Available: www.ict.usc.edu/press_new/ww.html. Accessed: February 21, 2001.

[28] University of Southern California, "War Is Virutal Hell" (press release). Online. Available: www.ict.usc.edu/press_new/wired.html. Accessed: February 21, 2001.

[29] Adapted quote by Warner Croft, Partner, Anderson Consulting, in J. Michael Brower, "Military Turns to Virtual Classroom," *Training and Simulation Industry and Technology Trends* (November 1999), p. 47.

[30] "Training Funding Crunch Means More Soldiers Are in Simulators," *Training and Simulation Industry and Technology Trends* (November 1999), p. 6.

[31] Quote by Brig. General Stephen M. Seay, in Bill Gregory, "Training System Acquisition Chiefs' Priorities," *Training and Simulation 2000* (Winter 1999), pp. 22-23.

[32] Ibid.

[33] Quote by Major General David F. MacGhee, Jr., Director of air and space operations for the Air Command at Langley Air Force Base, Virginia, in Harold Kennedy, "'War in a Box' Not Real Enough for Air Force Combat Training," *Training and Simulation Industry and Technology Trends"* (November 1999), p. 10.

[34] Bill Gregory, "Training System Acquisition Chiefs' Priorities," *Training and Simulation 2000,* p. 22.

[35] Interview by Vanessa C. Mitra with Aubrey White, Program Manager, Institute of Advanced Technology, The University of Texas at Austin, Austin, Texas, February 27, 2001.

[36] Ferrell interview.

[37] Army and Alumni Career Program Online, *Job Links.* Online. Available: http://www.acap.army.mil/acap/listings.htm. Accessed: April 9, 2001.

[38] Telephone interview by Vanessa C. Mitra with Theresa Remtula, Technology Specialist, Ft. Leonard Wood Army Career and Alumni Program, Ft. Leonard Wood, Missouri, February 6, 2001.

[39] Telephone interview by Vanessa C. Mitra with Jeanie Kellas, Manager, Ft. Leonard Wood Army Career and Alumni Program, Ft. Leonard Wood, Missouri, February 20, 2001.

[40] Ibid.

[41] U.S. Department of Labor, Veterans' Employment and Training Service (VETS), *Use Your Military Experience and Training (UMET).* Online. Available: http://umet-vets.dol.gov/. Accessed: July 31, 2001.

[42] Ibid.

[43] "Vehicle Design Begins in Virtual Cave," *Training and Simulation Industry and Technology Trends* (November 1999), p. 50.

Chapter 10. Innovations in Technology-Based Solutions for Workforce Service Delivery in Other States

Introduction

The Workforce Investment Act (WIA) of 1998 aims to increase the quality and availability of the workforce in part through the creation of one-stop workforce service systems in each state. This federal legislation builds on approaches that leading states had already pioneered. WIA explicitly charges states with the task of developing a network of workforce centers that provide regional information on working conditions and job availability, as well as services to help match clients with jobs. This includes the maintenance of databases of client and employer profiles to assist with job searches and placement, skills and training workshops, and access to continuing education courses through partnerships with local community colleges and other providers of training and education.

Recognizing the problem of limited access to these centers and the opportunities presented by the Internet, most states have either developed or have the goal of establishing a Web-based workforce service delivery system. Such systems can be accessible 24 hours a day, seven days a week, to any job seeker, employer, or service provider from any computer with Internet access. Thus, state employment security agencies (SESAs) have been made responsible for the development of their own information technology systems for the streamlining and provision of universal access to workforce services. In effect, the states have become laboratories to experiment with various models for the delivery of workforce services through computer-based technology.

This chapter examines the technology and service features of some of the first states to use electronically oriented workforce development systems. For this study, we selected states recognized as leaders in the application of various technologies in workforce development services and analyzed what has made those systems effective and efficient. Although information technology is used across the full spectrum of workforce services, this chapter focuses on three areas: job information and matching services, customer tracking and accountability, and skill assessment tools.

The chapter describes collaborative efforts among state agencies and initiatives at the national level to support the development of technology-based innovations in workforce service delivery. Our final section explores the potential that adoption of an extensible markup language (XML) standard could have to improve the efficiency and effectiveness of labor market data exchange.

Major Challenges to Providing Effective Services

A significant challenge to providing effective workforce services is obtaining adequate funding for the one-stop system. Even combining the resources of state employment and welfare

147

programs into one system, as Texas has done, does not cover the costs of implementing all the required services and developing and maintaining a collaborative system.[1] Furthermore, WIA precludes federal funds being used for capital improvement, even to improve operating systems.[2] As a result, the ability of states to upgrade system technologies and resolve incompatibilities between state- and local-level systems or different state agency programs may be seriously hampered.

Cost issues are exacerbated by the devolution of workforce development programs from the federal to the state level. There is a tension between the state-by-state approach to developing technology-based solutions and the economics of information technology (IT) development. Assigning each state the task of developing its own IT system for one-stop service delivery essentially fragments the pool of economic resources available for these efforts. Yet the IT industry exhibits ever-increasing returns to scale: high startup costs coupled with low distribution, replication, and adaptation costs lead to a natural advantage for ever-larger resource pools. The natural solution is for states to form alliances and cost-sharing structures and for the federal government to play some part in the coordination. This indeed is what is happening.

States have also faced issues relating to proprietary ownership of technologies developed for these systems. Contracting for services can be an efficient means of developing solutions. Often, a state will enter into a contract with a private firm for the development of all or part of a technology. This introduces a new potential tension. States, in their desire to facilitate universal and efficient access to workforce services, want to provide information that is freely open to the public, comprehensive, customizable, and generally unfettered by strings or conditions. However, private firms, in their drive for profits, need to find ways of collecting revenue from the process. The firms have an interest in keeping their intellectual property secrets from their competitors and therefore are generally not willing to allow their client states to share technologies with other states. This clearly runs against the efficiency benefits that come from states pooling their resources.

Several important obstacles remain to full implementation of an online one-stop network. Compatibility among many state and local systems is insufficient. Also inadequate is public knowledge on the use and benefits of a computer-based system. Training is needed to eliminate misperceptions and to acquaint job seekers and employers so that they can use the system easily. In the case of programs and features involving collaborations with other agencies, lack of interagency coordination and low priority given to WIA-related tasks by the partnering agencies have resulted in slow development and responses to changes in technology.

Still another challenge has been to design systems that are compatible with service needs at the local levels, while being plugged into a broad network of information that can be accessed by large numbers of providers. The workforce system needs to be connected to databases covering large geographical regions for the provision of timely, comprehensive, and accurate labor market information. Such interfaces should facilitate flexibility by supporting America's highly mobile culture with wider labor market opportunities open to every individual. Job seekers need organized access to an increasingly large and complex world of information. However, these interfaces must also present a localized, customized feel, as the primary importance for the individual is information regarding the immediate employment environment. Users need the capability to narrow the data and focus on specific areas to facilitate choice and engender a sense of community within the process. The systems must address the unique local needs covered by units as small as neighborhoods; and frontline staff at one-stop centers, as well as other contributors to the workforce system, need to be able to update the database directly. Alleviation of the tensions between these local and universal systems requires the creation of a seamless structure that integrates wide scales of databases. Still, incompatibilities among federal, state, and local technologies for distribution of workforce services and case management remain obstacles.

Finally, in addition to technological and governmental barriers, political issues such as privacy must be considered. Many local centers and state agency programs are reluctant to share data with others in the system in order to protect their clients' privacy and ensure that they actually end up providing the services to their clients.

State-Level Innovations in Technology for Workforce Service Delivery

Job Information and Matching Services

An overall goal of state workforce service delivery systems is to provide a single, integrated means of connecting job seekers and employers to the job market.[3] Websites operated by state labor or workforce departments generally provide labor market information on every region in the state served by its workforce centers, including unemployment rates, welfare, occupations, demographics, salary ranges, and access points for further skills or education, as well as links to related federal sites. Job seekers are able to browse through current openings posted on the site, submit resumes, and access links to career preparation sites or programs. Employers can advertise new openings, view resumes of current applicants, and obtain certain other business services. Several states offer space for service providers to advertise their training programs.

By the end of 1999, 15 states had implemented more fully integrated, computer-based workforce systems. Five of these—all with proven results and features exceeding WIA requirements—are discussed here.

Texas

Texas has been at the forefront of workforce system innovations throughout the 1990s. Texas was one of the first states to plan and implement a consolidated state workforce system through the passage of House Bill 1863 in 1995; its services are administered through 28 workforce development areas, more than any other state under the new WIA legislation. More than any prior state or federal measure, H.B. 1863 defined the roles of job seekers and employers in the workforce system and delegated responsibilities to state legislative, workforce, and education agencies.[4] According to a report on state workforce investment plans, Texas was the first state to establish reserves for state and local grants (to maintain funding in the event of a revenue shortage), one-stop workforce centers, incumbent worker projects, operator criteria and partner funding requirements for workforce centers, standards for core measures and customer satisfaction, designs for a state-automated management system, and a common data system to interface with programs in various state departments.[5]

Despite these achievements, the designs have yet to realize their full potential. Incompatibilities among state and various regional systems and insufficient funding have hindered coordination efforts among different agencies, as well as efforts to reach groups in rural areas. Texas could begin to remedy this by modifying its system to include features offered in other leading states.

Utah

Utah was the first state to consolidate all employment-related programs into a single system of one-stop centers. In 1996, the Utah State Legislature passed House Bill 375, creating the Department of Workforce Services, which oversaw administration of all service programs and the creation of the one-stop network. The department also established a "no-stop" goal of increasing widespread access to services via the Internet from homes, businesses, libraries, and schools. The department's website served as the entry point for all online one-stop services until the July 2000 launch of the new Utah Workforce System (UWORKS), which fully integrates job market information, job seeker and employer databases, and training modules into one interactive program. Potential employees can browse through statewide job postings and obtain information on further education and training opportunities, skill development workshops, and online general skill tutorials. Employers can post new openings and view resumes of job seekers who are system users. Service providers can post advertisements to both employers and job seekers. All UWORKS users access the system through private individual accounts, and skills training programs are downloadable. There are also Web links to job sites offering search assistance presentations on topics such as writing resumes and cover letters, interviewing techniques, and general workplace behavior.

UWORKS is largely customer driven. It is the first fully automated system responsive to customer needs. Utah has received several requests from other states to obtain the technology to incorporate into their systems. As of 2001, North Dakota, South Dakota, and Alabama had established system collaborations with UWORKS to enhance their service delivery programs.[6]

Florida

Florida has been a leading state in workforce services since the late 1980s. The Workforce Florida Act of 1996 established the current system, which is centered on the missions of three programs: Work and Gain Economic Self-Sufficiency (WAGES), First Jobs/First Wages, and the High Skills/High Wages Program.

Work and Gain Economic Self-Sufficiency (WAGES) is Florida's welfare-to-work program, administered through local boards. First Jobs/First Wages is an initiative that enlists the support of community, business, and educational institutions to provide education and workplace experiences for young people preparing to enter the workforce. High Skills/High Wages provides education and more advanced skills training for high-paying, high-responsibility jobs and career advancement. The State Workforce Development Board collaborates with the Departments of Education, Elder Affairs, Veterans' Affairs, Labor and Employment Security, Children and Families, Juvenile Justice, Management Services, and Corrections to oversee the administration of 61 workforce service programs.[7]

Information technology has played a big role in increasing the range and efficiency of these services, while producing striking results. Florida's Employment Community is an online resource that provides labor market information, trends and statistics, and connection means for job seekers, employers, and training service providers. Opportunities for further education and financial aid are also posted, as are advertisements from training service providers, including IT certification. This site currently focuses exclusively on high-tech sector employment; however, plans are under way to expand it into a full-service job bank.[8] Meanwhile, Florida provides search services for job seekers and employers through the site myflorida.com, which includes a skills-matching feature for job seekers. Statewide labor market information, including present and projected trends and statistics, is available via the Florida Research and Economic Database (FRED).[9] During program year 1999, 72.5 percent of job seekers using these systems found employment.[10] In addition, Florida places special emphasis on youth services and promotes career awareness in high school students through NEXT, a career advising and job resource magazine for teens that is also available online.[11] NEXT allows students to be better informed about the skills needed for jobs in their fields of interest and can lead to experiences that give students a head start toward better opportunities in their chosen fields.

Washington

Washington has consistently been regarded as one of the leading states in online resources since it first received federal funding to implement one-stop services.[12] The Washington Interactive Labor Market Access (WILMA) system site provides viewers with information and statistics on education, employer listings, census information, income, labor force, industries, economic indicators, and profiles of each county, including both present estimated figures and projections for the next ten years. WorkSource, the one-stop network, provides links to a wide array of other job search and career assistance resources. Included are listings of Internet access points; social service assistance programs and agencies; search vehicles for state, nationwide, and international job openings; websites of major high-tech employers; federal employment databases; and application and career planning sites. Similar to Utah's "no-stop" approach, these resources greatly increase the opportunities for connecting employers and job seekers.

Kentucky

Kentucky has two programs, both established through the Empower Kentucky initiative of 1997, that facilitate service delivery by means of strong interagency coordination: the Employ Kentucky Network and the Commonwealth Access and Resource System (CARE). The Employ Kentucky Network is an Internet-based system linking the Kentucky Cabinet of Workforce Development with the Employment Services, Adult Education and Literacy, Vocational Rehabilitation, and Technical Education Departments, and the Department for the Blind.[13] CARE is an electronic data collection system for common information on customers for state and community services. Through CARE, users need only go through one-time registration and assessment, while scheduling, planning, monitoring, state-community communication and agency service coordination are made easier.[14] Access is also simplified through links to existing systems. As a result of these collaborative efforts, job seekers, employers, and service providers are connected with a wider array of services accessible from a greater number of locations, and duplication of services among the agencies is greatly reduced.

Progress is being made toward establishing a single, comprehensive system capable of providing efficient and effective services on a large scale. New tools and programs are connecting various state agencies to each other and local networks are emerging. Greater numbers of community centers, increasing Internet access points, and private system accounts storing individual records are also helping to make this comprehensive system become a reality. However, equity still presents a considerable hurdle. Whether or not a client receives a particular needed service often depends on whether he or she falls into a targeted population group designated eligible for that service. If states can develop and enact more specific provisions and goals toward services such as assessment, case management, career counseling, on-the-job training, and postemployment services, and focus on population groups generally receiving lower attention or priority, greater progress could be made.

Customer Tracking and Accountability

Common gaps in online one-stop systems are lack of effective technology for maintenance of customer records and incompatibility among different state or regional systems. WIA requires states to report levels of entry, retention, and earnings in adult, youth, and dislocated worker programs, as well as customer satisfaction rates for both employers and individuals. Many states have the goal of developing an integrated accountability system to interface with other state systems, reduce duplication of services among multiple-agency services, and maximize the level of accuracy of this information. But they lack access to needed funds, hardware, or software to accomplish this goal. Such a system would greatly increase the accuracy of both client and employer records, eliminating the need for repeated data entry and thus preventing inadvertent repetition of services to individual customers and reducing costs. It would also increase the capacity for measuring effectiveness of the workforce system by facilitating client tracking, as well as staff efficiency and data exchange with other systems. An additional challenge is presented by the difficulty in obtaining timely, accurate, and consistent information for internal management and external reporting purposes.

Three states, discussed here in detail, have implemented innovative, relatively comprehensive systems for customer tracking and accountability systems.

Florida

Florida tracks customers and measures program effectiveness through the Florida Education and Training Placement Information Program (FETPIP). Established in 1988, FETPIP follows up on former students and participants of workforce and social service programs based on information provided by workforce, corrections, and training programs for migrant agricultural workers, apprenticeship programs, colleges and universities, and school districts. This information is linked with data from the U.S. Postal Service, Agency for Workforce Innovation, and Departments of Education, Defense, Corrections, Labor and Employment Security, Personnel Management, Management Services, Children and Families, and Revenue to report accountability in terms of employment rates, earnings, program effectiveness, and levels of public support. The system identifies the occupations of former students and major codes and intentions toward postsecondary education of current students, determines whether families have received Temporary Assistance to Needy Families (TANF), and provides information on whether former inmates return to prison. Effectiveness of all WIA-related services was evaluated by FETPIP in each required category. In program year 1999, Florida exceeded negotiated performance levels in each category at the statewide level.[15]

FETPIP-based performance data are also used to determine funding levels for certain state-funded programs. The state can receive WIA or education performance bonuses if federally prescribed performance measures are met. Florida universities, community colleges, K-12 schools, and the Department of Corrections can receive bonus and incentive payments based on placement levels of students after graduation and of inmates after release from incarceration.[16]

Washington

The Executive Policy Council in the state of Washington mandates reporting of service outcomes. To this end, Washington has issued a proposal to integrate a customer tracking and accountability system into its one-stop network. The Skills Knowledge Information and Employment System (SKIES) is modeled on the tracking services provided in Utah's UWORKS system. SKIES will enhance Washington's existing system by interfacing with other state and local systems and supporting related local and regional needs. Duplication of services to customers and excessive data processing will be reduced, while the portability and accessibility of the one-stop system will be increased.[17] With automated tracking, customer information will be more accurate, up-to-date, and easy to access, and system efficiency can be more accurately assessed based on outcomes. System interconnections will allow more widespread reporting of the effectiveness of not only individual programs but also collaborative efforts among multiple state agencies.

Texas

Career Development Resources,[18] a division of the Texas Workforce Commission, operates an Automated Student and Adult Learner Follow-up System (ASALFS). This system is used to measure the accountability of education and workforce programs. It contains quarterly earnings records from the unemployment insurance system received from the Texas Workforce Commission, as well as information from the Texas Education Agency, the Texas Higher Education Coordinating Board, the Department of Criminal Justice, the Schools for the Blind and Deaf, and selected participating private universities. These records contain information on client background, services received, and the status of clients after leaving the program, which helps determine the effectiveness of these services. The records are then linked to resource databases electronically. By centralizing these informational resources, the ASALFS helps to reduce duplication of services and reduces data exchange costs.[19]

In Austin, the Capital Workforce Development Board, the City of Austin, and Austin Business College are the key players in an initiative developing a local, Internet-based customer tracking and accountability system to serve Travis County. The system acts as a relational database, accessible from any Internet-equipped computer. It will allow all workforce and educational centers to share data, including client profiles, center records, and regional statistics easily and efficiently, thereby facilitating interagency coordination. A member of the workforce board working closely with the project stressed that the main goal was "to create a secure and interactive system that will be less of a hassle to the user, and decrease foot traffic in our workforce centers." He added that the main barrier to implementing the Austin system at the state level is a philosophical one. "Many centers don't want to share their data. You could do unthinkable things with someone's social security number." [20]

Although the Texas system measures effectiveness on a categorical program basis, it could go further with respect to efficiency, taking levels of both state and federal funding into particular consideration. If the Austin system or some alternative version could be modified and implemented at the state level, results could be reported more easily and could facilitate future coordinated efforts between agencies. Establishing state standards for individual program performance would also allow for better assessments of efficiency and effectiveness.

Skill Assessment

Commonly missing in existing electronic workforce systems are tools to determine a job seeker's readiness for a particular job. Although WIA provides access to skills training for those adults who do not secure employment at good wages in core and intensive services, it does not specify a requirement for skill assessment tools. Job seekers must possess not only required skills but also knowledge of appropriate workplace behavior and expectations to succeed in the marketplace. An applicant's character or attitudes can be a key consideration in his or her candidacy for a job. Seldom is assessment of a job seeker's level of preparation available, let alone any diagnosis of what further training may be required. Incompatibilities between workforce and educational technologies and limited funding for workforce-educational collaborations present challenges to providing increased access to further education and training opportunities.

From its High Tech Employment Center, Florida provides links to websites offering academic-based skill tests. These assessments are games or questionnaires that test a job applicant's knowledge of basic skills and general workplace behavior. In some cases, the sites match an applicant with a particular field of employment or industry, based on his/her responses. Washington also has a link from the WorkSource site to a state-supported career guidance tool. This assessment of applicants' interests and abilities is an exploratory tool for gathering information on different fields and offering recommendations about what types of work the applicant might fit best. [21]

The job-matching process in Texas could benefit considerably from providing more links to similar assessments from workforce center websites, especially assessments created by employers who use the services of these workforce centers. In conjunction with skill requirements for specific positions, these assessments could reduce the service needs of many job seekers by refining their career search.

Interstate Collaboration and National-Level Developments

State workforce agencies may increase the efficiency of developing and delivering technology-based solutions by entering into collaborations and partnerships with each other. As the Internet and other IT phenomena evolve, the industry has become increasingly consolidated around a few key producers. Large corporations have come to dominate several of the most prominent areas of IT development: operating systems (Microsoft), databases (Oracle), office software (Microsoft) Internet browsers (Microsoft), and e-commerce (Amazon). This trend shows the advantage of pooling resources and capitalizing on increasing returns to scale. A program or system of software programs can be replicated and adapted at costs far below development, due to the electronic nature of computer code and the increasing move toward modularity with "object-oriented" computer programming.

In this section, we examine some initiatives and alliances that are emerging among state, national, and private agencies for developing and sharing technology-based solutions for workforce service delivery. Several of these efforts began in the mid-1990s or earlier, well ahead of passage of the Workforce Investment Act.

O*NET

The Occupational Information Network (O*NET), under development by the O*NET Consortium, led by the U.S. Department of Labor, is a comprehensive, indexed listing of worker and employment categories. It is intended to serve as a standard for referencing job information for the development of services that use such information in both the private and public sectors. Such a standard, if widely adopted, should enable more rapid, efficient sharing of information across wide-ranging workforce information systems that utilize the same data.

O*NET is the dynamic, technology-based replacement to the static Dictionary of Occupational Titles (DOT)—the DOL's taxonomy of job categories that has been in use for decades. In contrast to the DOT, which classified occupations according to their relationship to people, data, and things, O*NET is based on knowledge, skills, and abilities. The online system was designed for rapid adaptation to changes in job descriptions and fields of employment. In addition to the database itself, there is a Web-based application. Up-and-coming features of the application include the O*NET Interest Profiler, Work Locator, Importance Locator, and Ability Profiler—a suite of tools that will assist job seekers in making career choices.

DOL continues to develop O*NET. In early 2001, O*NET was developing an automated service based on the process of generating the report, called *Skills Match*, for the one-stop operating system.[22] The O*NET database is being expanded. The DOL will randomly sample businesses, adding 200-300 new job titles each year, with the expectation of replenishing the database every five years. A national survey was conducted in 2001. The O*NET database is organized into six main areas: Worker Characteristics, Worker Requirements, Experience Requirements, Occupational Characteristics, Occupational Requirements, and Occupation-Specific Requirements.[23]

Several states already use the O*NET database. For example, California's Employment Development Department (CAEDD) used O*NET tools to survey and analyze the needs of a specific group of unemployed workers and produce a report for those individuals on the best ways to market their job skills and obtain reemployment. CAEDD claims that O*NET helped them to expand their services and assist these workers to find jobs faster.

America's Career Kit

America's Career Kit is another suite of four Internet tools designed to provide assistance to the states in developing online, technology-based solutions to the requirements of the Workforce

Investment Act of 1998. It was developed as a collaborative effort between the American Association of Community Colleges (AACC), the U.S. Department of Labor, the Council for Excellence in Government, and 15 states, led by Minnesota.[24] The tools include America's Job Bank (AJB), America's Career InfoNet (ACIN), America's Learning Exchange (ALX), and America's Service Locator (ASL). AJB is a labor exchange technology that allows job seekers to post resumes and businesses to post job announcements. The service is designed to integrate seamlessly with state job exchanges by allowing a subset of its database to serve as state-specific exchanges—for example, the Texas Job Bank—with the same look and feel. ACIN is a labor market information clearinghouse that provides information on wages and employment trends across occupations and industries, as well as skills, knowledge, and employment experience requirements for most occupations, and cost of living data. There is also an extensive, well-organized list of links to other employment information services. ALX is a database of learning providers searchable by state, subject, and delivery method.[25]

One problem with America's Job Bank has been the issue of proprietary ownership of the rights to the intellectual property by Applied Theory, the firm that developed it under federal contract. This has raised issues for states that have the choice of incorporating this technology into their own systems. For example, the Minnesota Department of Economic Security, in developing Minnesota's Job Bank, initially had hoped to utilize the software code from America's Job Bank in the development of its system, but this was unfortunately not the case. This relationship also involved compatibility issues: transfer of data from one system to another is limited. Even though Minnesota's was patterned after America's Job Bank, AJB could not provide certain specific information due to Applied Theory's attempt to control the reference as part of its revenue-generating strategy.[26]

America's Workforce System

America's Workforce System (AWS) is a one-stop operating system designed by America's Workforce Technology Solutions (AWTS). The system is intended as an electronic backbone for one-stop centers. A primary advantage for employing such a system statewide is that such standardization allows easy access to databases and rapid transfer of information across a wide geographical area. Thus, states may comply with provisions in WIA for streamlining and providing universal access to services. AWS was set up to be adapted to and work with varying data systems; this flexibility allows it to be integrated with other workforce development technologies such as America's Job Bank.[27]

AWTS is based in Topeka, Kansas, and receives its funding through an agreement between the National Association of State Workforce Agencies (NASWA) and the Kansas Department of Human Resources. NASWA contracts with AWTS to develop an annual work plan with the organization's members. State employment and securities agencies then contract with NASWA for work specified in the annual plan.

State employment security agencies enjoy many benefits when they subscribe to AWTS services. Foremost among these is cost sharing. Those who are not associated with AWTS pay the entire cost of supporting computer systems for employment and training programs. As indicated in the following comparison, the cost savings can be substantial, especially for smaller states.

For roughly the cost of one full-time equivalent position, a SESA may have the use of systems used to capture data, maintain operations, and meet reporting needs. In contrast, SESAs not using AWTS services are reported to use from 7 to 23 positions for the same purpose, with costs ranging from $350,000 to over $1 million per year. An additional benefit of using AWTS systems is that SESAs do not have to spend the tremendous amount of effort needed to keep up with changing federal reporting standards. AWTS has staff assigned to monitor federal reporting requirements and ensures timely inclusion of these requirements into their systems.[28] As of January 2002, twenty-one states, including Texas, subscribed to these services.[29]

America's Job Link Alliance

America's Job Link Alliance was initially formed to help Ohio and Kansas maximize their returns on investment in information systems and to share successful strategies and best practices for the creation of information technology solutions for workforce service delivery. Since its inception in November 2000, Oklahoma, Vermont, Missouri, and New Mexico have joined the alliance.[30] Members agree to share resources and lessons learned and to cooperate in several areas. Where appropriate, they participate together in the creation of technologies, the production of marketing materials to promote these technologies, and the development of training programs for frontline workers with the systems. They also agree to combine purchasing power for the procurement of services from other organizations for the development of technologies.

Kansas' development of a statewide integrated workforce development system through America's Job Link Alliance illustrates the power of innovation through collaboration. The Kansas State Department of Human Resources analyzed and evaluated existing systems and chose OhioWorks based on specific elements of the design and its proven success. Kansas was able to adapt the Ohio system to create Kansas JobLink in only four months. A Kansas spokesman explained the advantages: "Their new system communicates with others Kansas had previously invested in and includes interfaces and links to existing Workforce Investment Act core partner legacy systems."[31]

The systems being used by Ohio and Kansas include modules for online job and skill matching, resume preparation, case management, employer job listing, service provider registry, federal reporting, and labor market information. Due to the modularity of the original design, any participating state may pick and choose from the services it prefers.[32]

Ohio is also currently developing an online tool for administration of unemployment insurance systems that will be available to all member states. With this service, the Kansas Department of Human Resources expects to increase the effectiveness and equity of its workforce services. By ensuring that individuals with Internet access can obtain unemployment insurance services without tying up additional human resources, the agency can be more focused on those who truly need them (i.e., those without effective Internet access).[33]

Currently, there are no financial obligations with being a member of the alliance. To join, a state agency must only express an interest in using the programs developed by member states and sign a memorandum of understanding stating their intention to utilize programs developed under the alliance and agree to share their own developments with other member states.[34]

The alliance is considering a more integrated, cost-sharing structure for the future. Kansas, having a larger technical support structure than smaller states participating in the alliance, may agree to host services for those states in exchange for subscription fees. The concept is that only one technical support system is needed to perform the core maintenance and maintain database development for a system that is essentially the same, with minor adaptations, across the member states. The host state would also be responsible for employing the skilled technicians needed for this task. Currently, taking on these functions separately, both Ohio and Kansas, the two largest states in the alliance, depend on Accenture Corporation for the same services. Combining the resources of several states would allow them to achieve this without private sector assistance.[35]

DOL considers the alliance to be one of the most promising developments and has granted $500,000 to assist with system development costs. America's Job Link Alliance is also in the process of obtaining an additional $2 million from DOL to continue the program.[36]

The experience of the alliance suggests two opportunities for Texas. The Texas Workforce Commission could join America's Job Link Alliance to take advantage of the cost-sharing benefits it bestows, or Texas could actively seek partner states to form its own coalition for the same purpose.

Open Standards for Data Exchange

Significant developments in information technology may affect the efficiency, effectiveness, and equity of workforce service delivery in the near future. It is always hazardous to predict upcoming innovations in technology and an even greater challenge to predict the impact of such change on society. Indeed, venture capitalists gamble great sums of money on such predictions, and they frequently lose. While any definitive or comprehensive overview of prospective technological developments is beyond the scope and resources of our research, the following section focuses on an example of one innovation that may have an impact in workforce arena. It concerns the development of an open technical standard for communication over the Internet, called XML, promulgated by the World Wide Web Consortium. The World Wide Web Consortium (W3C) is an international body whose mission is to "lead the World Wide Web to its full potential by developing common protocols that promote its evolution and ensure its interoperability."[37] Among other advantages, XML has the potential to enhance the availability and organization of labor market information. XML applications in e-learning education and training programs are already built into the common standards of the Sharable Courseware Object Reference Model (SCORM), promoted by DoD and a consortium of federal agencies, private firms, and academic institutions, as discussed in chapter 9 of this report.

XML

XML is an Internet communications standard that is quietly making an impact in many industries. XML, which stands for extensible markup language, is related to HTML, the common standard for creating Web documents, but it embodies a significantly more powerful functionality: meta-data.

Meta-data is data about data. In a Web-page document, normal HTML code includes the text that would appear on the page, along with "mark-up" tags (hence the name, hyper-text *mark-up* language) that describe how the text should appear on the page and what images should be included with the text. But HTML says nothing about what the text actually means or refers to. XML, in contrast, does not specify how text or other data appears in a Web browser; rather, it is a standard for creating a set of tags that themselves describe the *meaning* of text to be transferred over the Web. Using XML an industry may establish a framework of meta-tags that are specifically tailored to meet the needs of the industry.

The usefulness of XML can be intuitively grasped with quick glance at a sample of XML for the publishing industry:

```
<Book>
<Name>The Complete XML Guide</Name>


<Author>
<Name>John Smith</Name>


<Title>Jr.</Title>
</Author>


<Year>2000</Year>
<Publisher>John Wiley &Sons</Publisher>
<PubCity>New York</PubCity>


<Edition>First</Edition>
</Book>[38]
```

It is easy to see that the meta-data tags describe the publishing information for a book about XML. Indeed, one of the goals of XML is that the code itself be readable without processing by a browser. But the real advantage of an XML standard comes from the way it can be read by a browser. When all players within a specific industry employ the standard, functionality can be programmed into software applications that interpret and process this information. No one needs to preside over a process of determining the meaning of the content for the purpose of ushering data into the proper pigeonholes of a database or sorting through what data are relevant to a search criterion and what are not. The system just "knows" where the data should go and what is relevant. XML is independent of any system or any vendor, which means that it enhances the nonproprietary aspects of the Internet. A number of industries, including aerospace, automotive, telecommunications, and computer software, have been effectively using standards similar to XML to share information for years.[39]

The current development of an XML standard for online education content illustrates the potential of this type of standardization and may serve as a model for the workforce development system. A group called IMS Global Learning Consortium[40] is developing an XML standard that could revolutionize the way educational content on the Internet is catalogued and located, and this could serve as a model for innovations in workforce service delivery. Theoretically, if such a standard is adopted universally, it will vastly improve the efficiency and effectiveness of educational content cataloguing systems and reduce the time it takes consumers to locate educational resources. Simple tools exist that allow educational content to be packaged or marked up with XML meta-tag documents. One of these is the LRN toolkit, developed by Microsoft Corporation, one of the members of the IMS Consortium.

To understand the power of this idea, imagine a student seeking information about volcanoes for a book report. Typically a Web search will yield tens of thousands of results, many of which may pertain to volcanoes in *some* way, but are focused on tourism, personal information, or simply contain the word "volcano" somewhere within the text. If educational content were universally marked up with the IMS standard, the search process would be greatly streamlined and lead the student directly to the content he or she needs. The browser would be able to automatically sort through all search results, determine which are germane to the student's research on volcanoes by selecting those sites marked up with the IMS standard and that are categorized as pertaining to volcanoes, and present only those results. Given the mountains of Web pages typically served by a search, this would yield a vast increase in the efficiency and effectiveness of students' research efforts, not to mention a great reduction in their frustration. This system may even permit a continually updated and precise index of *all* educational content on the Web.

Such a standard could revolutionize the workforce system. First, consider the number of job openings that are posted directly by employers over the Internet. In May 2001, America's Job Exchange had 1.9 million job postings and 440 million resumes.[41] The proliferation of job banks created by the private sector and by state workforce agencies complicates the situation. Despite several attempts to consolidate U.S. labor market information on the Internet, employment information is still largely dispersed. Job seekers must search extensively for employment information. A universally accepted XML standard for marking up Internet-posted job vacancies could achieve a similar goal that the IMS project is seeking for educational content on the Web: a continuously and automatically updated, and complete catalog of all Web-based job postings.

This would require the development of a simple tool for producing an XML document that would be available free for employers to use in the creation of Web-based job postings. It would also require universal or near universal acceptance by employers, which admittedly is no easy feat. Openness of the standard, availability of free tools for simple implementation of the standard by businesses, and a public awareness campaign regarding the benefits of universal adaptation for all stakeholders would all be necessary for a successful implementation of this type of standard in the workforce system.

The DOL could spearhead the formation of a consortium of state agencies involved in workforce development, technical colleges, and IT industry leaders to develop such an XML standard for employment information. By facilitating the consolidation of labor market information, such a standard would allow job seekers to spend their time more efficiently searching for jobs. At the same time, it would enable employers to disseminate vacancy announcements to a wider audience, allowing for better fits in the matching process.

Conclusion and Recommendations

States have begun to capitalize on the opportunities presented by new technologies to improve their workforce services while providing more efficient access. Overlap and limitations of state agency programs are being considerably reduced, while the boundaries separating state and local systems, as well as systems in different states, are thinning, thanks to coordinated efforts.

Recommendation 10-1: The Texas workforce system should continually assess the progress made toward its goals, identify services not meeting set performance measures and population groups not receiving the full range of needed services, and adopt innovations in technology that may offer means of improving these services and reaching these groups. Technology itself will not provide complete or final solutions. States must consistently reassess the structure and functions of every program within every state and local agency and consolidate or reorganize as needed to minimize duplication and fragmentation while maximizing collaborative efforts and communication means between workers and employers.

Recommendation 10-2: Texas should collaborate with other states to share the costs of developing and implementing innovations in information technologies used in the workforce system. Texas can gain a lot from collaborating with other states to improve workforce service technologies. As one of the nation's leading states in workforce development, Texas also has much to contribute. The nature of IT development exhibits significant increasing economic returns to scale. Texas could participate in multiple-state coalitions to extend the scope of labor market information presented while reducing system costs. The "no-stop" vision of Utah and Washington could provide an excellent basis for technological modifications and improvements to the state system that would increase the opportunities for connecting job seekers and employers. An agency coordination program similar to Kentucky's CARE could further reduce the duplication while facilitating the distribution of agency services and increasing possibilities for collaborative programs. Florida's FETPIP offers an excellent model for a tracking and accountability system that measures program effectiveness and efficiency. It can also be used to help determine funding needs. Texas should consider joining America's Job Link Alliance or establishing its own coalition with other states to save money through sharing costs.

Recommendation 10-3: Texas should advocate for workforce and education agencies to implement XML standards for labor market information and job matching. Just as adoption of the SCORM standards has promoted interoperability and improved efficiency and compatibility of computer-based education and training programs, so there is a need for standards in labor market information and job-matching programs. XML or some other advanced technology may offer the means of achieving a system that is more effective and efficient for both employers and job seekers.

Recommendation 10-4: In implementing innovations in information technology, concerns about privacy and confidentiality of information must be appropriately addressed. Care must be taken while carrying out these changes to uphold concerns of individual participants of the system regarding privacy of information in order to assure their rights and so that the chance of public opposition can be minimized. Only when all the technical, structural, and personal issues are

161

addressed can the maximum level of efficiency, equity, and effectiveness of workforce services be achieved.

Notes

[1] Daniel O'Shea and Christopher T. King, *Restructuring Workforce Development Initiatives in States and Localities*, Report No. 12 (Albany: The Nelson A. Rockefeller Institute of Government, April 2001), p. 20.

[2] Workforce Florida, *Workforce Florida Strategic Plan*, 2001-2002. Online. Available:http://www.wages.org/wages/wfi/partners/stratplan/stratplan-full.pdf. Accessed May 7, 2001.

[3] Center for Public Policy Priorities, *The Workforce Investment Act of 1998*. Online. Available: http://www.cppp.org/products/policypages/91-110/91-110html/PP96.html. Accessed May 7, 2001.

[4] Ray Marshall Center for the Study of Human Resources, *Workforce Development Evaluation in Texas: An Assessment* (September 1996), pp. 1-7.

[5] National Governors' Association Center for Best Practices, *WIA Early Implementation State Workforce Investment Plans* (March 27, 2000). Online. Available: http://www.nga.org/cda/files/WIAMATRIX.pdf. Accessed May 7, 2001.

[6] Utah Department of Workforce Services, *Utah's Workforce System*. Online. Available: http://www.dws.state.ut.us/PI/UWORKS/UWORKS.htm. Accessed May 7, 2001.

[7] Florida Legislature, Office of Program Policy Analysis, and Government Accountability, *Review of the Workforce Development System*. Report no. 99-34. Online. Available: http:www.OPPAGA.state.fl.us/reports/econ/r99-34s.html. Accessed May 7, 2001.

[8] Florida Employment Community Web Site. Online. Available: https://www.myfloridajobs.com/wagesct/wagesprod/empcenter/about.cfm. Accessed May 7, 2001.

[9] Florida Agency for Workforce Innovation, *Florida Research and Economic Database*. Online. Available at http://fred.labormarketinfo.com/. Accessed May 7, 2001.

[10] Workforce Florida Strategic Plan, 2001-2002. Online. Available:http://www.wages.org/wages/wfi/partners/stratplan/stratplan-full.pdf. Accessed May 7, 2001.

[11] Florida Trend *NEXT*. Online. Available: http://www.floridanext.com/. Accessed May 7, 2001.

[12] Tod Newcombe, "Reinventing Welfare for the Digital Age," *Government Technology* (April 2000). Online. Available: http://www.govtech.net/publications/gt/2000/apr/digitalstates2/digitalstates2.phtml. Accessed May 7, 2001.

[13] The Commonwealth of Kentucky, *Employ Kentucky Network*. Online. Available: http://www.state.ky.us/agencies/gov/empower/saccess/care.htm. Accessed May 7, 2001.

[14] Ibid.

[15] Florida Department of Education, *First Year WIA Performance: Outcome Data*. Online. Available: http://www.firn.edu/doe/bin00078/fetpip/pdf/wreports.pdf. Accessed: May 7, 2001.

[16] Email from Jay Pfeiffer, Director, Florida Education Training and Placement Information Program, to Daniel Starr, April 6, 2001.

[17] Washington State Employment Security Department, *Acquisition Approval Request to Procure System Integrator Services to Implement a Customer Tracking and Accountability System* (May 1999).

[18] Career Development Resources was formerly entitled the Texas State Occupational Information Coordinating Committee (Texas SOICC).

[19] Texas State Occupational Information Coordinating Committee, *Automated Student and Adult Learner Follow-Up System, Final Report 1999* (Austin, Tex., 2000), pp. 1-11.

[20] Telephone interview by Daniel Starr with Paul Ellis, President, Austin Business College, Austin, Texas, April 9, 2001.

[21] Workforce Training and Education Coordinating Board, *Washington Career Guide*. Online. Available: http://www.wa.gov/careerguide/career/assess/. Accessed May 7, 2001.

[22] Ibid.

[23] National O*NET Consortium, *O*NET*. Online. Available: http://www.onetcenter.org/. Accessed May 7, 2001.

[24] Interstate Conference of Employment Security Agencies, *Workforce ATM*. "ALX Connects. Vol. 2. Issue 3." Online. Available: http://www.icesa.org/articles/template.cfm?results_art_filename=alxapr.htm. Accessed: May 7, 2001.

[25] America's Workforce Network, *America's Career Infonet*. Online. Available: http://www.acinet.org/acinet/ Accessed May 7, 2001.

[26] Telephone interview by Michael Faust with Constance Feltz, Project Team Leader, Minnesota Department of Economic Security, St. Paul, Minnesota, March 28, 2001.

[27] America's Workforce Technology Solutions, *America's Workforce System*. Online. Available: http://www.awts.org/html/america.html. Accessed: May 7, 2001.

[28] Ibid.

[29] Email from Stan Voth, America's Workforce Technology Solutions, Topeka, Kansas. "AWTS Membership," to Robert W. Glover, January 25, 2002.

[30] Telephone interview by Michael Faust with David McEachern, Director of Management Information Services, Kansas Department of Human Resources, Topeka, Kansas, May 3, 2001.

[31] Interstate Conference of Employment Security Agencies, *Workforce ATM,* "Information Technology Committee Meeting Notes." Online. Available: http://www.icesa.org/articles/template.cfm?results_art_filename=itnovdecmin.htm. Accessed: May 7, 2001.

[32] McEachern interview.

[33] Ibid.

[34] Ibid.

[35] Ibid.

[36] Ibid.

[37] Available: www.w3.org/Consortium/.

[38] DM Review, "Meta Data and Data Administration: XML: The Global Meta Data Standard." Online. Available: http://www.dmreview.com/editorial/dmreview/print_action.cfm?EdID=1845. Accessed: May 7, 2001.

[39] IMS Global Learning Consortium, Inc., *IMS Global Learning Consortium Inc.* Online. Available: http://www.imsproject.org. Accessed: May 7, 2001.

[40] The original name of this initiative was the Instructional Management System (IMS) project. Over time, the organization has dropped the full name and just uses the acronym IMS. Visit their website for further details: http://www.imsproject.org/.

[41] America's Workforce Technology Solutions, *America's Job Bank.* Online. Available: http://www.ajb.org. Accessed: May 7, 2001.

Chapter 11. Implementing Information Technology through Partnerships

The growing importance of quality training and development programs has forced public and private sector stakeholders to reevaluate their roles in education and workforce preparation. The interdependence between the public and private sectors is increasingly being recognized and the interests of both need to be addressed in shaping workforce development initiatives. Both sectors can benefit from partnerships, allowing them to share information, practices, and resources.

A common theme running through this report is the use of partnerships to implement technological innovations in workforce systems. A remarkable array of examples of partnerships has been discussed, ranging from the coalition of representatives from the businesses, education, and community groups that developed Entertech to the multistate coalitions used to finance development of state innovations in information technology.

Faced with economic losses, industries have placed significant pressures on the public sector to remedy this situation. While the lack of a qualified workforce has affected all industries, ranging from health care to manufacturing, the most urgent demands have been from the high-tech industry.

As Texas evaluates public support for adult education and employment training programs, corporations and service providers must respond to new funding provisions, increased employer requirements, and technological changes in the workplace. With unique expertise in the field of adult training and the skills needed to enter the field, high-tech companies can enhance the effectiveness of training programs by sharing their knowledge and resources. In order for cross-sector partnerships to achieve success, the implementation of programs must focus on efficiency, equity, and effectiveness. In this context, efficient programs will allow participants to gain new skills as they are being applied in their field. With an emphasis on access to the latest technology and information, partnerships can allow trainees to become acclimated into the workforce at a faster rate. A commitment to equity requires that partnerships focus on the reasons Texans are leaving the educational system without the skills necessary for entering the workforce. By creating opportunities for traditionally disadvantaged groups, the partnerships can attack the problem at its source while largely increasing the availability of skilled employees. The effectiveness of these partnerships can be directly measured by the increase in employable workers. The benefit of this to the public sector is economic growth for the future. By increasing the number of skilled employees, Texas can attract new businesses and restore the faith of existing companies. The private sector will be able to reduce employee shortages and realize its production and earning potential. In order to maximize the effectiveness of cross-sector partnerships, it is necessary to examine the elements that make up successful partnerships, the improvements that can be made on existing partnerships, and the uses of technology that can foster these improvements.

Background

The rapid growth of technology-based industries relies on a steady stream of qualified workers. In order to meet these needs, individual service providers and employers who rely on them must form a network in which the skill demands of industry are clearly articulated, so the training provided is aimed at fulfilling those needs.

According to the American Society for Training and Development (ASTD), training expenditures continue to grow, employers are relying more on in-house staff to provide training, and the use of learning technologies is leveling off.[1] Findings from the report were based on the results of ASTD's Benchmarking Service, an annual process that collects information from 501 organizations of various types on the nature of their training expenditures and practices. The data indicate the following:

- Firms in the health-care and government sectors provided training to the highest percent of eligible employees.

- The trade, technology, and transportation and public utilities sectors provided training to the lowest percent of eligible employees.

- Most training money is spent on technical processes and procedures and information technology skills.

- Organizations are delivering less of their training in the classroom. The overall decline over time corresponds closely with the increases in technology-delivered training.

Individual firms have been actively trying to meet training demands. The Employment Policy Foundation estimates that across all industries business spent $62.5 billion in formal, direct training costs in 1999 compared to $18.7 billion in 1994 (in 1999 dollars). An additional $180 billion was spent on unplanned and unstructured informal training.[2]

Partnerships must be based on an involvement and investment that is proportionate to each partner's benefits. The current programs, however, are unbalanced in both interests and input. One sector usually serves as a "silent partner," providing funding without taking an active role in the implementation. These programs need to take on a more cooperative approach and emphasize achieving the common goals of both sectors. By combining resources, both economic and intellectual, training providers can focus on areas that need immediate attention to meet the rising demands of employers.

Why Partnerships?

Much of the discussion surrounding public-private partnerships in workforce training and development focuses on the issues of responsibility, cost, and benefit. The public sector's responsibility begins with education. State and local governments are faced with the task of operating a public K-12 system that will prepare students with the basic skills necessary to enter the workforce or continue into higher education. This responsibility extends to the postsecondary education with the expectation that the knowledge gained will increase employment opportunities.

Unfortunately, due to deficiencies in the educational system, unequal opportunities, and socioeconomic disadvantages, too many students leave the public education system without obtaining these necessary skills.

Texas has begun to recognize the responsibilities of providing educational programs to prepare people for the workforce. The Texas Council on Workforce and Economic Competitiveness (TCWEC) is required by statute to "promote the development of a well-educated, highly skilled workforce in [the] state and to advocate the development of an integrated workforce development system that provides quality services addressing the needs of business and workers."[3] Private industries depend on the public sector to provide prospective employees with basic skills in mathematics and reading. There is an implied expectation that a potential employee possesses certain skills that will allow the individual to be trained for a specific function or duty. The need for a workforce that can be trained with specific skills quickly is essential in rapidly changing fields. Texas business leaders in high-tech fields have made policy makers aware of the skill shortages in the existing workforce. About 34,000 information technology (IT) jobs in Texas went unfilled in 2000, including 800 in state government.[4]

Faced with this reality, businesses have three choices: take an economic loss and a large risk by relocating to an area with a potentially more qualified workforce, import skilled employees from other states and countries, or get involved on a proactive level by participating in workforce development. The first option would be detrimental to the state's economy and costly to the industries. The second option is also costly to the industry. Hiring skilled employees from abroad is even more costly and is subject to federal regulations, especially under the H-1B visa program. The third choice embodies a long-term vision of creating partnerships that help develop a new workforce with the skills necessary to grow within an industry. The programs involved in these partnerships benefit the public sector by providing the funds, resources, and inputs necessary to make sure that workforce services are applicable to an existing job market. Private industries benefit by ensuring that the growth of their business is not hindered by a lack of qualified or trainable employees. By working together, both sectors are able to design training programs around their needs. Given the shared benefits of these programs, the costs involved should be seen as investments by both parties in reaching their larger goals.

Corporate Universities

Corporate universities have changed the way workers at some companies obtain additional training and education. According to a survey by Corporate University Xchange (CUX), the number of corporate universities has quadrupled since the early 1980s to more than 1,600 by the year 2000.[5] This growth reflects the shift for some companies away from traditional colleges and universities to in-house programs for education and training. Corporate universities must demonstrate their impact on individual and corporate performance by linking the firm's strategic plans to the development of curricula for sponsored learning and training programs.[6] By raising their emphasis on employee development, companies can ensure that their employees have competitive skills, as well as knowledge about the firm's products and services. Technology-based solutions have made continuing education more accessible. In the ever-changing technology world, these programs are becoming a necessity in more sectors of the economy to get their employees up to speed on technology. Online learning can be provided by corporate universities at a relatively low cost, anytime, anywhere in the world, and in different languages. Most Web-based learning materials use books, CD-ROMs, and emailed or Web-posted assignments, and they facilitate chat-room style discussions among teachers and students to engage learners.

Employees view corporate universities as a plus in terms of their impact on career development.[7] According to Jeanne Meister, president of CUX, "Rather than coming straight from academia, chief learning officers are versed in technology."[8] Besides enhancing the skills of employees, corporate universities are used to train customers, suppliers, and distributors.

The rise in corporate universities presents both opportunities and challenges for traditional universities. On the one hand, corporate universities meet the demand for continuing education and provide a chance for universities to forge new partnerships with companies. However, they also create competition for traditional universities. A decade ago, if the company desired, the Harvard Business School could provide a management course offered from its regular course listings. Today, more companies are treating universities as their vendors, demanding courses tailored to their specific needs at competitive prices. Many companies are finding that they can do a better job of providing their own education and training to employees at lower costs.

Corporate universities operate in a variety of ways. Some hire full-time staff to teach courses, whereas others rely on in-house expertise. Many draw upon university faculty members and other experts to work as consultants who instruct participants in the classroom and over the Internet. Although corporate "campus" models vary, the virtual model based on on-line learning is becoming increasingly common.

In 1997, Hughes Training began setting up corporate universities and developing training for businesses. This Arlington-based company, best known for making flight simulators to train pilots, modified its curriculum to meet the needs of its non-aerospace clients using technology to deliver educational services. One of Hughes's largest clients, General Motors University, utilized these technology-based solutions to provide classroom training and simulated production-line tasks, virtual classrooms with employees linked to teachers interactively through TV screens, and a CD-ROM interactive program for educating top-level GM managers from Switzerland to Brazil. GM found that it was less costly to train employees online than it was to fly them to Detroit or fly the instructors to various plants. Thus, GM subsequently installed downlinks in 42 production plants across North America to accommodate the training needs of its employees.

The growth of in-house educational institutes and corporate universities is spreading beyond manufacturing and financial businesses. A recent survey by *Corporate University Review* found that health care, communications, transportation, utility, retail, and agricultural businesses have also been establishing corporate universities. Joseph DiGregorio of Georgia Tech attributes the rise of corporate universities to firms' recognition of two things over the past decade. First, what the academic institutions have had to offer in many cases has not always been of good quality, nor has it achieved the expected impact on their employees. Second, higher education is a $300 billion a year business—and growing. It offers an attractive potential market to corporations.

One author estimated that in 1999, 44 percent of postsecondary education was directed toward serving the needs of nontraditional, working adult students, who need to keep up with new developments in their field or need to be retrained.[9] To address these workforce needs, a number of corporate universities are offering courses to the public. For example, people can enroll at Barnes and Noble University in free online courses. They can also take courses from Dell Learning at any of its websites. However, corporate universities have to pay attention to measuring outcomes and must be able to demonstrate to managers that an investment in education results in a tangible return. Courses offered by some corporate universities use built-in evaluation tools, including learning management systems that embed pre-and post-assessments into the training to enable managers to see which courses their employees are taking, as well as how they have done.[10] For example, Motorola University uses in-house skills and innovative techniques to assess courses. An Evaluation Services Team measures how effectively the company's training and educational programs are working.

Many corporate universities are finding that the most effective approach is to team with a university to take advantage of the expertise that academia can offer. Sixteen percent of all corporate education partnerships are with traditional colleges and universities.[11] As of 2001, almost half of the 140 corporate universities offered college academic credit for some courses and degree programs in partnership with local or national universities.

Dell Learning offers courses and training materials on its Intranet, available around the world at any time to its employees. It includes interactive courses that can be downloaded directly to an employee's laptop computer, lectures "broadcast" by experts, and an online library of reference materials. The Computer Operator Training and Qualification program for Network Operating Center employees on the Dell University website allows an employee to target the appropriate test objectives based on qualification level and product or system.

The amount of money that online learning generates has attracted for-profit ventures, such as the University of Phoenix, a public corporation with shares traded on the New York Stock Exchange. Traditional universities have to become more business-minded, responsive, and competitive. New York University has even launched a for-profit online subsidiary. Most established universities are moving into the distance learning market.

Some companies, such as Texas Instruments (TI), provide employees with a combination of both in-house and outside training. The company encourages continued education for its employees by offering an education assistance program that reimburses employees for tuition at an accredited university.[12] An additional avenue for employee training is TI's Virtual University, a program with a formal, established curriculum that contracts with professors from leading universities to conduct business school seminars at various company sites.

Exchanging Information

Vendor Selection

According to ASTD, "Organizations are delivering less of their training in the classroom, increasing technology-delivered training by outside vendors."[13] Selection criteria and methods for choosing outside vendors for educational products are shared among different companies to increase efficiency and effectiveness in the selection process. For example, the Dell Corporation uses the Functional Requirements Specification (FRS) Template to select vendors. Dell starts by setting up the logistics of the program's description, trying to identify the purpose of the proposal, the scope with systems and subsystems that will and will not be included as a part of the system, and definitions, acronyms, and abbreviations of the document. The template is an electronic screening device that selects the vendor that is most compatible with Dell's operations, systems, and needs. This process is economical because it reduces the costs of having a company design its own product. Only 5 to 10 percent of Dell's training programs are internally designed. Even the training that is developed "internally" usually involves contract resources. According to Darin Hartley, former director of Dell E-learning, "The ideal situation to get training and related services is off-the-shelf, when the product can be bought and implemented right out of the box."[14]

The vendor questionnaire used by TI employs a similar approach. TI goes beyond Dell's FRS by asking questions related to the pricing of the product in comparison with the market, the potential vendor's opinion about its primary competitor and what it does best, and the vendor's history, ownership, and the possibilities of customizing courses offered by vendors into different languages.

Government agencies have recently adopted similar procedures to select service providers. In accordance with the Federal Acquisition Streamlining Act in 1994 and the Clinger-Cohen Act in 1996, the federal government prefers commercial items over those custom manufactured to government specifications. As a result, the government is now implementing information systems based on commercial software solutions, in contrast to the past, when government systems "had to be different" and were written from scratch by teams of systems integrators.[15]

Vendor selection may offer a fruitful for forming partnerships, allowing both public and private partners to develop an electronic, multi-attribute utility model that will measure the variables offered by vendors to both the public and private sectors. Variables such as training objectives, scope, outcomes, faculty, location, flexibility of delivery, and budget can be quantified and measured to allow both sides to find similar effective training providers that best fit their needs and abilities.[16] By sharing information in partnerships based on common goals and abilities, programs can be implemented more quickly because private companies have already removed many of the obstacles for the public sector, including costs.

Certification Issues

Due to the fact that investments such as training and development are so difficult to measure and evaluate, they are often considered costs on the organizational balance sheet. The lack of evaluation standards makes it almost impossible to answer the question of how training affects an organization's effectiveness.

Led by the U.S. Department of Defense (DoD), representatives from federal agencies, academic institutions, and industry have worked to develop a common specification for instructional software to make possible interoperability in training programs used across government agencies and the private sector. The DoD announced the release of a version of a common specification, called the Sharable Courseware Object Reference Model (SCORM).[17] This new specification provides the foundation for how the DoD and others will use learning and communications technologies to build and operate in the learning environment of the future. Through the Advanced Distributed Learning (ADL) initiative, developers are producing prototypes and content that meet the new SCORM specification requirements. Doing so is essential to refining SCORM and to creating sufficient amounts of reusable and platform-independent learning in order to educate, train, and aid performance better, faster, and at a cheaper cost.

Several organizations with a strong interest in government training technology have collaborated under the ADL initiative to address training technology issues. These partners include the Office of the Secretary of Defense's ADL Initiative, the Department of Labor's Federal Learning eXchange, the National Guard Bureau's DTTP Project, The Graduate School, USDA, and the National Academy of Public Administration's (NAPA) Center for Human Resources Management (CHRM).[18] By forming this collaboration, each agency with its complementary role in the development, delivery, and distribution of training technologies can leverage its scarce resources to maximize the benefits for its own agency, the entire federal sector, and the public.

ASTD has worked closely with several companies to develop a set of parameters to measure the efficiency of training programs. The program, now available to any member organization free of charge in the ASTD Measurement Kit, consists of two parts. The first part focuses on measuring the organization's investment in training. It includes questions on training expenditures, outsourcing practices, training content, methods of instruction, evaluation practices, and human resource practices as well as basic questions about the organization itself, such as number of employees, total payroll, and the industry in which the organization does business.[19]

The second part is designed to measure training outcomes. It introduces two sets of core evaluation questions, designed to be benchmarked across organizations and course types. The first set can be administered to trainees immediately following a training course and evaluates their initial reaction to the course. The second can be administered to trainees and their supervisors some months after the training in order to evaluate the effect of training on job performance.[20]

The results of collaboration between private and public sectors in setting unified criteria for training and development services can eliminate inconsistencies and also provide higher standards for outside vendors to reach.

Strategic Philanthropy in Education

Given the complaints of employers that some of today's workforce lack skills, especially in computer basics, industry has inherent interests in forming partnerships with the public school system. This is perhaps one of the most beneficial forms of public-private partnerships in that the public school system helps prepare the workforce of tomorrow. Faced with the challenge of producing a viable workforce to meet the skill demands of high-tech employers, few school systems have sufficient funds, equipment, or experienced instructors to respond adequately on their own. However, high-tech firms have all of the above. With regard to technology-based education, our nation's elementary and secondary schools spend 5 percent per student of what the private sector spends per employee.[21] Traditionally, a philanthropic relationship between private companies and public schools involved donating funds or computers. What is often overlooked is the fact that the equipment donated does not always come with instructions on how it can be used to teach students. Teachers who are not always proficient with the equipment often have full discretion as to how the equipment is used. As a result, the equipment is often not used as intended, or at least not to its full potential. Companies need to view their involvement in public schools as an investment and therefore they should expect to see results. These companies work with schools in partnerships. High-tech firms need to create an open dialogue with schools and clearly establish their needs. The overall shift in perception is to change the relationship with schools from recipients of donations to active partners. The partnership could establish and improve workplace learning. In order to be most effective, an industry's leaders can join together in industry-led sectoral coalitions. By consolidating common interests, industries can combine their resources and work with schools to form a curriculum that will train students to become part of a larger workforce, rather than training students to work for a particular company.

Private Funding for Cooperative Projects

Industry and community consortia are also forming to allow for a greater combination of resources and to encourage the creation of vendor-neutral training programs that will benefit a more diverse group of potential employees. For example, the Austin Idea Network is a project started by a group of Austin high-tech entrepreneurs and community leaders. Its goal is to improve central Texas, helping to relieve strains caused by the region's growth by mobilizing leaders in the high-tech community to drive projects that meet community needs. As stated in the organization's mission, projects must be consistent with the elements of sustainable community development programs and should be able to make a measurable contribution within 12 to 18 months of implementation.[22] In response to the demand for a workforce better able to meet the needs of employers in the technology industry, the network developed a program in partnership with the Austin Independent School District (AISD). Originally entitled DigiKids, the program aimed to place a computer in the households of all students in AISD. In its pilot phase, DigiKids planned to offer computers and training for all teachers and students at one grade level. To provide training for teachers, parents, and students, DigiKids partnered with the Community Technology and Training Center (CTTC), a program operated at Austin high schools in low-income neighborhoods during evenings and weekends.

Another goal of the Austin Idea Network has been to strengthen educational resources in East Austin by forming a partnership with Houston-Tillotson College (HT), an independent, church-related, historically African American institution. The goal of the partnership is to connect HT to entrepreneurs and executives in the business community. This plan includes increasing internships and job opportunities for students, expanding technology resources on campus, and increasing corporate relationships with the college.

The Alliance for Higher Education, a Texas affiliate of the American Council on Education (ACE), is a consortium of universities, businesses, hospitals, and public school districts that utilize distance learning. Operated by the Cecil and Ida Green Education and Information Network, the Alliance links entities across Texas and especially in the Dallas/Fort Worth Metroplex. Each year, the network enables thousands of employees of Alliance companies, including many from Texas Instruments to receive academic credit and earn college degrees for coursework taken without leaving the workplace. Founded in 1974, the Alliance offers the College Credit Recommendation Service (CCRS).[23] The CCRS has enabled thousands of employees throughout the world to receive college credit for formal education in the workplace. Through the CCRS, college and university faculty evaluate the workplace training offered by business, industry, labor unions, professional associations, and government agencies, and make college credit recommendations where appropriate. Corporations report that with their training reviewed for college credit they achieve the following benefits: validating the quality of training, emphasizing a commitment to high-quality education by translating formal courses into college credit recommendations, and giving organizations a competitive edge. Participation in ACE and CCRS provides online links to other training organizations and to the nation's universities.

To help create a well-prepared workforce, the Technical Workforce Development Office at Texas Instruments works directly with the SEMATECH Skills Standards Task Force to create a standard set of skills for semiconductor technicians and to help selected two-year schools enhance their ability to train people in these skills. TI assists schools with curriculum development, scholarships, internships, equipment donations, and other classroom resources. In the Dallas-Fort Worth area, TI's contribution of sophisticated research lab equipment served as a catalyst for the launch of the Metroplex Research Consortium for Electronic Devices and Materials. The consortium provides educational opportunities for 4,500 students at Southern Methodist University, the University of North Texas, the University of Texas at Arlington, and the University of Texas at Dallas. Real-time semiconductor technologies, such as the digital signal processor (DSP) and analog chips, are driving improvements in communications, entertainment, and information technology. In 1999, TI established a collaborative university network called the DSP Leadership University Program, with three leading universities in the DSP field: Rice University, Georgia Tech, and MIT. In addition to receiving a basic grant of $1 million to fund DSP research over three years, each university will benefit from TI's insight into market needs. The network is expected to create a unique synergy among leading researchers, accelerating progress in areas of DSP applications and algorithms development.

Recommendations and Conclusions

The existing programs that allow for public-private partnerships in training and development are not meeting the demands of employers and are not focusing on changing the system. The need has been demonstrated, and the solutions are available. The existing programs need to combine their most positive attributes and work together to achieve success. High-tech industries are not and should not be the only entities combining resources with the public sector. Other fields such as health care, agriculture, and finance can use the following recommendations to foster partnerships with government and not-for-profit agencies to create a stable and lasting workforce.

Recommendation 11-1: *The Texas Workforce System should make effective use of various partnerships and collaborations to implement innovations in information technology.* The wide variety of partnerships described in the chapters of this report testifies to the power of collaborations for implementing innovations in information technology in workforce services.

Recommendation 11-2: Texas community colleges and technical institutes should seek private sector partners willing to share facilities and equipment, thereby providing students with access to up-to-date equipment. Educators often face insurmountable expenses in recreating and maintaining up-to-date high-tech work environments in on-campus laboratories. Private partners can also aid in locating and retaining qualified instructors. The proposed partnership could follow the format of the Skills Development Fund. However, the funds would go to the business as well as the college. In return, instruction would partially be conducted at the business, taught by knowledgeable experts from the industry. Students would be able to learn on the current equipment from someone who has firsthand knowledge of how the technology is used. Students would be able to experience the job as well as learn the skills. Classroom learning would be modeled after corporate universities, using methods such as simulation software and tutorial instruction. The program could be conducted at the worksite, on the college campus, or at home if distance learning is an appropriate tool. This type of partnership combines the benefits of classroom instruction with the hands-on experience of OJT without the high costs to community colleges and employers. The instruction and equipment could be revised to maintain pace with changes in the industry. Industries producing products with short life cyles, such as semiconductor manufacturing and aviation machinery, are only two examples in which such partnerships would be beneficial.

Recommendation 11-3: Educators should seek input from industry, especially in high-technology fields, in developing curriculum standards and expectations for student learning. Companies often donate equipment without setting expectations. Schools need to determine the best uses for computers in the classroom and make sure that teachers have the training to effectively use the equipment. Educators complain that they are not computer technicians and companies say that they are not educators. Educators and high-technology companies need to form a consensus regarding the intended purpose of the computers. To maximize benefits on both sides, the two groups should develop methods that simplify the delivery system of basic educational skills while introducing students to basic concepts and equipment used in IT.

Educators in high schools should be approaching relationships with high-tech companies as a way of fostering contextual learning, opportunities for problem solving, and career awareness within the curriculum. High schools, postsecondary institutions, and employers can collaborate to better prepare students for college and careers. By integrating worksite learning with classroom learning, students can learn to apply what they know and understand it more deeply. Providing education with clearly defined real-world applications can deepen understanding, as well as increase student self-confidence and motivation, which in turn can improve school completion rates. By introducing these skills to students in high school and helping to strengthen their preparation, employers can attract disadvantaged and minority youths that may not have otherwise been exposed to industry practices, technology, and job-related skills. This will improve equity in education and training.

Recommendation 11-4: Texas government should address its own needs for IT workers. Taking advantage of the recent economic downturn, the public sector can recruit and train its own talented IT professionals in an institute or academy following the lessons and examples of corporate universities in the private sector. To its credit, the Office of the State Comptroller has already implemented a pilot project, Information Technology (IT) Academy, to train state employees for IT jobs. This promising initiative should be continued and improved over time. In this endeavor, there may be opportunities to establish partnerships with corporate universities, beginning with an open exchange of information and resources.

The public and private sectors have different cultures and operate under different procedures and timetables. Business needs to help the public sector improve the way technology-based solutions are introduced and implemented. The interdependence of public and private training programs cannot be ignored. Cross-sector collaboration between the public and private sectors can develop a successful and sustainable workforce by combining the best attributes of both sectors.

For partnerships to be effective, each partner must be an active participant, each must have an investment, and each must expect results. A partnership cannot be based on a funding contribution alone. There must be combined input as to what each partner needs and an agreed-upon strategy for utilizing the resources of both partners in meeting these needs. While the current system has provided some good ideas, these can be improved upon to develop a workforce that is equipped to fill the positions of today and tomorrow.

The public sector needs to engage businesses in sharing best practices, combining resources, and developing educational and training programs. This will allow the public sector to overcome traditional obstacles in creating an able and ready workforce. The benefits of having an employable workforce will provide economic growth to participating businesses and the localities in which they are located.

Notes

[1] American Society for Training and Development (ASTD), *The 2000 State of the Industry Report.* Online. Available: www.astd.org. Accessed: May 3, 2001.

[2] Employment Policy Foundation, *Upgrading Workplace Skills: $300 Billion Annual Investment* (Washington, D.C., April 10, 2000), p. 4. Online. Available: http://www.epf.org/research/newsletters/2000/ib000410.pdf. Accessed: May 3, 2001.

[3] Texas Government Code Annotated, Sec. 2308.101, (1) & (2).

[4] Texas Comptroller of Public Accounts, *Comptroller Carole Keeton Rylander's Texas IT Academy Recruits Applicants,* March 20, 2000 (press release). Online. Available: http://www.window.state.tx.us/news/00322ita.html. Accessed: March 18, 2001.

[5] Corporate University eXchange (CUX). Online. Available: www.corpu.com. Accessed November 20, 2000.

[6] Concept Sytems, Inc., *Corporate Universities.* Online. Available: http://www.conceptsystems.com/applications/corpuniv/corpuniv.htm. Accessed: May 3, 2001.

[7] Mary Gotschall, "Transforming Adult Education by Leveraging Knowledge throughout the Enterprise." *Fortune Magazine,* Education Section. Online. Available: http://www.timeinc.net/fortune/sections/corpuni/corpuni.htm. Accessed: December 5, 2000.

[8] Jeanne Meister, "The Brave New World of Corporate Education," *The Chronicle of Higher Education* (February 9, 2001). Online. Available: http://chronicle.com/free/v47/i22/22b01001.htm. Accessed: May 3, 2001.

[9] Stephen Budiansky, "Education with a Bottom Line," *American Society for Engineering Education PRISM Magazine* (October 1999). Online. Available: http://www.asee.org/prism/oct99/html/cover_story.htm. Accessed: May 3, 2001.

[10] Click2Learn, *Learning Management System.* Online. Available: www.click2learn.com Accessed: May 3, 2001. Also see Dell Computer Corporation, *Dell Learning.* Online. Available: http://www.dell.com/us/en/gen/corporate/dellu.htm www.dell.com. Accessed: December 3, 2000.

[11] Meister, "The Brave New World of Corporate Education."

[12] Texas Instruments, *Benefits: Training and Development.* Online. Available: http://www.ti.com/recruit/docs/development.shtml. Accessed: February 10, 2001.

[13] Leslie Eaton, "Labor Department Study Describes Need for IT Skills for Most Workers." *New York Times* (October 20, 1999). Online. Available: .http://www.nytimes.com/yr/mo/day/news/national/regional/ny-computer-skills. Accessed: November 20, 2000.

[14] Interview by Svetlana Negrustuyeva with Darin Hartley, Former Director of Dell E-Learning, Austin, Texas, December 1, 2000.

[15] Steve Charles, "Sizing up the Federal Opportunity." Fedmarket.com. Online. Available: http://www.fedmarket.com/vtools/articles/federal_opportunity.html. Accessed: March 2, 2001.

[16] David Gruber, *We're Education . . . .You're Semiconductors* (Philadelphia: Public/Private Ventures, January 2000).

[17] Advanced Distributed Learning, *DoD Officially Releases SCORM,* March 28, 2000 (press release). Online. Available: http://www.adlnet.org/index.cfm. Accessed: May 6, 2001.

[18] Advanced Distributed Learning, *Federal e-Learning Showcases in Dallas TX,* May 8, 2001 (press release). Online. Available: http://www.adlnet.org/index.cfm. Accessed: May 6, 2001.

[19] American Society for Training and Development, "Measurement Kit: Tools for Benchmarking and Continuous Improvement." Online. Available: http://www.astd.org/virtual_community/research/measure/measurement_kit_main.html. Accessed: May 3, 2001.

[20] Ibid.

[21] Dr. Jennifer House, Vice President of Strategic Relations, Classroom Connect, Inc. Testimony before the House Commerce Committee, Subcommittee on Telecommunications and the Internet, on behalf of the Software and Information Industry Association. Washington, D.C., March 8, 2001. Online. Available: http://www.siia.net/sharedcontent/govt/issues/edu/ClassroomConnectTestimony.pdf. Accessed: May 3, 2001.

[22] Austin Idea Network, *The Network's Mission.* Online. Available: http://austinideanetwork.org/home.htm. Accessed: March 25, 2001.

[23] Alliance for Higher Education, *American Council on Education (ACE) Offers College Credit Recommendation Services (CCRS).* Online. Available: http://www.allianceedu.org/html/ace_acreditation.html. Accessed: April 28, 2001.

Chapter 12. Conclusions and Recommendations

This report has presented the results of research on applications of information technology to improve the Texas workforce system. The workforce system plays vital roles in assisting employers and job seekers by providing key services, such as job-matching, assessment, career counseling and case management, training and retraining, and outplacement services.[1] In all of these areas, information technology can be a resource for enhancing equity, effectiveness, and efficiency in the delivery of services.

Texas policy makers have begun to recognize the challenges that information technology poses to the state's education and workforce systems. The *Special Commission on 21st Century Colleges and Universities*, appointed by then–Lieutenant Governor Rick Perry, described the rapid development of a knowledge-based economy and profound changes in Texas demographics, especially pointing out the need to raise the achievement, skills and knowledge of Hispanic and African American students across Texas.[2] The Texas Higher Education Coordinating Board has developed a plan for postsecondary education to close the gaps in participation rates, graduation rates, excellence, and research by 2015.[3] The report of the *e-Texas Commission*, issued in December 2000, further emphasized challenges in the workplace brought on by the New Economy and changes in technology.[4]

Our study focused on ways that information technology can be part of the solution to the challenges that it raises. Information technology offers considerable promise to improve labor exchange through the Internet; to enhance education and training through distance learning and e-learning; to support to support and train workforce staff; to provide more up-to-date, accurate information to consumers of workforce education and training; to offer career guidance and counseling; and to implement evaluation and accountability systems. In short, information technology offers an important resource to improve the entire range of workforce services—from front-line assistance for job seekers walking into a workforce center to evaluation systems to assess service effectiveness.

However, information technology is no panacea. Rarely is information technology a stand-alone solution. Information technology offers tools to extend human capabilities, not to replace them. Usually, human intervention in some form needs to accompany the technology to be effective. Stated another way, technology is more often a complement to rather than a substitute for human intervention. Many individuals who enter a local workforce center will need some assistance or tutoring from a professional staff member to be able to use a computer effectively. In another example, the trend in e-learning is toward "blended learning," which combines aspects of direct human interaction found in traditional instruction with distance learning.

Improving Effectiveness, Efficiency, and Equity in Workforce Services

Information technology can improve the *effectiveness* of workforce services. In the arena of electronic job matching, for example, the technologies extend the reach of employers in publicizing the job openings they post. Likewise, job seekers can cast their net more widely to search for a job, or they can design an electronic job search that is specifically customized to their needs.

Information technology can improve *efficiency*. As the U.S. military has demonstrated, computer-based instruction (CBI) and simulation training have accelerated learning times and increased efficiency. Use of the Internet by the military has reduced printing costs. Likewise, the military has saved on travel costs by using distance learning technologies. With computers, learning applications can be designed to assess what learners already know and what they need to know and prescribe customized programs of learning. In job matching, employers utilize special software to simplify the process of sorting through resumes more efficiently.

There are also hopeful signs that new information technologies can improve *equity* in workforce services. For example, early research on the use of electronic systems for job search has revealed that given access to computer and the Internet, minorities are *more* likely than whites to use these technologies to search for a job. This should come as no surprise. Computers do not discriminate on the basis of racial or ethnic status in job matching. Effective distance learning can offer rural Texans the same education and training opportunities that their urban counterparts have enjoyed.

Findings and Recommendations

The following is a brief summary of our key findings and recommendations, explaining how they fit within the large vision of a more equitable, efficient, and effective workforce development system to serve Texas. Our recommendations are all numbered, with the first number identifying the chapter in which the recommendation is discussed and the second number designating the place of the recommendation within the order of the chapter.

Improve Access to Information Technology

Unquestionably, the ability to access and use information technology will be vital to success in competing in modern workplaces. Access to computers and the Internet is essential for every Texan. However, market forces alone will not assure such access. There is a role for government in making access to information technology available to everyone. Access to technology in a real sense is a public good. Facilitating effective access for all to the new information technology is one of the most important roles for the public sector.

There are numerous dimensions to the access issue. Many interrelated types of access problems exist. There is access of minorities and the poor and the disabled to computers and the Internet, and access of rural areas to broadband technology.

Our opening discussion in chapter 2 focused on one aspect of that access—assuring access for rural Texas to broadband communications technology. Rural areas across Texas pose special problems of access. Powerful Internet resources, especially broadband access, should be widely and equitably available and affordable for all learners. Texas needs to make the extension of broadband access for all learners a central goal of telecommunications policy. A good start on this policy can be found in the provisions of the Texas Public Utility Regulatory Act:

> It is the policy of this state to ensure that customers in all regions of this state, including low-income customers and customers in rural and high cost areas, have access to telecommunications and information services, including interexchange services, cable services, wireless services, and advanced telecommunications and information services, that are reasonably comparable to those provided in urban areas and that are available at prices that are reasonably comparable to prices charged for similar services in urban areas.[5]

The implications of such a policy meaningfully implemented are to provide access to computers and the Internet in schools, libraries, community centers, and other public places. Through Texas Infrastructure Fund (TIF) grants and other endeavors, broadband infrastructure should be extended to rural and other underserved areas.

Our study makes several specific recommendations regarding access for rural Texans, summarized as follows:

Recommendation 2-1: As a matter of state policy, Texas should promote effective access to information technology for all Texans.

Recommendation 2-2: Texas state agencies should implement the specific recommendations of the Texas PUC made in its January 2001 study, "Availability of Advanced Services in Rural and High Cost Areas."

Recommendation 2-3: The State of Texas should allow local governments to compete for grants from the Telecommunications Infrastructure Fund (TIF).

Recommendation 2-4: Texas should allow cities and counties to fund telecommunications-related initiatives by giving them the authority to issue bonds or increase local sales taxes for such projects.

Recommendation 2-5: To promote access to distance learning, the State of Texas should require providers of telecommunications and Internet services to make special provisions (such as free supply of appliances, connections, etc.) for marginalized groups so that they can benefit from distance learning courses.

Pedagogy and Effectiveness

Effective pedagogy is a critical component to the future success of computer-based education. Computer-based education and training programs are abundant, yet few of these instructional programs are based on effective instructional techniques. We know little about their quality and effectiveness. Without effectiveness, computers just become an expensive and glitzy alternative to traditional, instructor-led education. Training centers, public schools and colleges, and not-for-profit organizations are making large investments in computer systems to deliver education and job training, even though the current consensus is uncertain regarding their effectiveness. Education and job training could benefit tremendously from more effective application of computers to instruction. Participants can be helped who may not have succeeded under traditional classroom approaches to instruction.

Chapter 3 discusses the potential advantages of computer-based instruction, examining two examples of well-designed courseware. It then reviews various barriers to developing pedagogically effective computer programs. It makes recommendations to overcome these barriers and promote the spread of effective computer-based instructional programs, based on sound pedagogy. These recommendations are as follows:

Recommendation 3-1: The federal government should increase research and development (R&D) funding to support the development and dissemination of effective pedagogical instruction.

Recommendation 3-2: The federal government should establish a standards body to develop and publish criteria for pedagogical effectiveness and for use in rating instructional programs.

Recommendation 3-3: Education and the public sector should increase the demand for pedagogically effective programs.

Internet Job Matching

Chapter 4 examines the impact of the Internet on effective job matching for job seekers. The use of the Internet to post and find jobs is rapidly expanding. Both employers and job seekers have benefited from using the Internet to satisfy their workforce needs. Job seekers are finding that automated labor exchange websites can complement more traditional methods of searching for a job. These include general commercial, company, Web engines, newspaper-sponsored community, specialized, or niche websites, as well as government-sponsored websites. This chapter reviews some of the more popular websites along with their features and characteristics. It explores key impacts of Internet-based job-matching services and makes the following recommendations:

Recommendation 4-1: Policy makers at all levels—federal, state, and local—in partnership with leading information technology firms, should expand and intensify efforts to make access to computers and the Internet truly universal.

Recommendation 4-2: Public and private sponsors of Internet-based labor exchange should give greater attention to "opportunities for learning" as a primary field in the job-matching process.

Recommendation 4-3: Workforce policy makers and practitioners at all levels should devote serious attention to reinventing and continuously improving labor exchange over the next few years in light of the new and expanding role played by online automated services.

Recommendation 4-4: The U.S. Department of Labor, in collaboration with state workforce agencies, local workforce boards, and other actors, should develop, refine, and offer training on both the use of computers and the effective use of online labor exchange services.

Recommendation 4-5: The U.S. Department of Labor, state workforce agencies, local workforce boards, and other actors in the public and private sectors should continually assess their existing LMI and labor exchange systems to ensure that they are appropriate, useful, and understandable to employers and job seekers with varying levels of education and skill.

Applications of Information Technology in Texas Workforce Centers

Chapter 5 examines the existing system of Texas Workforce Centers. Workforce centers—also known as "career centers" or "one-stop centers"—are located in cities and rural communities across Texas. The centers have been successful at matching many unemployed people with jobs. However, various groups, such as individuals with low levels of literacy or without experience in using computers, the disabled, and individuals without access to transportation, are often inadvertently excluded. Workforce centers can be improved through the implementation of information technology, together with a human touch. Most technological solutions are complements rather than substitutes for human interaction. Problem areas for these workforce centers are examined in detail and recommendations for improvement are offered, including establishing virtual centers, such as Worksource in Austin has recently done.

Recommendation 5-1: Texas workforce centers should strive to stay technologically modern and up to date.

Recommendation 5-2: Literacy training and employability skills or "soft skills" training should be widely available.

Recommendation 5-3: The Texas workforce system should implement online or virtual workforce centers to provide services over the Internet.

Recommendation 5-4: Problems of incompatibilities between local, state, and federal systems must be overcome.

Support and Training for Caseworkers and Other Workforce Staff

Chapter 6 profiles the role of case managers in the Texas workforce development system and examines how information technology can be used to support them in accessing and delivering services to their clients. The case manager is often the primary contact for individuals seeking workforce services. It is important to determine what can be done to assist case managers in providing services more effectively. A key challenge in integrating the workforce and welfare systems is not only placing applicants into jobs, but promoting careers that both foster skill development and provide advancement opportunities. There is a need for greater cross training of workforce and welfare systems staff, especially staff whose experience has been limited to a particular program. Such compartmentalization hinders the ability of the workforce system to provide effective services. Enhancing the case manager's capacity with technology-based solutions will enable front-line staff to better serve and support customers' needs. Further, information technology solutions can provide case managers with essential training on the applicable federal and state welfare and workforce development services and requirements.

Our specific recommendations include the following:

Recommendation 6-1: Local workforce boards and other agencies that provide case management services (including DHS and TWC) should use a mix of push and pull technology to support workforce and case management staff and help them keep abreast of current trends in Texas relating to best practices and examples of workforce and welfare services.

Recommendation 6-2: Texas should reconfigure the EnterTech software module or use the EnterTech approach to develop training for case managers in all aspects of the workforce and welfare systems.

Recommendation 6-3: Texas should implement computer-based case management systems to improve the delivery of services.

Preparing a Workforce for the New Economy

An important issue in workforce development is preparing our students with the appropriate academic and technological competence to work in the New Economy. School districts and postsecondary institutions in the Greater Austin area have made efforts to grow a workforce for the New Economy. Four initiatives are profiled as examples: the implementation of national information technology standards into a new "Computer Science 2000" curriculum: the Assured Experiences program in Round Rock Independent School District, which integrates technology K-12; the High Tech Educator Network; and the national Tech-Prep program, which has documented success across Texas. All four programs demonstrate the importance of high technology in Austin, the willingness of schools to embrace technology, and of industry to be involved through intermediary organizations, such as the Capital Area Tech Prep Consortium, ARIES Alliance, and Capital Area Training Foundation. These efforts to apply technology are essential to deliver a workforce that is prepared to work in the New Economy.

Recommendation 7-1: School districts should introduce students earlier to information technology tools through integrating their use into school tasks as a regular part of the curriculum.

Recommendation 7-2: Texas schools should make use of vendor-neutral curricula, designed to provide students with transferable knowledge and skills that do not limit learners to working for particular company or particular brands of equipment.

Recommendation 7-3: Texas education and training entities should use nationally recognized industry skills standards, such as those provided by the National Workforce Center for Emerging Technologies, to improve cooperation and alignment between industry needs and schools.

Recommendation 7-4: Texas secondary schools should establish additional written articulation agreements with postsecondary institutions to promote continued learning beyond high school.

Postsecondary Institutions, Workforce Development, and Distance Learning

Chapter 8 explores the use of technology to enhance workforce development by Texas postsecondary institutions. Labor shortages in high-demand occupations in the health-care and information technology industries during the late 1990s focused greater attention on how community and technical colleges and public universities can contribute to workforce development. Two priority concerns for Texas are the demographic changes in the state and the increasingly competitive, global knowledge economy. An overview of current problems and gaps within the educational system is given, as well as technology-based solutions utilized by postsecondary institutions for workforce development. Our recommendations focus on providing increased funding and support for postsecondary education, expanding industry-education alliances, and advancing information technology strategies, especially distance learning, as demonstrated in the Virtual College of Texas.

Recommendation 8-1: Postsecondary institutions should expand distance learning, using cable and broadcast television, satellite networks, Internet and Web-based courses, and interactive video technologies. Special focus should be placed on reaching underserved rural communities.

Recommendation 8-2: The federal and state governments should increase funding for technology resources and facilities and for technology training of faculty and staff at postsecondary institutions. The private sector may also be a resource in this initiative.

Recommendation 8-3: Postsecondary institutions should provide incentives to recruit and retain qualified faculty and staff who teach technology courses. This includes restructuring incentives for faculty to develop and teach courses online.

Recommendation 8-4: Public universities and community colleges should engage with private industry in public-private partnerships to improve the linkages between industry needs and postsecondary curricula, so that Texas workers can be equipped workers with the appropriate education and training to work in the New Economy.

Recommendation 8-5: Texas postsecondary institutions should secure additional funding for the recruitment and retention of Latino and African American students, especially in mathematics, science, and technology. Also, these institutions should provide programmatic and financial support to help ensure that these students graduate.

Learning from the U.S. Military

Perhaps the greatest single untapped source of proven techniques and approaches that can be adapted for wider use is the U.S. military. An enormous public investment in applying learning technologies has been made in the military over many years. The military has been developing and using state-of-the-art technology-based approaches to education and training for widely varying populations for many years, and doing it well. More needs to be done both to capture and disseminate lessons from their experiences and to ensure the diffusion of these approaches in nonmilitary sectors, both public and private.

The military has been active in developing and using technology for job training programs and standards, as well as for job matching. The military is currently promoting the development of technical standards for distance learning programs. The initiative, entitled Advanced Distributed Learning (ADL), is a collaboration among federal government agencies, the military, the business community, and academic institutions. The adoption of a single technical standard for all technology-based learning programs will help e-learning programs to become more interoperable (i.e., having compatible communication and operating systems), durable, reusable, adaptable, and affordable.

In addition to the development of standards, the military has accumulated significant experience in using computer-based instruction (CBI) and simulation-based training. Such experience should be examined and leveraged by the civilian sector in order to implement successful training practices more broadly. CBI and simulation have enhanced the equity, efficiency, and effectiveness of workforce delivery services in the military. To help assure equity, the military makes no distinctions between individuals, based on low or high levels of achievement, economic background, race, or gender: all must be trained and utilized. The military has saved money by using CBI and simulations, thereby increasing efficiency. The military has found CBI and simulations to be effective training methods that enhance decision-making abilities. Critical moments in the training session can be later reviewed and evaluated. Understanding these benefits and their application to the civilian sector can assist the development and implementation of successful job training and matching programs.

Our recommendations in this area are as follows:

Recommendation 9-1: The Texas workforce system should learn from the experience of the military in training and using technology.

Recommendation 9-2: The Texas workforce system should adopt and promote the use of ADL specifications and guidelines, Sharable Courseware Object Reference Model (SCORM).

Recommendation 9-3: Training programs need to incorporate feedback from the population that the training aims to assist.

Innovations and Learning in Other States

The U.S. Department of Labor and various states have developed numerous promising Internet-based approaches and systems to improve the delivery of workforce information and services for programs funded under the Workforce Investment Act of 1998. Chapter 10 reviews technological developments in three categories of services: (1) job information and matching systems, (2) customer tracking and accountability tools, and (3) skills assessment tools.

State workforce agencies face challenges in implementing effective services on the Internet, particularly in securing the financial and human resources necessary for developing and maintaining online systems. Several states have joined interstate collaborations to share costs and information to develop these expensive technologies. In addition, various tools have been developed at the national level to facilitate development. Innovative technologies are being developed or used in states across the nation, financed by various cost-sharing structures.

Recommendations that come from this review are the following:

Recommendation 10-1: The Texas workforce system should continually assess the progress made toward its goals, identify services not meeting set performance measures and population groups not receiving the full range of needed services, and adopt innovations in technology that may offer means of improving these services and reaching these groups.

Recommendation 10-2: Texas should collaborate with other states to share costs of developing and implementing innovations in information technologies used in the workforce system.

Recommendation 10-3: Texas should advocate for state workforce and education agencies to implement XML standards for labor market information and job matching.

Recommendation 10-4: In implementing innovations in information technology, concerns about privacy and confidentiality of information must be appropriately addressed.

Partnerships and Collaboration: Keys to Successful Implementation

Implementing information technology is most effectively accomplished through partnership arrangements for many reasons. A remarkable variety of partnerships and collaborations established for various purposes was identified in our research, including the following:

- Entertech used a coalition of representatives from local businesses, community organizations, and education to advise staff on each stage of the development of the Entertech program. The Office of the Governor of Texas also collaborated by providing a portion of funding for Entertech.

- The ARIES project in Austin to grow a local IT workforce began with the formation of a nonprofit collaboration between schools and business representatives.

- The High-Tech Educator network in Central Texas has demonstrated how the technology knowledge and skills of teachers can be upgraded through partnerships with industry.

- The Army University Access Online (AUAO) is a partnership between the U.S. Army and 24 colleges and universities to offer college credits to participating soldiers in more than 87 programs.

- Several corporate universities have partnered with traditional universities to offer courses for college credit.

- The Advanced Distributed Learning (ADL) initiative, spearheaded by the U.S. Department of Defense to develop the SCORM common standards for learning software, is a major collaboration of federal agencies, private firms, and academia.

- The various collaborations among states to develop and share information technologies, such as America's Workforce System and America's Job Link Alliance, offer models of partnerships for cost sharing in the development and implementation of innovations in workforce services.

- The Virtual College of Texas is a collaboration of more than 50 community and technical colleges to offer distance learning courses for college credit and continuing education across Texas.

The strongest partnerships are based on mutually beneficial relationships between two or more entities that have reached agreement on clear goals and objectives of the particular endeavor.

Our recommendations in this area are as follows:

Recommendation 11-1: The Texas workforce system should make effective use of various partnerships and collaborations to implement innovations in information technology.

Recommendation 11-2: Texas community colleges and technical institutes should seek private sector partners willing to share facilities and equipment, thereby providing students with access to up-to-date equipment.

Recommendation 11:3: Educators should seek input from industry, especially in high-technology fields, in developing curriculum standards and expectations for student learning.

Recommendation 11-4: Texas government should address its own needs for IT workers. Taking advantage of the recent economic downturn, the public sector can recruit and train its own talented IT professionals in an institute or academy, following the lessons and examples of corporate universities in the private sector.

Concluding Observations

The Value of Standards

Achieving consensus and implementing various kinds of standards are topics that appeared in several sections of our report. Some examples of standards include the following:

SCORM. A collaborative of federal agencies, private firms, and educators led by the U.S. Department of Defense in its Advanced Distributed Learning Initiative (www.adlnet.org) produced the Sharable Content Object Reference Model (SCORM). SCORM a set of technical specifications that enable sharable, durable, and reusable learning content and interoperability. SCORM allows e-learning content to be used across multiple end-user devices.

XML Standards. XML allows developers to define their own tags that instruct applications how to interpret the data.

Industry Skill Standards. In any workforce preparation program, it is important to identify vendor-neutral skill standards on which employers agree. Industry skill standards provide the basic framework around which curriculum content and pedagogy can be designed. Skill standards that are widely accepted and used for hiring and promotion decisions by industry offer a powerful guide to education and training providers and to learners regarding what they need to know. The skill standards for information technology developed by the National Workforce Center for Emerging Technologies offer an excellent example.

Quality Standards for Pedagogy in Computer-Based Instruction. If consensus can be developed on high-quality standards through the National Research Council or some other credible agency, they can provide guidance for software developers and consumers. Such standards should include universal design features to accommodate access for the disabled.

Need for Increased Funding

Another area that is a prerequisite for technology-based solutions is additional funding for designing, implementing, and maintaining the system. In short, increased funding is needed to build a technology infrastructure for the Texas workforce system. Increased funding is also required for certain selected purposes, such as to finance research and development costs of producing and disseminating appropriate pedagogy to make effective use the full power of computers and information technology. Additional funding at public universities and community colleges is needed to promote and support the fields of mathematics, the sciences, and technologies. We recommend more funding for groups that are disproportionately affected by inequities in the workforce development system. They need to receive access to technology and opportunities to ensure that they obtain the skills required to be successful in the workforce of the New Economy.

Information Technology: Great Potential, Great Challenges

While technology has great potential for good, it also can have adverse consequences. Technology can place individuals without effective access to computers, the Internet, video, and other computer-related technologies at an even greater disadvantage. Issues of computer literacy and access to technology must be considered when one is making recommendations regarding the use of information technology. Workforce development services must be available to all. If a particular technology excludes certain groups of people or treats them differently, solutions must be found to reduce or alleviate inequities.

Information available on the Internet can bring potential harm to the very people the workforce system is trying to serve. The Internet is a free-for-all, where content is not monitored for accuracy or legitimacy. Unsuspecting individuals can easily be misled by inaccurate information and make undesirable decisions as a result. Care and thought must be given to all the possible technology solutions so as not to eliminate any group or increase the likelihood of clients accessing bad or misleading information.

Information technology—especially providing access to computers and the Internet—has compelling public aspects that call for a larger role for government.

Information Technology: No Substitute for Human Intervention

Technology is more often a complement, rather than a substitute for, human interaction. When technology solutions are implemented, stakeholders should consider how to best balance technology and human interaction. In many cases, clients of the workforce system may be unable to utilize technology to access workforce services. Having staff available to assist the new or unfamiliar user is imperative. Without this, the system will not work. Technology solutions can enhance the equity, efficiency, and effectiveness of workforce development, but it must not so at the expense of human interaction. An assessment of where and when human interaction is desirable needs to occur *before* technology solutions are implemented.

Given the stake that the public and private sectors have in building a skilled workforce, both sectors must take on new roles and a new relationship where the practices are more closely aligned so that workforce challenges can be better met. Government agencies must become a catalyst for action among employers, not just providers of services, and employers must become true partners in workforce preparation. The public sector needs to create and support an infrastructure that builds on the strengths of public and private organizations. Government needs to encourage the private sector to support training and career advancement while also leveraging the resources and expertise of employers. The private sector needs to work with the public sector to develop standards and credentials for skills that workers must possess to be successful in the workforce.[6]

Promoting Efficiency, Effectiveness, and Equity

In order for a workforce development system to achieve its many goals, services must be delivered equitably, efficiently, and effectively. Information technology provides new opportunities for state governments to increase the efficiency, effectiveness, and equity in the delivery of workforce development services.

Texas needs to take the next step in the evolution of workforce development services to ensure service delivery is equitable, efficient, and effective. Our report has raised questions and issues with the existing workforce system in Texas and suggested a variety of policy recommendations to improve the system, especially through making use of emerging information technology.

Notes

[1] Texas Workforce Commission, *What Is the Texas Workforce Commission?* Online. Available: http://www.twc.state.tx.us/twcinfo/whatis.html. Accessed: April 10, 2001.

[2] Office of the Governor, State of Texas, Special Commission on 21st Century Colleges and Universities, *Higher Education in the 21st Century. Moving Every Texan Forward* (Austin, Tex., January 2, 2000).

[3] Texas Higher Education Coordinating Board, *Closing the Gaps by 2015* (Austin, Tex., October 2000).

[4] Texas State Comptroller, *E-Texas: Education, Excellence, Efficiency, Effectiveness* (Austin, Tex., December 2000).

[5] Public Utility Regulatory Act, TX. UTIL. CODE ANN., Section 51.001(g) (Vernon 1998 and Supp. 2000), *as cited in* Public Utility Commission of Texas, *Report to the 77th Texas Legislature: Availability of Advanced Services in Rural and High Cost Areas* (Austin, Tex., January 2001).

[6] National Governors Association, Center for Best Practices, *Demand Side Strategies for Workforce Development*. Online. March 1997. Available: http://www.nga.org/Workforce/DemandSide3.htm. Accessed: January 11, 2001.

Bibliography

Advanced Distributed Learning (ADL). *About ADL*. Online. Available: http://www.adlnet.org. Accessed April 8, 2001.

——————. *About SCORM*. Online. Available: http://www.adlnet.org/ourstory/scorm.cfm. Accessed: April 8, 2001.

——————. *DoD Officially Releases SCORM,* March 28, 2000, Press Release. Online. Available: http://www.adlnet.org/index.cfm. Accessed: May 6, 2001.

——————. *Federal Learning Showcases in Dallas Texas.* May 8, 2001, Press Release. Online. Available: http://www.adlnet.org/index.cfm. Accessed: May 6, 2001.

——————. *MIT Open Knowledge Initiative, ADL Co-Laboratory, and IMS Cooperate to Advance Learning Technology,* Press Release, July 11, 2001. Online. Available: http://www.adlnet.org/news_events/news/full_story.cfm?News_Id=89&News_Type=1&Filter=1,2,5. Accessed: August 2, 2001.

Alliance for Higher Education. *American Council on Education (ACE) Offers College Credit Recommendation Services (CCRS).* Online. Available: http://www.allianceedu.org/html/ace_acreditation.html. Accessed: April 28, 2001.

America's Workforce Network. *America's Career Infonet.* Online. Available: http://www.acinet.org/acinet/. Accessed: May 7, 2001.

America's Workforce Technology Solutions. *America's Job Bank.* Online. Available: http://www.ajb.org. Accessed: May 7, 2001.

——————. *America's Workforce System.* Online. Available: http://www.awts.org/html/america.html. Accessed: May 7, 2001.

American Society for Training and Development (ASTD). "Measurement Kit: Tools for Benchmarking and Continuous Improvement." Online. Available: http://www.astd.org/virtual_community/research/measure/measurement_kit_main.html. Accessed: May 3, 2001.

——————. "The 2000 State of the Industry Report." Online. Available: http://www.astd.org. Accessed: May 3, 2001.

Army and Alumni Career Program Online. *Job Links.* Online. Available: http://www.acap.army.mil/acap/listings.htm. Accessed: April 9, 2001.

195

Army University Access Online (AUAO). *More About AUAO.* Online. Available: http://eARMYU.com/public/public_about-auao_more-about-auao.asp. Accessed: August 13, 2001.

——————. *Partners.* Online. Available: http://eARMYU.com/public/public_about-auao_partners.asp. Accessed: August 13, 2001.

——————. *Resources: FAQ's.* Online. Available: http://eARMYU.com/public/public_resources_faqs.asp. Accessed: August 13, 2001.

Austin Idea Network. *The Network's Mission.* Online. Available: http://austinideanetwork.org/home.htm. Accessed: March 25, 2001.

Austin's Living Wage Coalition. *The Living Wage.* Online. Available: http://www.main.org/alwc/myth.htm. Accessed: May 2, 2001.

Barnow, Burt S., and Christopher T. King. "Information and Communications Technology and Workforce Service Delivery: A Comparative Look." In *Global Restructuring, Training and the Social Dialogue,* eds. Torkel Alfthan, Christopher T. King, and Gyorgy Sziraczki. Geneva, Switzerland: International Labor Organization, 2001.

Bell, Stephen H. "The Prevalence of Education and Training Activities among Welfare and Food Stamp Recipients, New Federalism, National Survey of America's Families." Washington, D.C.: Urban Institute, October 2000.

Bennett, William J., and David Galernter. "Improving Education with Technology: Why Two Former Skeptics Have Joined the Revolution." *Education Week* (March 4, 2001), p. 68.

Berge, L. Zane, *Sustaining Distance Training.* San Francisco: Jossey-Bass, 2001.

Bethoney, Herb. "Spec Unites Learning Systems." *PC Week Labs, eWeek* (June 27, 1999). Online. Available: http://www.zdet.com/. Accessed: November 5, 2000.

Blurton, C. *Human Development: Information and Communication Technologies and Social Processes.* New York: United Nations Development Program, 2000.

Bolt, David, and Ray Crawford. *Digital Divide: Computers and Our Children's Future.* New York: TV Books, 2000.

Bortnick, Steven M., and Michelle Harrison Ports. "Job Search Methods and Results: Tracking the Unemployed, 1991." *Monthly Labor Review,* vol. 115, no. 12 (December 1992), pp. 29–35.

Brown, Carrie H. *Closing the Gaps: How Tech-Prep Programs Have Increased Participation and Success in Texas Schools, A Five Year Study.* Beaumont, Tex.: Region 5 Education Service Center, February 2001.

196

Brown, Carrie, and Rob Franks. "Tech-Prep 101." Paper presented at the Texas State Tech-Prep Conference, Austin, Texas, March 19, 2001.

Budiansky, Stephen. "Education with a Bottom Line." *American Society for Engineering Education PRISM Magazine* (October 1999). Online. Available: http://www.asee.org/prism/oct99/html/cover_story.htm. Accessed: May 3, 2001.

Business Wire. "IBM and Hispanic Association of Colleges and Universities Join Forces to Address the Digital Divide" (March 5, 2001). Online. Available: Lexis-Nexis Academic Universe, http://web.lexis-nexis.com/universe/. Accessed: March 10, 2001.

C/Net Coverage Website. *Who Started the Net?* Online. Available: http://coverage.cnet.com/Content/Features/Techno/Networks/ss05.html. Accessed: April 24, 2001.

Cappelli, Peter, Laurie Bassi, Harry Katz, David Knoke, Paul Osterman, and Michael Useem. *Change at Work.* New York: Oxford University Press, 1997.

Carnevale, Anthony P. "Beyond Consensus: Much Ado about Job Training." *Brookings Review* (Fall 1999), pp. 40, 42.

Center for Public Policy Priorities. *Working but Poor.* Austin, Tex., March 1999.

—————. *The Workforce Investment Act of 1998.* Online. Available: http://www.cppp.org/products/policypages/91-110/91-110html/PP96.html. Accessed: May 7, 2001.

Chapman, Gary. "Industry Needs New Take on the 'Digital Divide.'" *Austin American-Statesman* (February 23, 2001).

Charles, Steve. "Sizing up the Federal Opportunity." Fedmarket.com. Online. Available: http://www.fedmarket.com/vtools/articles/federal_opportunity.html. Accessed: March 2, 2001.

Cisco. *Training and Certification.* Online. Available: http://www.cisco.com/warp/public/10/wwtraining/. Accessed: April 12, 2001.

City of Grand Prairie, Texas. *Texas Smart Job Fund.* Online. Available: http://www.ci.grand-prarie.tx.us. Accessed: March 18, 2001.

Click2Learn. *Learning Management System.* Online. Available: www.click2learn.com. Accessed: May 3, 2001.

Commission on Technology and Adult Learning. *A Vision of E-Learning for America's Workforce.* Alexandria, VA: American Society for Training and Development and the National Governors Association Center for Best Practices, 2001.

197

Commonwealth of Kentucky. *Employ Kentucky Network*. Online. Available: http://www.state.ky.us/agencies/gov/empower/saccess/care.htm. Accessed: May 7, 2001.

Compaine, Benjamin M., ed. *The Digital Divide: Facing a Crisis or Creating a Myth*. Cambridge, MA: MIT Press, 2001.

CompTIA. *Certification*. Online. Available: http://www.comptia.com/certification/index.htm. Accessed: March 23, 2001.

Concept Systems, Inc. *Corporate Universities*. Online. Available: http://www.conceptsystems.com/applications/corpuniv/corpuniv.htm. Accessed: May 3, 2001.

"Content, Technology, Services." *E-Learning Magazine*. Online. Available: http://www.elearningmag.com. Accessed: March 20, 2001.

Coopers and Lybrand. *Transformation of Higher Education in the Digital Age*. MA, 1998.

Corporate University Exchange (CUX). Online. Available: http://www.corpu.com. Accessed: November 20, 2000.

Corporation for a Skilled Workforce. Reinventing One-Stop Systems to Flourish in the Internet Environment, Comment by Larry Good, 2000 (Pamphlet).

Croft, Warner. Partner, Anderson Consulting. Quoted in J. Michael Brower, "Military Tunes to Virtual Classroom." *Training and Simulation Industry and Technology Trends* (November 1999), p. 47.

Dell Computer Corporation. *Dell Learning*. Online. Available: http://www.dell.com/us/en/gen/corporate/dellu.htm. Accessed: December 3, 2000.

Eaton, Leslie. "Labor Department Study Describes Need for IT Skills for Most Workers." *New York Times* (October 20, 1999). Online. Available: http://www.nytimes.com/yr/mo/day/news/national/regional/ny-computer-skills. Accessed: November 20, 2000.

E-Learning and Training Labs. *The EnterTech Project: Changing Learning and Lives*. Austin, Tex.: IC^2 Institute, The University of Texas at Austin, 2002.

Ellis, Richard, and B. Lindsay Lowell. "Core Occupations of the U.S. Information Technology Workforce." Report 1 of the IT Workforce Data Project, United Engineering Foundation (January 1999). Online. Available: http://www.uefoundation.org/report1.html. Accessed: November 11, 2000.

Emery, Gail Repsher. "Army Project Boosts E-Learning Prospects." *Washington Technology*, vol. 16, no. 8, July 16, 2001. Online. Available: http://www.washingtontechnology.com/news/16_8/federal/16859-1.html. Accessed: August 3, 2001.

Employment Policy Foundation. "Upgrading Workplace Skills' $300 Billion Annual Investment." Washington, D.C., April 10, 2000, p. 4. Online. Available: http://www.epf.org/research/newsletters/2000/ib000410.pdf. Accessed: May 3, 2001.

Encyclopedia Britannica Online. "Social Service." Online. Available: http://members.eb.com/bol/topic?eu=117546&sctn=2. Accessed: March 11, 2001.

EnterTech. *Introduction*. Online. Available: http://www.utexas.edu/depts/ic2/et/ intro.html. Accessed: March 5, 2001.

——————. *Assessment and Evaluation Strategies for the Learner Report*. Online. Available: http://www.utexas.edu/depts/ic2/et/eval/stueval.html. Accessed: April 24, 2001.

——————. *EnterTech Reports*. Online. Available: http://www.utexas.edu/depts/ic2/et/report.html. Accessed: April 24, 2001.

——————. *Knowledge, Skills and Abilities Required for Entry-level Jobs in the Technology Industry and the Related Supply and Service Industries*. Online. Available: http://www.utexas.edu/depts/ic2/et/ksa/ksa.html. Accessed: April 2, 2001.

——————. Online. Available: http://www.utexas.edu/depts/ic2/et/. Accessed: April 10, 2001.

——————. *Target Learner Characteristics Report*. Online. Available: http://www.utexas.edu/depts/ic2/et/learner/intro.html. Accessed: April 5, 2001.

Federal Benchmarking Consortium. *Best Practices in One-Stop Customer Service: Serving the American Public Study*. Washington, D.C.: U.S. Government Printing Office, November 1997.

Fletcher, Dexter, for the Under Secretary of Defense for Personnel and Readiness, Readiness and Training Directorate. *Development and Assessment of ADL Prototypes*.

Fletcher, J. D., and Paul R. Chatelier. "Training in the Military." In *Training and Retraining: A Handbook for Business, Industry, Government, and the Military*, eds. Sigmund Tobias and J. D. Fletcher. New York: Macmillan, 2000.

Florida Agency for Workforce Innovation. *Florida Research and Economic Database*. Online. Available: http://fred.labormarketinfo.com/ Accessed: May 7, 2001.

Florida Department of Education. *First Year WIA Performance Outcome Data*. Online. Available: http://www.firn.edu/doe/bin00078/fetpip/pdf/wreports.pdf. Accessed: May 7, 2001.

Florida Employment Community. Online. Available: https://www.myfloridajobs.com/wagesct/wagesprod/empcenter/about.cfm. Accessed: May 7, 2001.

Florida Legislature. Office of Program Policy Analysis, and Government Accountability. *Review of the Workforce Development System Report no. 99-34*. Online. Available: http:www.OPPAGA.state.fl.us/reports/econ/r99-34s.html. Accessed: May 7, 2001.

Florida Trend. *NEXT*. Online. Available: http://www.floridanext.com/. Accessed: May 7, 2001.

Freeman, Peter, and William Aspray. *The Supply of Information Technology Workers in the United States*. Washington, D.C.: Computing Research Association, 1999.

Friel, Brian. "A College of One." *Government Executive Magazine* (August 1, 2001). Online. Available: http://www.govexec.com/features/0801/0801managetech2.htm. Accessed: August 3, 2001.

Galston, William. "The U.S. Rural Economy in Historical and Global Context." In *Back to Shared Prosperity: The Growing Inequality of Wealth and Income in America*, ed. Ray Marshall. Armonk, N.Y.: M. E. Sharpe, 2000.

Ganzglass, Evelyn, Martin Jensen, Neil Ridley, Martin Simon, and Chris Thompson. *Transforming State Workforce Systems: Case Studies of Five Leading States*. Washington, D.C.: National Governors Association, Center for Best Practices, 2001

Gardner, Gregg Shai. "Silicon Wadi." *The Jerusalem Post* (December 24, 2000), Economics Sec., p. 9. Online. Available: http://web.lexis-nexis.com/universe/. Accessed: March 6, 2001.

Gibbons, Andrew S., and Peter G. Fairweather. "Computer-Based Instruction." In *Training and Retraining: A Handbook for Business, Industry, Government, and the Military*, eds. Sigmund Tobias and J. D. Fletcher. New York: Macmillan Reference USA, 2000.

Goldberger, Susan, and Richard Kazis. *Revitalizing High Schools: What the School-to-Career Movement Can Contribute*. Washington, D.C.: American Youth Policy Forum, Institute for Educational Leadership, Jobs for the Future, and National Association of Secondary School Principals, 1995.

Gotschall, Mary. "Transforming Adult Education by Leveraging Knowledge throughout the Enterprise." *Fortune Magazine*, Education Sec. Online. Available: http://www.timeinc.net/fortune/sections/corpuni/corpuni.htm. Accessed: December 5, 2000.

Gregory, Bill. "Training System Acquisition Chiefs' Priorities." *Training and Simulation 2000.* p. 22.

Grubb, Norton W., Norena Badway, Denise Bell, Bernadette Chi, Chris King, Julie Herr, Heath Prince, Richard Kazis, Lisa Hicks, and Judith Combes Taylor. *Toward Order from Chaos: State Efforts to Reform Workforce Development Systems.* Berkeley, Calif.: National Center for Research in Vocational Education, January 1999.

Gruber, David. *We're education . . . .you're semiconductors.* Philadelphia: Public/Private Ventures, January 2000.

Haas, Carl T., Robert W. Glover, Richard L. Tucker, and R. Kevin Terrien. *Impact of the Internet on the Recruitment of Skilled Labor.* Austin, Tex.: Center for Construction Industry Studies, The University of Texas at Austin, Report no. 17. February 2001.

Horrigan, John. Senior Research Specialist, Pew Research Center Internet Project, Class Presentation at the Lyndon B. Johnson School of Public Affairs, Austin, Texas, March 8, 2001.

HotJobs.com. *TMP Worldwide, HotJobs Reiterate Dual Positioning: Reinforces Value, Differentiation Can Unleash Untapped Market,* Press Release July 17, 2001. Online. Available: http://www.hotjobs.com/htdocs/about/news/071701.html/ Accessed: August 6, 2001.

Human Internet Guide for Beginners. Online. Available: http://www.learnthenet.com /english/glossary/pull.htm. Accessed: March 6, 2001.

IMS Global Learning Consortium, Inc. *IMS Global Learning Consortium Inc.* Online. Available: http://www.imsproject.org. Accessed: May 7, 2001.

Independent Schools Association of the Central States. *Technology Newsletter.* Online. Available: http://www.isacs.org/monograph/techletterNov2000.html. Accessed: May 5, 2001.

Interstate Conference of Employment Security Agencies. "ALX Connects." *Workforce ATM,* vol. 2, no. 3. Online. Available: http://www.icesa.org/articles/template.cfm?results_art_filename=alxapr.htm. Accessed: May 7, 2001.

——————. "Information Technology Committee Meeting Notes." *Workforce ATM.* Online. Available: http:// www.icesa.org/articles/template.cfm?results_art_filename=itnovdecmin.htm. Accessed: May 7, 2001.

Katsinas, Stephen G. "Community Colleges and Workforce Development in the New Economy." Winter 1994. Online. Available: http://scholar.lib.vt.edu/ejournals/CATALYST/V24N1/katsinas.html. Accessed: April 2, 2001.

King, Christopher T. "Federalism and Workforce Policy Reform." *Publius: The Journal of Federalism,* vol. 29, no. 2 (Spring 1999), pp. 53-71.

Kuhn, Peter, and Mikal Skuterud. "Job Search Methods." *Monthly Labor Review,* vol. 123, no. 10 (October 2000), pp. 3–11.

Lawson, Leslie O., and Christopher T. King. "The Reality of Welfare-to-Work: Employment Opportunities for Women Affected by Welfare Time Limits in Texas." Report prepared for the Urban Institute, Washington, D.C., September 1997.

Lemmond, L. E. "Where Are Our Spring 2000 High School Graduates Today?" Paper presented at the Texas Tech-Prep Conference, Austin, Texas, March 19, 2001.

Lidsky, David. "Online Content: The Web Delivers News, Sports, Weather, and Even Software Come to Your Desktop." *PC Magazine Online.* Online. Available: ZDNet, http://www.zdnet.com/pcmag/feastures/push/_open.htm. Accessed: March 6, 2001.

MacGhee, Major General David F., Jr. Director of Air and Space Operations for the Air Command at Langley Air Force Base, VA. Quoted in Harold Kennedy, "'War in a Box' Not Real Enough for Air Force Combat Training." *Training and Simulation Industry and Technology Trends* (November 1999), p. 10.

Mack, Raneta Lawson. *The Digital Divide: Standing at the Intersection of Race and Technology.* Durham, N.C.: Carolina Academic Press, 2001.

Maxwell, N., and V. Rubin. *High School Career Academies: A Pathway to Educational Reform in Urban School Districts.* Kalamazoo, Mich.: W. E. Upjohn Institute for Employment Research, 2000.

McDonald, Tim. "Internet Penetration Sets New U.S. Record." February 14, 2001. *News FactorNetwork.* Online. Available: http://www.newsfactor.com/perl/story/7497.html. Accessed: April 24, 2001.

McPherson, Robert. "Designing a Local Workforce Services Delivery System." Vol. 4. Austin, Tex: Ray Marshall Center for the Study of Human Resources of the LBJ School of Public Affairs, The University of Texas at Austin. February 1997.

Meares, Carol Ann, and John F. Sargent, Jr., *The Digital Work Force: Building Infotech Skills at the Speed of Innovation.* Washington, D.C.: U.S. Department of Commerce, Office of Technology Policy, June 1999.

Meister, Jeanne. "The Brave New World of Corporate Education." *The Chronicle of Higher Education.* February 9, 2001. Online. Available: http://chronicle.com/free/v47/i22/22b01001.htm. Accessed: May 3, 2001.

"Meta Data and Data Administration: XML: The Global Meta Data Standard." *DM Review.* Online. Available: http://www.dmreview.com/editorial/dmreview/print_action.cfm?EdID=1845. Accessed: May 7, 2001.

Midland College. *The Midland Advanced Technology Center.* Online. Available: http://www.midland.cc.tx.us/~atc/index.html. Accessed: March 10, 2001.

Minoli, Daniel. *Distance Learning Technology and Applications.* Norwood, Mass.: Artech House, Inc., 1996.

Moy, Allison. "Papers on 'Welfare-to-Work' and 'Workforce Investment Act.'" *2001 Practitioner's Guide to Federal Resources for Community Economic Development.* Prepared by the National Congress for Community Economic Development, February 2001.

Nathan, Richard P., and Thomas L. Gais. *Implementing the Personal Responsibility Act of 1996: A First Look.* Albany: The Rockefeller Institute of Government, State University of New York, 1999.

National Commission on the High School Senior. *The Lost Opportunity of Senior Year: Finding a Better Way.* Washington, D.C., January 2001.

National Governors Association. Center for Best Practices. March 1997. *Demand Side Strategies for Workforce Development.* Online. Available: http://www.nga.org/Workforce/DemandSide3.htm. Accessed: January 11, 2001.

—————. Policy Position. HR-36. *Welfare Reform Policy.* Online. Available: http://www.nga.org/nga/legislativeUpdate/policyPositionDetailPrint/1,1390,554,00.htm. Accessed: April 3, 2001.

—————. *WIA Early Implementation State Workforce Investment Plans* (March 27, 2000). Online. Available: http://www.nga.org/cda/files/WIAMATRIX.pdf. Accessed: May 7, 2001.

National O*NET Consortium. *O*NET*. Online. Available: http://www.onetcenter.org/. Accessed May 7, 2001.

National Research Council (U.S.). Committee on Workforce Needs in Information Technology. *Building a Workforce for the Information Economy*. Washington, D.C.: National Academy Press, 2001.

Newcombe, Tod. "Reinventing Welfare for the Digital Age." *Government Technology* (April 2000). Online. Available: http://www.govtech.net/publications/gt/2000/apr/digitalstates2/digitalstates2.html. Accessed: May 7, 2001.

Nielsen/NetRatings. *Information provided by Allen Weiner, Vice President of Analytical Services, NetRatings*. Online. Available: http://www.NetRatings.com. Accessed: February 22, 2001.

North Central Texas WorkForce Online. Available: http://www.dfwjobs.com/joblinks.html. Accessed: February 14, 2002.

Northwest Center on Emerging Technologies. *Building a Foundation for Tomorrow*. Bellevue, Washington, 1999.

NSF Revised Project Plan for Proposal No. 0101726, "Computer Science 2000/ARIES Alliance," in response to memo of April 25, 2001 from Dr. R. Corby Hovis. Obtained from Mary Jo Sanna, Director of Education, May 11, 2001.

O'Shea, Daniel, and Christopher T. King. *Restructuring Workforce Development Initiatives in States and Localities*. Albany: Nelson A. Rockefeller Institute of Government, Report no. 12, April 2001.

Parnell, Dale. *The Neglected Majority*. Washington, D.C.: The Community College Press, 1985

Pindus, Nancy, Robin Koralek, Karin Martinson, and John Trutko. *Coordination and Integration of Welfare and Workforce Development Systems*. Report prepared for the U.S. Department of Health and Human Services, Office of the Assistant Secretary for Planning and Evaluation, March 20, 2000. Online. Available: http://aspe.hhs.gov/hsp/coord00/. Accessed: February 13, 2001.

Ports, Michelle Harrison. "Trends in Job Search Methods, 1970–92." *Monthly Labor Review*, vol. 116, no. 10 (October 1993), pp. 63–67.

Powers, Tom. *TIF: Progress and Future*. Opening Keynote Address to 1999 Texas Distance Learning Association Conference, 1999.

Public Utility Commission of Texas. Report to the 77th Texas Legislature: Availability of Advanced Services in Rural and High Cost Areas. Austin, Tex., January 2001.

Rangarajan, Anu. *Keeping Welfare Recipients Employed: A Guide for States Designing Job Retention Services*. Doc. no. PR98-20. Princeton, N.J.: Mathematica Policy Research, Inc., June 1998.

Ray Marshall Center for the Study of Human Resources. *Workforce Development Evaluation in Texas: An Assessment*. Austin, Tex., September 1996.

Reese, R. Anthony. Assistant Professor, University of Texas Law School. Class presentation, *Converting Technology to Wealth*, at the IC^2 Institute, The University of Texas at Austin, February 20, 2001.

Runzheimer International. *Survey and Analysis of Employee Relocation Policies and Costs*. 7th ed., 1999.

SACC Training and Development Committee. *The Report on Distance Learning,* 2000.

Samuelson, Robert J. "Debunking the Digital Divide," *The Washington Post* (March 20, 2002), p. A-33.

Scientific Learning Corporation. *Results*. Online. Available: http://www.scientificlearning.com/scie/index.php3?main=results_intro&cartid=. Accessed: April 22, 2001.

Seay, Brigadier General Stephen M. Quoted in Bill Gregory, "Training System Acquisition Chiefs' Priorities." *Training and Simulation 2000* (Winter 1999), pp. 22–23.

Shaffrey, Ted. "U.S. Army Hires 'Star Trek' Veteran to Create Soldier Simulation." *Westside Weekly* (February 18, 2001). Online. Available: http://www.ict.usc.edu/press_new/ww.html. Accessed: February 21, 2001.

Sheppard, Harold L., and A. Harvey Belitsky. *The Job Hunt: Job-Seeking Behavior of Unemployed Workers in a Local Economy*. Baltimore: Johns Hopkins University Press, 1966.

Southern Regional Education Board. *Electronic Campus*. Online. Available: http://www.electroniccampus.org. Accessed: March 12, 2001.

State of Texas Human Resources Management. *The Report on Distance Learning,* 2000.

Telecommunications Infrastructure Fund (TIF). Board Annual Report, January 2001, p. 3. Online Available: http://www.tifb.state.tx.us/other/Annual%20Report%20Jan15.00.doc. Accessed: May 2, 2001.

—————. "Texas Libraries Receive Technology Funds." March 1, 1999 (press release). Online. Available: http://www.tifb.state.tx.us/grantloan/LibraryInfo/LB3PressRel.htm. Accessed: May 2, 2001.

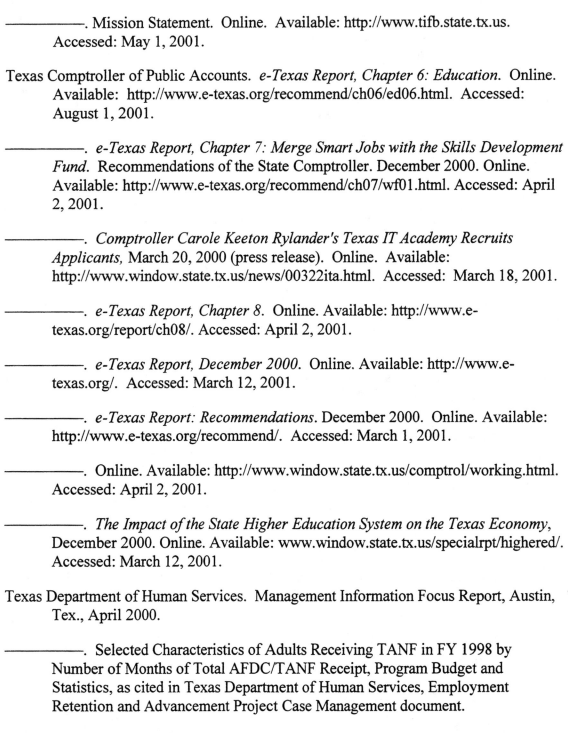

—————. Mission Statement. Online. Available: http://www.tifb.state.tx.us. Accessed: May 1, 2001.

Texas Comptroller of Public Accounts. *e-Texas Report, Chapter 6: Education.* Online. Available: http://www.e-texas.org/recommend/ch06/ed06.html. Accessed: August 1, 2001.

—————. *e-Texas Report, Chapter 7: Merge Smart Jobs with the Skills Development Fund.* Recommendations of the State Comptroller. December 2000. Online. Available: http://www.e-texas.org/recommend/ch07/wf01.html. Accessed: April 2, 2001.

—————. *Comptroller Carole Keeton Rylander's Texas IT Academy Recruits Applicants,* March 20, 2000 (press release). Online. Available: http://www.window.state.tx.us/news/00322ita.html. Accessed: March 18, 2001.

—————. *e-Texas Report, Chapter 8.* Online. Available: http://www.e-texas.org/report/ch08/. Accessed: April 2, 2001.

—————. *e-Texas Report, December 2000.* Online. Available: http://www.e-texas.org/. Accessed: March 12, 2001.

—————. *e-Texas Report: Recommendations.* December 2000. Online. Available: http://www.e-texas.org/recommend/. Accessed: March 1, 2001.

—————. Online. Available: http://www.window.state.tx.us/comptrol/working.html. Accessed: April 2, 2001.

—————. *The Impact of the State Higher Education System on the Texas Economy,* December 2000. Online. Available: www.window.state.tx.us/specialrpt/highered/. Accessed: March 12, 2001.

Texas Department of Human Services. Management Information Focus Report, Austin, Tex., April 2000.

—————. Selected Characteristics of Adults Receiving TANF in FY 1998 by Number of Months of Total AFDC/TANF Receipt, Program Budget and Statistics, as cited in Texas Department of Human Services, Employment Retention and Advancement Project Case Management document.

Texas Government Code Annotated, Sec. 2308.101, (1) & (2).

Texas Higher Education Coordinating Board, the Texas Education Agency, and the Texas Department of Commerce. "TECH-PREP in Texas, Education that Works: Status Report: A Snap-Shot of the Impact of the Tech-Prep Initiative in the Governor's 24 Planning Regions." Report prepared by Carrie Hughes Brown, Director of Tech-Prep/School-to-Work Initiative Management Project, Beaumont, Texas, April 1996.

Texas Higher Education Coordinating Board. *Closing the Gaps by 2015*. Austin, Tex., October 2000.

—————. *Report on the Performance of Texas Public Universities*, Austin, Tex.March 2001.

—————. *Texas Public Community and Technical Colleges, 2000 Statewide Factbook*. Online. Available: www.thecb.state.tx.us/CTC/ie/ctcsf/. Accessed: March 11, 2001.

Texas House of Representatives, Economic Development Committee. Interim Report to the 77th Texas Legislature, November 2000.

Texas Instruments. *Benefits: Training and Development*. Online. Available: http://www.ti.com/recruit/docs/development.shtml. Accessed: February 10, 2001.

Texas Office of the Governor. Special Commission on 21st Century Colleges and Universities. *Higher Education in the 21st Century…Moving Every Texan Forward*. Austin, Tex., January 2, 2000.

Texas State Occupational Information Coordinating Committee. *Automated Student and Adult Learner Follow-Up System, Final Report 1999*.

Texas State Technical College. *About e-Commerce Technology Program*. Online. Available: http://www.set.tstc.edu/DeptInfo/AboutECT.htm. Accessed: March 9, 2001.

Texas Workforce Commission. *How Texas Works: 2000 Annual Report* (inside cover). Austin, Tex., 2000.

—————. *The Workforce Investment Act (WIA) of 1998*. Online. Available: http://www.twc.state.tx.us/svcs/jtpa/wiajtpa.html. Accessed: April 1, 2001.

—————. *What is the Texas Workforce Commission?* Online. Available: http://www.twc.state.tx.us/twcinfo/whatis.html. Accessed: April 10, 2001.

"Training Funding Crunch Means More Soldiers are in Simulators." *Training and Simulation Industry and Technology Trends* (November 1999), p. 6.

Turner, Shannon, and Donise W. Pearson. "Fast ForWord Learning Intervention Programs: Four Case Studies." *Texas Journal of Audiology and Speech Pathology*, vol. 13 (Spring/Summer 1999). Online. Available: http://www.scientificlearning.com/scie/index.php3?main=abs/sciepublished&cartid=. Accessed: April 22, 2001.

U.S. Congress. House Commerce Committee, Subcommittee on Telecommunications and the Internet. "Education Technology." Testimony on behalf of the Software and Information Industry Association by Dr. Jennifer House, Vice President of

207

Strategic Relations, Classroom Connect, Inc. Washington, D.C., March 8, 2001. Online. Available: http://www.siia.net/sharedcontent/govt/issues/edu/ClassroomConnectTestimony.pdf. Accessed: May 3, 2001.

U.S. Congress. House Committee on Ways and Means, Subcommittee on Human Resources. "Time on Welfare and Welfare Dependency." Testimony by LaDonna Pavetti, Research Associate, The Urban Institute, March 23, 1996. Online. Available: http://www.urban.org/welfare/pavtes.htm. Accessed: February 2, 2001.

U.S. Congress. House. Workforce Investment Act. H.R. 1385, 105th Congress, 2nd Session (1998).

U.S. Department of Commerce, Economics and Statistics Administration, Census Bureau. *Home Computers and Internet Use in the United States: August 2000.* Current Population Report P23-207. Washington, D.C., September 2001.

—————. *Computer Use in the United States: October 1997.* Current Population Report P20-522. Washington, D.C., September 1999.

U.S. Department of Commerce, Economics and Statistics Administration, and National Telecommunications and Information Administration. *Falling through the Net: Toward Digital Inclusion. A Report on Americans' Access to Technology Tools,* October 2000. Online. Available: http://www.ntia.doc.gov/ntiahome/fttn00/Falling.htm. Accessed: April 2, 2001.

U.S. Department of Education. *E-Learning: Putting a World-Class Education at the Fingertips of All Children.* Washington, D.C., December 2000.

U.S. Department of Health and Human Services. "Coordination and Integration of Welfare and Workforce Development Systems." Literature Review on Service Coordination and Integration in the Welfare and Workforce Development Systems, by Karin Martinson, January 1999. Online. Available: http://aspe.hhs.gov/hsp/coord00/appa.htm. Accessed: April 2, 2001.

U.S. Department of Labor. Employment and Training Administration. *Benefits and Costs of Job Corps.* Research on Evaluation Monograph Series 01-M. Washington, D.C., 2001.

—————. *The Impacts of Job Corps on Participants' Employment and Relations Outcomes.* Research on Evaluation Monograph Series 01-K. Washington, D.C., 2001.

—————. *The One-Stop Center System.* Fact Sheet. Online. Available: http://www.doleta.gov/programs/factsht/one-stop.htm. Accessed: April 2, 2001.

_____. "Final Report: Creating Workforce Development Systems That Work." Washington, D.C., November 1, 1997.

U.S. Department of Labor. Employment and Training Administration, Veterans' Employment and Training Service (VETS). *Use Your Military Experience and Training (UMET)*. Online. Available: http://umet-vets.dol.gov/. Accessed: July 31, 2001.

U.S. Department of Labor, Office of Policy. *A Nation of Opportunity: Building America's 21st Century Workforce*. A Report Prepared by the 21st Century Workforce Commission. Washington, D.C., June 2000.

U.S. General Accounting Office, Health, Education, and Human Services Division. "Welfare Reform: Improving State Automated Systems Requires Coordinated Federal Effort," April 2000, GAO/HEHS-00-48.

U.S. Office of Technology Assessment. *Power On: New Tools for Teaching and Learning*. Washington, D.C.: U.S.Government Printing Office, 1989.

University of Southern California, "War is Virtual Hell." Online. Available: http://www.ict.usc.edu/press_new/wired.html. Accessed: February 21, 2001.

University of Texas at Austin, IC^2 Institute. Austin Technology Incubator. Online. Available: http://www.ic2-ati.org. Accessed: March 12, 2001.

University of Texas at Austin, IC^2 Institute. Cross-Border Institute for Regional Development. Online. Available: http://www.ic2.org/cbird.html. Accessed: March 10, 2001.

Utah Department of Workforce Services. *Utah's Workforce System*. Online. Available: http://www.dws.state.ut.us/PI/UWORKS/UWORKS.htm. Accessed: May 7, 2001.

"Vehicle Design Begins in Virtual Cave," *Training and Simulation Industry and Technology Trends* (November 1999), p. 50.

Virginia Department of Social Services. *Temporary Assistance for Needy Families*. Online. Available: http://www.dss.state.va.us/benefit/tanf.html. Accessed: April 5, 2001.

Virtual College of Texas. *Operations Manual*, p. 3. Online. Available: http://www.vct.org. Accessed: July 25, 2001.

_____. Online. Available: http://www.vct.org. Accessed: March 9, 2001.

Walsh, John, Miriam Johnson, and Marged Sugarman. *Help Wanted: Case Studies of Classified Ads*. Salt Lake City: Olympus Publishing, 1975.

Washington State Employment Security Department. *Acquisition Approval Request to Procure System Integrator Services to Implement a Customer Tracking and Accountability System*, May 1999.

Web-Based Education Commission. *The Power of the Internet for Learning: Moving from Promise to Practice* (December 2000). Report to the president and the Congress of the United States. Online. Available: http://www.webcommission.org. Accessed: March 22, 2001.

Webopedia Website. Online. Available: http://www.webopedia.com. Accessed: April 25, 2001.

Welch, David. "Different Drill: Hughes Training Learns New Tricks as It Targets Corporate Clients." *Fort Worth Star Telegram* (October 22, 1997).

Western Governors University. *About WGU: Frequently Asked Questions*. Online. Available: http://www.wgu.edu/wgu/about/faqs.html. Accessed: August 1, 2001.

——————. *Western Governors University Earns Accreditation from the Distance Education and Training Council*, Press Release, June 13, 2001. Online. Available: http://www.wgu.edu/wgu/about/release58.html. Accessed: August 1, 2001.

——————. *What We Are*. Online. Available: http://www.wgu.edu/wgu/about/whatwe.html. Accessed: August 1, 2001.

White House, The. "From Digital Divide to Digital Opportunity: The Importance of Bridging the Digital Divide." Online. Available: http://clinton4.nara.gov/WH/New/digitaldivide/digital3.html.

White, Ronald D. "More Job Seekers, Firms Use the Net: But Effectiveness of the Web Sites Remains Unclear." *Los Angeles Times* (March 18, 2001).

Wilson, Lois S., Katharine Golas, and Harold F. O'Neil, Jr. "Basic Skills Training." In *Training and Retraining: A Handbook for Business, Industry, Government, and the Military,* ed. Sigmund Tobias and J. D. Fletcher. New York: Macmillan Reference USA, 2000, p. 492.

Workforce Florida. *Workforce Florida Strategic Plan, 2001–2002*. Online. Available: http://www.wages.org/wages/wfi/partners/stratplan/stratplan-full.pdf. Accessed: May 7, 2001.

Workforce Information System of Texas (TWIST) System in Texas. Online. Available: http://www.Sybase.com/detail/1,3693,204205,00.html. Accessed: March 6, 2001.

Workforce Training and Education Coordinating Board. *Washington Career Guide*. Online. Available: http://www.wa.gov/careerguide/career/assess/. Accessed: May 7, 2001.

Zerh, Mary Ann. "Rural Connections." *Education Week,* vol. 20, no. 35 (May 10, 2001).

Interviews

Angel, Linda. Strategic Planner and Manager, Excellence, Marketing, Creativity and Capital (EMC2), Central Texas Workforce System, Killeen, Texas. Telephone interview by Robert W. Glover, October 16, 2001.

Bearley, Crystal. Career Specialist, Capital of Texas Workforce Center, Austin, Texas. Interviewed by Tanya Cruz and Tina Ghabel, February 27, 2001.

Collis, John. Career Counselor, Texas A&M Corpus Christi, Corpus Christi, Texas. Interviewed by Madge Vásquez, November 21, 2000.

Dorrer, John. Deputy Director, Workforce Development Program, National Center on Education and the Economy, Washington, D.C. Telephone interview by Tanya Cruz, March 16, 2001.

Dorsey, Anne. Assistant Director, Texas Skills Standards Board, Austin, Texas. Interviewed by Susan Vermeer, May 9, 2001.

Duncan, David. Director, Governmental Relations, Texas Workforce Commission, Austin, Texas. Interviewed by Piper Stege and Jema Turk, March 31, 2001.

Ellis, Paul. President, Austin Business College, Austin, Texas. Telephone interview by Dan Starr, April 9, 2001.

Feltz, Constance. Project Team Leader, Minnesota Department of Economic Security, St. Paul, Minnesota. Telephone interview by Michael Faust, March 28, 2001.

Ferrell, Bruce. Captain, Army National Guard Force Readiness Officer, Austin, Texas. Interviewed by Vanessa C. Mitra, November 13, 2000.

Fluharty, Gerry. Special Initiatives/ Products Specialist, Killeen One-Stop Center, Killeen, Texas. Interviewed by Piper Stege and Jema Turk, November 2, 2000.

Garcia, Ron. Principal, South Grand Prairie High School, Grand Prairie, Texas. Interviewed by Susan Vermeer and Robert W. Glover, February 19, 2001.

Gosset, Kristin. Executive Director, Austin Idea Network, Austin, Texas. Interviewed by Kevin Heinz and Svetlana Negrustuyeva, February 21, 2001.

Groening, David. Private Consultant and Project Manager, Austin, Texas. Interviewed by Piper Stege and Jema Turk, April 12, 2001.

Grossenbacher, Bill. Director, Career Centers, ACS State and Local Solutions, Inc. (formerly Lockheed Martin Corporation). Austin, Texas. Interviewed by Piper Stege and Jema Turk, May 23, 2001.

Hartley, Darin. Former Director, Dell E-Learning, Austin, Texas. Interviewed by Svetlana Negrustuyeva, December 1, 2000.

Husbands, Fitz. Director, High Schools That Work and Tech Prep, and Robert Franks, Director, Tech Prep Programs, Texas Higher Education Coordinating Board, Austin, Texas. Interviewed by Susan Vermeer and Madge Vásquez, March 19, 2001.

Jackson, Melinda. Project Manager, EnterTech Austin, Texas. Interviewed by Kathryn Supinski, February 21, 2001.

Kellas, Jeanie. Manager, Ft. Leonard Wood Army Career and Alumni Program, Ft. Leonard Wood, Missouri. Telephone interview by Vanessa C. Mitra, February 20, 2001.

Kincaid, Sharyl. Assistant Director, School to Career, Round Rock, Texas. Interviewed by Susan Vermeer, March 22, 2001.

Latham, Wendy. Grant Administrator for the Telecommunications Infrastructure Fund (TIF), Austin, Texas. Interviewed by Tina Ghabel, May 1, 2001.

Lopez, Ben. Program Specialist, Central Texas Workforce Center, Killeen, Texas. Email to Tina Ghabel, March 1, 2001.

Lucas, Michael, and Doug Smith. Committee Clerks. Human Services Committee, Texas House of Representatives, Austin, Texas. Interviewed by Piper Stege and Jema Turk, October 23, 2000.

Macias, Louis. Director, Workforce Administration, Texas Workforce Commission (TWC), Austin, Texas. Telephone interview by Tina Ghabel, March 15, 2001.

Martin, Sarah Ann. Policy Analyst. Department of Human Services. "Employment Retention and Advancement (ERA) Project: A New ERA in Welfare Reform." Email to Tanya Cruz, March 15, 2001.

Matula, Anne. Dean of Business, Del Mar College, Corpus Christi, Texas. Interviewed by Madge Vásquez, January 8, 2001.

McClure, Jim. Professional Development Coordinator, Capital Area Training Foundation, Austin, Texas Email to Susan Vermeer, May 10, 2001.

McCollough, Dale. Executive Director, Capital Area Tech-Prep Consortium, Austin, Texas. Interviewed by Susan Vermeer, March 20, 2001.

McEachern, David. Director of Management Information Services, Kansas Department of Human Resources, Topeka, Kansas. Telephone interview by Michael Faust. May 3, 2001.

McKimmy, Paul. Director of Workforce Development, Texas A&M Corpus Christi, Corpus Christi, Texas. Interviewed by Madge Vásquez, January 8, 2001.

Megateli, Abderrahmane. CBIRD Project Coordinator, IC^2 Institute, The University of Texas, Austin, Texas. Interviewed by Madge Vásquez, February 9, 2001.

Merjanian, Ara. Consultant, Austin, Texas. Telephone interview by Kathryn Supinski, March 2, 2001.

Minnich, Steve. Vice President, State and Local Solutions, Inc. (formerly Lockheed Martin Corporation), Austin, Texas. Interviewed by Piper Stege and Jema Turk, October 15, 2000.

Mireles, Brig. Transition Coordinator, Leander High School, Leander, Texas. Interviewed by Susan Vermeer, March 19, 2001.

Morris, Deborah. Assistant Deputy Commissioner, Planning Evaluation and Project Management, Texas Department of Human Services, Austin, Texas. Telephone interview by Tanya Cruz, March 14, 2001.

O'Shea, Daniel. Research Associate, Ray Marshall Center for the Study of Human Resources of the LBJ School of Public Affairs, The University of Texas at Austin, Austin, Texas. Interviewed by Tanya Cruz and Tina Ghabel, March 28, 2001.

Pfeiffer, Jay. Director, Florida Education Training and Placement Information Program. E-mail to Daniel Starr, April 6, 2001.

Rasco, Alan. Vice President, Workforce Development, Austin Community College, Austin, Texas. Interviewed by Madge Vásquez, December 8, 2000.

Remtula, Theresa. Technology Specialist, Ft. Leonard Wood Army Career and Alumni Program, Ft. Leonard Wood, Missouri. Telephone interview by Vanessa C. Mitra, February 6, 2001.

Reyna, Tadeo, Distance Learning Director and Dana Fahnholz, Distance Learning Coordinator, Texas A&M Kingsville, Kingsville, Texas. Interviewed by Madge Vásquez, January 10, 2001.

Roberts, Linda. Former Director, Office of Educational Technology, U.S. Department of Education, Austin, Texas. Interviewed by Kathryn Supinski, February 26, 2001.

Robertson, Phyllis D. Director, Warfighting Integration and Development Directorate, Ft. Sill, Oklahoma. Email to Vanessa C. Mitra, November 21, 2000.

Roe, Jim. Cisco Lab Teacher, Del Valle High School. Interviewed by Susan Vermeer, March 21, 2001.

Sabelli, Nora. National Science Foundation, Austin, Texas. Interviewed by Kathryn Supinski, March 6, 2001.

Sanna, Mary Jo, Project Director for Computer Science 2000/National Science Foundation, Capital Area Tech Prep Consortium, Austin, Texas. Interviewed by Susan Vermeer and Madge Vásquez, March 20, 2001.

Sexton, Andre. Captain, Field Artillery, U.S. Army, Ft. Sill, Oklahoma. Interviewed by Vanessa C. Mitra, April 4, 2001.

Stratton, Mike. Manager, Rundberg One-Stop Center, Austin, Texas. Interviewed by Piper Stege and Jema Turk, October 7, 2000.

Thomson, Ron. Director of Operations, Virtual College of Texas, Austin Community College, Austin, Texas. Email to Tina Ghabel, August 1, 2001.

Voth, Stan. America's Workforce Technology Solutions, Topeka, Kansas. E-mail to Robert W. Glover, January 25, 2002.

White, Aubrey. Program Manager, Institute of Advanced Technology, The University of Texas at Austin, Austin, Texas. Interviewed by Vanessa C. Mitra, February 27, 2001.

Glossary of Terms

Advanced Distributed Learning (ADL): An initiative begun by the U.S. Department of Defense which promotes "Anytime-Anywhere Learning," where systems are networked, platforms are interoperable, knowledge databases are made global, and virtual classrooms are utilized.

Asynchronous: Communication in which interaction between parties does not take place simultaneously. This term is often used to describe communications in which data can be transmitted intermittently rather than in a steady stream (synchronous).

Audio Graphics Conferencing: Connection of graphic display devices to allow participants to view high-resolution, still-frame visuals (including facsimile, slow-scan television and 35-mm slides) at different sites. In more sophisticated systems, participants can manipulate and change as well as view the visual or collaborate on the development of new files or documents.

Band: A range of frequencies between defined upper and lower limits.

Bandwidth: Usually measured in seconds, this is the maximum amount of data that can travel a communication path in a given time period.

Broadband: This is a shorthand term for high-speed, always-on Internet access. Specific technical definitions of broadband vary. According to the International Telecommunications Union, broadband means transmission capacity that is faster than primary rate ISDN (i.e., 1.5 or 2 megabites per second). The Federal Communications Commission defines broadband as transmission capacity of 200 kilobites per second or more because, in their view, this speed is sufficient to provide the most popular forms of broadband —to change Web pages as fast as one can flip through the pages of a book or to transmit full-motion video.

Browser: Software that allows you to find and see Internet resources on the World Wide Web (WWW). The term *browser* is often referred to as a Web browser.

Compact Disk Read-Only Memory (CD-ROM): A storage medium for digital data that generally holds up to 650 megabytes (mb) of information.

Computer-Based Training (CBT): The use of using interactive computer or video programs for instructional purposes.

Computer-Based Instruction (CBI): Also called computer-assisted instruction, this is a type of education in which a student learns by executing special training programs on a computer.

Digital Signal Processor (DSP): Refers to manipulating analog, or continuous, information, such as sound or photographs that have been converted into a digital form. DSP also implies the use of data compression, or sending the same amount of data in fewer bits (which means binary digit—the smallest unit of information), technique.

Digital Video Interactive (DVI): A format for recording digital video onto compact disc allowing for compression and full motion video.

Distance Education: The process of providing instruction when students and instructors are separated by physical distance and technology, often in tandem with face-to-face communication.

Distance Learning: A type of education in which students work on their own at home or at work and communicate with faculty and other student via email, electronic forums, video conferencing, and other forms of computer-based communication. Also, the term includes more traditional correspondence courses through mailed communications.

Efficiency: The output that results when compared to the amount of input. Input can be money and resources invested in the workforce system to accomplish its goals and responsibilities. Generally speaking, an efficient system is one with a high ratio of outputs to inputs. If a workforce system is very costly and produces little valued output—specifically, if few people attain and retain productive work—the system is not efficient.

Effectiveness: Producing a desired effect. As it relates to workforce development, the desired effect is to offer individuals and employers the opportunity to achieve and sustain economic prosperity. Effective initiatives emphasize the development of skills, knowledge, and competencies that lead to careers and self-sufficiency and stress the connection between learning and work.

E-Learning: Instructional content or learning experiences delivered through or enabled by electronic technology.

Electronic Mail (Email): Sending messages from one computer user to another over a network.

Equity: Just, impartial, and fair. For a workforce development system to be equitable, the system and services must not treat any individual or group with bias or favoritism, whether deliberate or accidental.

Extensible Markup Language (XML): This allows designers to create their own customized tags (or commands that specify how a document should be formatted), which enables the definition, transmission, validation, and interpretation of data between applications and between organizations.

High technology (high-tech): Refers to the latest developments in technology.

Hypertext Documents: The text available on the World Wide Web (WWW) that contains links, or highlighted words or phrases, to other documents. Hypertext is used to present information in which text, sounds, images, and actions are linked together in a way that allows you to move among and between documents.

Hypertext Markup Language (HTML): The computer language used to create hypertext documents.

Hypertext Transfer Protocol (Http): The transfer of hypertext (text that contains links to other documents) from one computer to another computer. The protocol is a set of standards used by computers to transfer this information over the Web.

Information Technology (IT): The study, design, development, implementation, support, or management of computer-based information systems. In practice, IT includes all production and all applications of hardware and software.

Internet: A worldwide collection of networks and gateways that use the TCP/IP suite of protocols to communicate with one another. At the heart of the Internet is a backbone of high-speed data communication lines between major nodes or host computers, consisting of thousands of commercial, government, educational, and other computer systems, that route data and messages. The genesis of the Internet was a decentralized network called ARPANET created by the Department of Defense in 1969 to facilitate communications in the event of a nuclear attack. The Internet has several uses, including the following: (1) to send and receive email; (2) to transfer digital files (including text, images, audio, or video files) from one computer to another; (3) to provide a means of researching and locating information for either government, educational, commercial uses; and (4) to communicate with other computers, either one at a time (instant message) or many at once (chat rooms or discussion groups).

Internet Protocol (IP): The international standard for addressing and sending data via the Internet. Most networks combine IP with a higher level protocol called Transport Control Protocol (TCP).

Interoperability: The ability of software and hardware on different machines from different vendors to share data.

Legacy System: An application in which an organization has already invested considerable time and money. Typically, legacy applications are database management systems running on mainframe or minicomputers.

Modem: A piece of equipment to allow computers to interact with each other via telephone lines by converting digital signals to analog for transmission along analog lines.

Multimedia: Any document that uses multiple forms of communication, such as text, audio, and/or video.

Network: A series of points connected by communication channels in different locations.

New Economy: Technology and global trade are driving massive efficiencies throughout the economy such that the broad economy can grow faster on a sustainable basis than historic rates without risk of inflation. A core technology driving this efficiency is the Internet.

Online: Active and in operation on the Internet. Also suggests access to a computer network.

Portable Document Format (PDF): A file type created by Adobe Systems, Inc., that allows documents to maintain the same layout and design as the original. Email, Web pages, and CD-ROMs can send PDF files. The document can be viewed on any computer that has Adobe Acrobat Reader software, which is a free service available for downloading from the Adobe site.

Portal: A portal is accessible through the Internet. It provides individuals a single point of entry for a host of activities, including email, educational materials, forums, search engines, and on-line shopping malls.

Pull Technology: The end user asks the server to send any new information to the desktop.

Push Technology: A server initiates contact with the client when new information is available and ready to be transmitted.

Satellite TV: Video and audio signals are relayed via a communication device that orbits around the earth.

School-to-Career: Systems, programs, or initiatives that improve the preparation and career awareness of students to facilitate their transition from school to work.

Server: A computer that handles requests for data, email, file transfers, and network services from other computers.

Simulation: The process of imitating a real phenomenon in a virtual or computer-based environment. Using mathematical formulas, advanced computer programs can simulate weather conditions, chemical reactions, atomic reactions, and even biological processes. In theory, any phenomenon that can be reduced to mathematical data and equations can be simulated on a computer.

Synchronous: Communication in which interaction between participants is simultaneous and occurring at regular intervals.

Tech-Prep: As defined in the 1990 Carl D. Perkins Vocational and Applied Technology Education Act, a Tech-Prep Education Program combines secondary and postsecondary education in a program which (1) leads to an associate degree or two-year certificate; (2) provides technical preparation in at least one field of engineering technology, applied science, mechanical, industrial, or practical art or trade, or agriculture, health or business; (3) builds student competence in mathematics, science, and communications (including through applied academics) through a sequential course of study; and (4) leads to placement in employment.

Telecommunication: The science of information transport using wire, radio, optical, or electromagnetic channels to transmit or receive signals for voice or data communications using electrical means.

Transport Control Protocol (TCP): Allows two hosts, which are computer systems that can be accessed by individuals using a computer at a remote location, to establish a connection and exchange streams of data. The TCP guarantees delivery of data and also guarantees that packets will be delivered in the same order in which they were sent.

Video Teleconferencing (VTC): Conducting a conference between two or more participants at different sites by using computer networks to transmit audio and video data. For example, a point-to-point (two-person) video conferencing system works much like a video telephone. Each participant has a video camera, microphone, and speakers mounted on his or her computer. As the two participants speak to one another, their voices are carried over the network and delivered to the other's speakers, and whatever images appear in front of the video camera appear in a window on the other participant's monitor.

Web-Based Training (WBT): Computer-based training delivered via the Internet.

World Wide Web (WWW): The multimedia part of the Internet. It is a system of Internet servers that support specially formatted documents. The documents are formatted in a language called HTML (Hypertext Markup Language) that supports links to other documents, as well as graphics, audio, and video files. Not all Internet servers are part of the World Wide Web. There are several applications called "Web browsers" that make it easy to access the World Wide Web, two of the most popular being Netscape Navigator and Microsoft's Internet Explorer.

World Wide Web Consortium (W3C): Founded in 1994 by Tim Berners-Lee, the original architect of the World Wide Web (WWW), this organization is an international consortium of companies involved with the Internet and the Web. The primary goal of W3C is to develop open standards so that the Web evolves in a single direction rather than being splintered among competing factions. This organization is the chief standards body for Http and HTML.

Sources Used for Glossary Definitions

Advanced Distributed Learning (ADL) Website, http://www.adlnet.org

Allison, J. L. *Distance Education at a Glance*, Moscow: University of Idaho

Army University Access Online, http://eARMYU.com

About: Internet for Beginners, Glossary, http://
www.learnthenet.com/english/glossary/glossary.htm

Ellis, Richard, and B. Lindsay Lowell. "Core Occupations of the U.S. Information
Technology Workforce." Report 1 of the IT Workforce Data Project, United
Engineering Foundation (January 1999). Online. Available:
http://www.uefoundation.org/report1.html. Accessed: November 11, 2000.

Texas Higher Education Coordinating Board, the Texas Education Agency, and the
Texas Department of Commerce. "TECH-PREP in Texas, Education that Works:
Status Report: A Snap-Shot of the Impact of the Tech-Prep Initiative in the
Governor's 24 Planning Regions." A report prepared by Carrie Hughes Brown,
Director of Tech-Prep/School-to-Work Initiative Management Project, Beaumont,
Texas, April 1996, p. 2.